Anne Marie Kanstrup, Tom Nyvang and Esben Munk Sørensen (eds.)

Perspectives on e-Government
Technology & Infrastructure, Politics & Organisation, Interaction & Communication

Aalborg University Press

Perspectives on e-Government
Anne Marie Kanstrup, Tom Nyvang, and Esben Munk Sørensen (eds.)

© Anne Marie Kanstrup, Tom Nyvang, and Esben Munk Sørensen (eds.) and Aalborg University Press, 2007

Cover: Nina Lilholt
Layout: Nina Lilholt
Printed by Publizon A/S, 2007
ISBN-13: 978-87-7307-786-3

Distribution:
Aalborg University Press
Niels Jernes Vej 6B
9220 Aalborg
Denmark
Phone: (+45) 96 35 71 40, Fax: (+45) 96 35 00 76
E-mail: aauf@forlag.aau.dk
www.forlag.aau.dk

All rights reserved. No part of this book may be reprinted or reproduced or utilized in any form or by any electronic, mechanical, or other means, now known or hereafter invented, including photocopying and recording, or in any information storage or retrieval system, without permission in writing from the publishers, except for reviews and short excerpts in scholarly publications.

Contents

Anne Marie Kanstrup & Tom Nyvang
Introduction..7

Background
Christian Richter Østergaard
The Digital North Denmark Programme – Promoting Regional Change?..........17

Lone Dirckinck-Holmfeld
Social Experiments and Participatory Research as Method........................51

Technology & Infrastructure
Jeremy Rose
Technology and Government: Extending the Double Dance of Agency...............73

Ole Brun Madsen
The Evolution of the Danish ICT Infrastructure Since 2000....................99

Politics & Organisation
Lars Torpe
Local Political Deliberations on the Internet 115

Jeppe Agger Nielsen
Digital Municipality Planning – Experiments with the Use of ICT-Tools in Democratic Processes. 131

Interaction & Communication
Ellen Christiansen
Inclusiveness as a Parameter in Design of Online Interaction with Public Authorities 155

Ann Bygholm
Communicating Across Sectors in Health Care – A Case of Establishing New Infrastructure 171

Tom Nyvang & Camilla Roseeuw Poulsen
Implementation of ICT in Government Organizations - User Driven or Management Driven? 193

Anne Marie Kanstrup & Pernille Bertelsen
Local IT-Support: Values, Characteristics, and Selection Methods 225

Authors 247

Introduction
Anne Marie Kanstrup & Tom Nyvang

This book is the first collaborative research publication from the Centre for Electronic Governance at Aalborg University. It is a central publication since it features the point of departure for the centre through papers presenting studies primarily taking place within the Digital North Denmark-project and secondarily taking place in other contexts but within the same themes. At the same time, it is an important publication in that it presents the three central research perspectives on e-Government: politics and organization, communication and interaction, technology and infrastructure. In other words, the aim and relevance of this publication is to set the ground for and point forward to future research from this outset.

Target Audience
The target audience is, in short, e-government researchers and reflective practitioners within e-government including developers, project managers, and e-government decision makers in general. To communicate our offer to the target audience it is however relevant to identify what we mean by reflective practitioners. The term reflective practitioner as used here here was coined by Schön (1983). He used it to describe professional problem solving in practice in a world in which a traditional technical rationality was insufficient to explain the success and failure of professional doing. In this case, reflective practitioners reflect-in-action while they are doing e-government and they may on occasions step back and reflect-on-action to revitalise their e-government practice. The aim of the book is to unfold some of the complexity of e-government by feeding tools for thinking into reflection-in-action and reflection-on-action – that is *not* to deliver a manual with list of steps towards e-government or comprehensive lists on dos and don'ts. The overarching argument is that the field is complex in the sense that a full understanding builds on contributions from three quite diverse fields of research: Technology & infrastructure, politics & organisation and communication & interaction. The book also aims to unfold specific

problems, challenges and opportunities as they arise in theoretical and empirical studies within each of the three themes. In the following sections, we take a closer look at the three perspectives and introduce the individual studies and papers within the perspectives.

Three Perspectives – and their interrelations

The book is - just as the Centre for Electronic Governance - structured by the three themes and perspectives on e-Government:

- **Technology and infrastructure** (concentrating on emerging internet-based and mobile technologies enabling governance, and on the physical and conceptual infrastructures that underpin these technologies).
- **Politics and organisation** (reflecting both the democratic dimension of digital governance and its location in government organisations with particular characteristics and ways of working).
- **Communication and interaction** (focusing on the roles of computer-mediated discourse, socio-technical interaction and technology-facilitated work in governance).

Central is here to point out that these perspectives are used to focus and structure research but that they are interrelated and powerful when put together (cf. figure I).

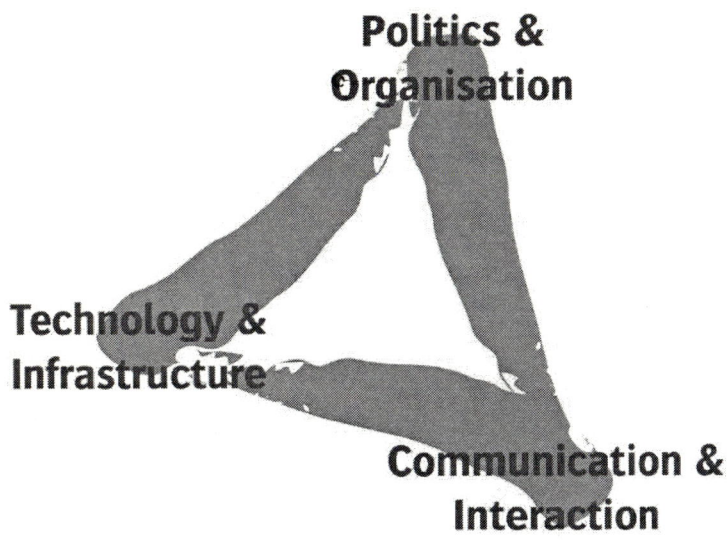

Figure 1: The three perspectives and interrelations for research in electronic governance.

Empirical Background

The empirical background for the Centre for Electronic Governance and a major part of the papers presented in this volume is the Digital North Denmark-project. In 1999, the Danish Government designated North Denmark a coming national IT lighthouse in its IT strategy. This decision was part of the national IT and Telecommunications Policy Strategy (Forskningsministeriet 2000). The policy was made with the aim to convert Denmark from an information society to a network society. A part of the strategy was to strengthen regions with an already proven IT-capacity and IT-development and North Jutland was selected as a cornerstone in the network society, to light up and show the way for the rest of Denmark (Forskningsministeriet 1999). In the years 2000-2003, the Ministry of Information Technology and Research invested DKK 170 mill. in the project. In addition to this came a regional co-financing from public and private enterprises of DKK 340 mill.

The project was named "The Digital North Denmark" and the overall goal was to explore the potentials of a network society for all citizens of North

Denmark. The democratic focus on "all citizens" resulted in an aim to establish a "wide ranging" IT-lighthouse which encouraged private companies, educational organisations, and even individual persons or communities to apply for funding and start experiments with Information and Communication Technology (ICT). Thus, the aim of the Digital North Denmark shifted from a focus on existing IT-strengths and their further development in the region to a focus on increasing IT-use in the region in order to strengthen the region as a whole and to create a "learning region" (Dalum & Pedersen 2004, 22-28).

The result was a total amount of 91 projects[1] categorised under the themes

- Digital administration (21 projects),
- Qualification and education (33 projects plus 11 projects on art and culture),
- IT industrial development (22 projects), and
- IT infrastructure (4 projects)

In addition, an independent participatory research group was established consisting of researchers from Aalborg University. The work in this participatory research group and not least the technological experimentation in the North Denmark in the years 2000-2004 has been an important basis and point of departure for the establishment of the centre for e-Government at Aalborg University – a cross disciplinary centre and research approach to electronic government which had its official opening at Aalborg University in April 2006. The first part of this book – the first two papers – presents this background: the Digital North Denmark-Project and the participatory research approach and experiences from the period.

The papers

The book is introduced with two papers presenting the empirical and methodological **background** of the centre:

Christian Richter Østergaard presents "The Digital North Denmark Programme - Promoting Regional Change?" - an analysis of the change strategy

---

[1] For further information see Dirckinck-Holmfeld et al. 2004 and http://www.detdigitalenordjylland.dk/en/welcome.htm.

in the Digital North Denmark and discusses the intended versus the implemented and realised strategy.

Lone Dirckinck-Holmfeld presents "Social Experiments and Participatory Research as Method" – a methodological reflection for participatory research as it has been carried out in the Participatory research group related to the Digital North Denmark as well as the perspectives this methodology brings for cross disciplinary participatory research in e-Government.

On this basis, papers are structured within the three themes: Technology & infrastructure, politics & organisation, and communication & interaction.

The theme **technology and infrastructure** is represented with two papers:

Jeremy Rose introduces this theme with the paper "Technology and Government: Extending the Double Dance of Agency". He theorises about the relation between information technology and government by introducing the concept of agency to e-government research.

Ole Brun Madsen presents "The Danish ICT Infrastructure Evolution Since 2000" - the importance of infrastructure in relation to e-government with reference to a large scale investigation of the needs and possibilities in a modern ICT infrastructure.

Within the theme **politics and organisation**, two papers present research results from the Digital North Denmark:

Lars Torpe introduces this theme with his paper "Local Political Deliberations on the Internet". He analyses the potentials of the Internet for political deliberation with focus on tools for citizen involvement and actual use and consequences of the tools.

Jeppe Agger Nielsen presents in "Digital Municipality Planning – Experiments with the Use of ICT-Tools in Democratic Processes" an investigation of the dialogue and communication possibilities in digital planning with reference to a case study in the municipality Hals.

Within the theme **communication and interaction**, four papers present research results from both the Digital North Denmark and related studies. The papers can be read as moving from a societal perspective with a paper focusing on citizenship (paper one) to an organisational perspective with two papers focusing on infrastructure (paper two) and implementation (paper three) to a use-perspective with a paper focusing on IT support (paper four).

Ellen Christiansen introduces this theme with the paper "Inclusiveness as a Parameter in Design of Online Interaction with Public Authorities " which discusses citizenship and e-Government and concludes by suggesting user driven innovation as a way for designing applications that enhance the experience of citizenship.

Ann Bygholm presents "Communicating Across Sectors in Health Care – A Case of Establishing a New Infrastructure" an analysis of the problems involved in application of ICT for communication and coordination in terms of the concept of infrastructure. The case being electronic exchange of information between municipality and hospital, and between municipality and the general practicing doctors.

Tom Nyvang and Camilla R. Poulsen present "Implementation of ICT in Government Organizations - User Driven or Management Driven?" reflections and analysis of two different strategies for implementing ICT in an organisation: A predominantly user driven and a predominantly management driven approach.

Anne Marie Kanstrup & Pernille Bertelsen present in their paper "Local IT-Support: Values, Characteristics, and Selection Methods" an analysis of local IT-support and suggest a method for identifying qualified candidates for IT-support positions in organisations.

References

Dalum, B. & Pedersen, C.Ø.R. (2004). DDN's historie, tilblivelse og profil (The History, Creation, and Profil of the Digital North Denmark). In: Dirckinck-Holmfeld, L. et al. (eds.). *Det Digitale Nordjylland - IKT og omstilling til netværkssamfundet? (The Digital North Denmark - ICT and change towards the network society)*. Aalborg: Aalborg Universitetsforlag 2004.

Dirckinck-Holmfeld, L. et al. (2004). *Det Digitale Nordjylland - IKT og omstilling til netværkssamfundet? (The Digital North Denmark - IT and conversion to the network society)*. Aalborg: Aalborg Universitetsforlag.

Forskningsministeriet (Ministry of Science, Technology and Innovation) (1999). *Det Digitale Danmark (The Digital Denmark)*. Forskningsministeriet (http://www.videnskabsministeriet.dk/cgi-bin/doc-show.cgi?doc_id=19166&doc_type=37&markwords=Det+digitale+danmark).

Forskningsministeriet (Ministry of Science, Technology and Innovation) (2000). *Omstilling til netværkssamfundet: IT- og telepolitisk redegørelse til Folketinget.* http://www.fsk.dk/fsk/publ/2000/omstilling.

Schön, D.A. (1983). *The Reflective Practitioner – How Professionals Think in Action.* Basic Book.

Part One
Background

The Digital North Denmark Programme – Promoting Regional Change?

Christian Richter Østergaard

> The Digital North Denmark (DDN) was a three-year IT-programme initiated in 2000 in the County of North Jutland, Denmark. This chapter analyses the history, planning, and intended versus realised implementation of DDN and investigates whether DDN promoted regional change. The theoretical framework is based on notions of radical, incremental, localised, and structural change. These are used to analyse the change from the initial profile to the implemented profile and the change in focus as well as the project types during the period. The profile of the programme changed from focusing on localised change targeting the producers of information and communication technology (ICT) in the region to initiating a radical change project focusing on the users. Dramatic external events also influenced the results. DDN was presented in 1999, when the ICT sector was booming, but it was implemented late 2000, when the ICT crisis had begun. The purpose of this chapter is to analyse how the shift from incremental to radical change has affected the programme and whether and how this shift may have had long-term consequences on the development perspectives for the regional ICT sector.

Introduction

The Digital North Denmark (DDN) was an IT-programme running from 2000 to 2003 in the North Jutland County in Denmark with national government support of € 23 million. The Danish government initiated the programme with the aim of further strengthening regions with an already proven information and communication technology (ICT) capability (Dybkjær and Lindegaard, 1999, p.96-100). The declared approach was to build on the existing competencies in industry as well as at universities. The national government chose two regions – Ørestaden, a new concentration of knowledge-based institutions near Copenhagen Airport, and North Jutland. The Copenhagen programme was basically concentrated on, literally, construction of a new IT University, a new-neighbouring science park and a new media centre for the public broadcaster, Danmarks Radio. The North Denmark programme was, on the other hand, organised as a large-scale experiment based on project-offers within four themes. The participants - meant to be project consortia of ideally private firms, public or private organisations as well as regional and municipal government bodies - could obtain a maximum national government support of one third of the total project sum.

The point of departure of the chapter is the theories of regional innovation policy based on localised change. Innovation policy is public action aimed to influence technical change and other kinds of innovation (Edquist, 1999). A policy programme is 'localised' if it is targeted to create incremental change in a region. It aims to reproduce and strengthen existing structures, but does not necessarily imply following deterministic trajectories, since unpredictable changes may occur and new variety is mainly directed and channelled by the existing environment (Dosi et al., 1988; Boschma, 2004). The challenge is to support the (positive) development path of the regional production system, while avoiding technological and institutional lock-in. It is not sufficient only to learn, but also important to unlearn at the company as well as at the policymaker level (Lorenzen, 2001).

The North Jutland region was chosen as 'IT-lighthouse' due to several reasons. It was considered to have a great ICT potential; it was well known for network cooperation between firms, university, science park and public organisations; it had experienced a process of structural change from being a crisis area in the 1980s to an ICT growth area in the 1990s, and it was home of a successful, international, visible, wireless communication cluster, NorCOM. The local university was considered to have been an important actor in the transformation process of the region and was intended to become a key player in establishing the 'IT lighthouse'. Since the 1980s, the region had been supported by several EU programmes and the county administration had proved to be quite experienced in organising support programmes based on project offers. The proven capability of cooperation between private and public organisations, the wireless cluster firms, and the university were considered as key features. The policy programme, however, faced some tension in the formulation of a goal: Could the successful cluster be used to develop other parts of the ICT sector, or should the programme be used to promote development broadly in the region?

During the implementation of the programme, this profile was significantly changed. The wireless cluster firms and the university were largely missing as participants and some of the large projects revealed a lack of cooperation between firms and public organisations. Dramatic external events also influenced the results. DDN was presented in 1999, when the ICT sector was booming, but implemented from late 2000, when the ICT crisis had begun.

The purpose of this chapter is to analyse how the shift from incremental to radical change has affected the programme and whether and how this shift may have had long-term consequences for the development perspectives for the regional ICT sector.

This chapter investigates how the profile of the programme changed from focusing on localised change targeting the producers of ICT in the region, into initiation of a radical change project focusing on the users. In addition to the more historical accounts for DDN, the actual implementation will also be analysed. The analyses of development perspectives for the regional ICT sector will focus on the participation of the university and the cluster.

The chapter contains a discussion of the theoretical approach. Then it presents an analysis of the structural change in the 1990s with an emphasis on the ICT sector, and analyses the history of DDN and the shaping of its final profile. Furthermore, it deals with the actual implementation and DDN's impact on the development perspectives of the ICT sector. Then the period after DDN is analysed. Finally, the conclusions are presented.

Incremental versus radical change in regional innovation policy

In recent years, a variety of regional policies have been used as tools for development of peripheral regions in Europe. The role of regional policy and its effectiveness has been debated in the literature (see e.g. Cooke, 2001; Lorenzen, 2001). One of the main issues is whether it is at all possible to create more fundamental change in the development trajectory of a region through public policy or whether the only realistic aim for policies is to improve existing structures and avoid lock-in, as stated by Edquist (1999):

> *"..'lock-in' failures imply a role for policy in adapting to shifts in new technologies and demand. This means that a key issue is the choice between supporting existing systems (with their historically accumulated learning and knowledge bases) and supporting the development of radically new technologies and supporting systems"* (Edquist, 1999, p.17)

Innovation is a complex phenomenon, embracing products, processes and services. It includes technological as well as organisational innovations (Edquist, 1999). It is also a pervasive phenomenon, which penetrates all aspects of economic life, and is a result of on-going processes of learning, searching and exploring (Lundvall, 1992). Thus innovation is a powerful explanatory factor behind differences in performance among regions. Regions with a successful innovative activity prosper while less innovative regions are lagging behind. Therefore, regions that want to catch-up must increase their innovative activity (Fagerberg, 2005).

Freeman and Soete (1997) classify innovations according to how radical and incremental they are compared to the existing technology. This approach can also be applied to the change in industry structure. The innovations are then classified according to how radical they are compared to the current structure.

Radical innovation is major change that represents a new technological paradigm. Radical change implies that the codes developed to communicate a cumulatively changing technology will become inadequate (Rogers, 1995). The producers that follow a given trajectory will have problems understanding and evaluating the potentials of the new paradigm (Lundvall, 1992, p. 58). *Radical* change creates a high degree of uncertainty in organisations and industry. It also sweeps away significant parts of previous investments in technical skills and knowledge, designs, production techniques, plants and equipment (Utterback, 1994, p. 200). The change is not necessarily delimited to the supply side. It may come from a change at the demand side and in the organisational or institutional structure. Incremental innovation, on the other hand, is gradual and cumulative.

Incremental innovations are only small changes in technology, organisations, processes, products or services. Subsequently *incremental* change refers to continuous improvements and changes in the current industry structure.

Boschma (2004) distinguishes between two ideal types of aims for regional policy: 'localised' versus 'structural' change. *Localised* change is following the development trajectory based on the existing structure in the region. The change is location-specific and determined by the past, which defines the limits. It is incremental and cumulative and reproduces and strengthens existing structures. The (positive) cumulative change and path dependence may, however, result in a lock-in, which at a later stage may produce negative effects. When a region is facing technological and institutional lock-in, it becomes vulnerable to external changes in the economy.

According to Maskell et al. (1998), each region has a set of capabilities that consist of the institutional background, the structure of industry, natural resources, knowledge and skills. These have been developed through a historical, interactive process. Further evolution relies on the creation, utilisation and reproduction of knowledge. Public and private organisations affect the regions through creation and demand of skills and knowledge. But the organisations are also outcomes of the existing structure and institutions in the region (Storper, 1997). New variety is thus mainly directed and channelled by the existing environment. Localised change is cumulative and path dependent, but not deterministic and predictable, and bound to end in a lock-in situation (Boschma, 2004).

Structural change is more dramatic. It is based on technological, organisational and institutional transformation and relies on creative destruction (Boschma, 2004). It implies a shift of the regional development trajectory. A lot of uncertainty is related to the structural change. The outcome is less predictable. The element of chance is high, since small historical events may be reinforced by agglomeration economics and spinoffs. Such processes are well known from the studies of regional industrial clusters (Krugman, 1991; Pedersen, 2005). But the speed of change is not necessarily high (Boschma, 2004). Structural change is not immediate, but new trajectories emerge and develop gradually. Structural change points at transformation of the industrial structure of a region. But new trajectories develop gradually or incrementally in most cases. It could be expected that many incremental changes may accumulate a structural change over time. However, the more radical the change is the greater the possibility that it may also require improvements of infrastructure, and organisational and social changes to succeed.

The goal of policy programmes can target 'long-run' structural change or focus on localised change. This distinction is, however, often blurred in reality – i.e. hidden in the rhetoric of the programme declarations. The notions of incremental versus radical innovation are easier to distinguish and to make operational. A policy programme based on experiments can exemplify this. When initiating a programme, it is possible for the policy makers to outline a goal and set a frame for the experiments. If it is based on project offers, the outcome is partly defined by the applicants. The policy makers can set some requirements in the tender material and carry out selection among the applications. This makes the potential outcome of the programme uncertain. The individual projects also have a higher degree of uncertainty, and some are likely to fail. Variety is created in the regional system since the organisations are involved in different search strategies. A localised policy programme based on experimentation at firm level would contain some projects focused on incremental and others on radical change. The latter are novel and could introduce new technologies or consumption patterns etc. Some of these could change the development trajectory for parts of the region and, over time, lead to a structural change. The radical and structural change is sometimes argued to be the most important for changes in the industry structure, while others argue that the cumulative impact of incremental changes is just as great and therefore the continuous incremental changes lead to structural change over time.

If we look at policies for structural change, there is a difference between national and regional policies. At the national level, polices are associated with creating new industries (becoming first mover) or catching up, and usually not directed towards specific regions. Public procurement appears to have been the most successful in this respect (Lundvall, 1992; Edquist, 1997). This instrument can also be effective at regional level, where a boost from public demand or a clear expression of will/support can reduce uncertainty related to innovation. The effect is of course not known ex ante, since the evolution is still uncertain. But as argued by e.g. Mowery and Nelson (1999), there have been successes as well as failures in public policies targeting radical changes in industry structure. Lundvall and Borrás (2005) point at limits for the public sector's competence in technology policy. They argue that technology policy might be pursued where the public sector operates as a major or lead user, while it should be more cautious when it comes to developing specific, new technologies for the market.

There is some tension between policy support of diversity and scale in an innovation system. The more open an innovation system is for impulses from outside the system, the less risk to miss promising new development paths that emerge outside (Fagerberg, 2005).

Innovation policy must take point of departure in the existing innovation system. The analytical basis of the innovation policy is a combination of 'what is good practice' and what are the characteristics of the innovation system (Lundvall and Borrás, 2005). Therefore, the innovation policy is often incremental since policy makers are more likely to take point of departure in existing development trajectories. Regional innovation policies are sensitive to the regional endowment, trajectories and context. Localised polices should take regional variety as a point of departure, and be based on a bottom-up strategy attuned to the needs and resources of the regions (Maskell et al., 1998; Cooke, 2001; Boschma, 2004). However, it is also necessary to mobilise the actors in the system to participate and interact to develop socially relevant and clear policy programmes that can be implemented successfully (Lundvall and Borrás, 2005, p. 614).

In summary, the theories state that there is a difference between regional policies, targeting incremental change, and radical change. The incremental change policy aims at strengthening the existing structure, while the radical change policy aims at changing this structure. However, from a regional policy perspective, it is necessary to take point of departure in the needs and competences of the regions, and to mobilise users and producers. There is no simple policy solution or recommendation, but initiating incremental change requires mobilisation of the targeted actors, while radical change involves more risk taking and requires willingness to change, but still implies mobilisation of regional actors.

The North Jutland region – from lagging behind to catching up

The North Jutland County is located at the northern tip of the peninsula of Jutland, the part of Denmark connected to the European continent. The population is around half a million people, slightly less than one tenth of the Danish total. Total employment was 246,500 persons in 1999, of which the private sector share was 163,500. The largest city is Aalborg, the fourth largest in Denmark, with 163,000 inhabitants. The region has traditionally been characterised as peripheral and lagging behind with an unemployment rate among the highest in Denmark. The industry structure has been dominated by more traditional industries, such as agriculture and food processing, fishery, tourism, shipyards, textiles, tobacco and cement. However, during the late 1980s and the 1990s, the region experienced a process of structural change with jobs moving from the traditional sectors to the service and the high-tech sectors. Although the firms in North Jutland are still specialised within the primary sector (i.e. an above national average employment share) and within the metal product industry, they are also specialised in especially mechanical engineering as well as in electronics. The latter has been among the features which indicate that the region has caught up. At present, the industry structure is in line with the average Danish 'non-metropolitan' counties. The two 'metropolitan' regions are the greater Copenhagen area and Aarhus. The region has undergone a structural change, but still has structural problems, and has an above average unemployment rate and a below average income compared to the Danish average (Dalum et al., 2005).

Aalborg University (AAU) plays an important role in North Jutland. It was established in 1974 and has today 13,000 students and 1,700 employees in Humanities, Engineering, Natural Sciences and Social Sciences. Until 2000, AAU was the one of only two universities in Denmark that offered the MSc in engineering and, in the 1990s, approximately fifty percent of the Danish MSc's in engineering graduated from AAU. From its establishment, AAU has been very active in cooperation with private firms and it participates in many networks and joint research projects. Almost 40% of the total number of graduates from the university got their first job in the region (Nielsen et al., 2002, p. 81).

From 1986, the region has been supported with several EU Programmes due to the crisis in North Jutland especially in fishing, shipbuilding from the last half of the 1980s and the structural problems with a high unemployment rate[1]. Especially the Objective 2-funds for Industrial Reconversion have been used to promote the structural change in the region[2]. In the period from 1986 to 1999, the region was supported with € 210 million from the EU, which generated additionally € 247 million in support from Danish public organisations and € 302 million from private firms. In comparison, the DDN programme was financed by € 23 million in public support and the current Objective 2 EU-programme running from 2000 to 2006 has received € 246 million in public support. The evaluation reports of the EU programmes indicate that the overall effect has been positive for the region, but due to their fragmented nature, the direct effect in terms of employment and indirect effects e.g. creation of networks is difficult to measure[3]. The direct effect of DDN is expected to be smaller than Objective 2 due to the difference in size. The North Jutland County administration has been the administrator of the EU programmes, i.e. organising the project offers, putting together the financing, attracting external partners, and other related tasks. Through this work, the County Administration created competencies and established a wide network to the different participating actors, which were useful in the DDN programme.

The ICT-sector in North Jutland before the DDN-programme

The ICT sector in North Jutland had experienced high growth during the 1990s. Employment grew with 63.5% from 1992 to 1999 compared with a growth of 33.7% at national level. Total ICT employment[4] was 8,300 in 1999, but the region has not been specialised in ICT employment. The specialisation indicator

---

[1] From 1980 to 1992, the average unemployment rate in North Jutland was 2.5-3 percentage points higher than the national average (Ministry of Industry, 1994).
[2] The programmes have been quite broad in their objectives, e.g. the Objective 2 programme for Industrial Reconversion has supported projects with physical investments in private companies, knowledge building projects in private companies, knowledge building projects with soft framework conditions, infrastructure, education in firms and education with soft framework conditions.
[3] Http://www.nja.dk/serviceomraader/erhvervogarbejdsmarked/euprogrammer/resultaterafnordjy skeeuprogrammer.htm
[4] The ICT sector is defined as the following industrial classification codes NACE/DB(93): 3001, 3002, 3130, 3210, 3220, 3230, 331020, 331030, 331090, 3320, 3300, 514320, 516410, 516520, 6420, 713310, 72.

increased from 0.7 to 0.8 during the period. The region has been catching up from a rather low level.

The structure of the ICT sector in North Jutland is different from the overall Danish structure, since 45% of the employment was in manufacturing compared to 25% at national level. Specialisation in ICT manufacturing increased during the 1990s from 1.05 to 1.5 concentrated on two segments, telecommunications equipment and electronic components. Table 1 reveals that especially employment growth in telecom hardware has been outstanding with an increase from a three to nearly six times larger employment share compared to the national average.

	Speciali-sation		North Jutland				Denmark	
			Employ-ment	Share of ICT	Development 1992-99	Change	Share of ICT	Development 1992-99
	1992	1999	(persons)	(%)	(1992=100)	(persons)	(%)	(1992=100)
Manufacturing	1.05	1.51	3,731	44.9	**150.3**	1,248	25.3	104.3
Office machinery	4.33	6.81	288	3.5	**116.1**	40	0.4	73.7
Computers	0.70	0.36	52	0.6	48.1	-56	1.5	94.4
Electronic components and wire	1.55	1.14	511	6.2	81.2	-118	4.6	110.2
Telecommunications equipment	3.13	5.92	1,936	23.3	**207.3**	1,002	3.4	109.5
Consumer electronics	0.27	0.89	467	5.6	392.4	348	5.4	120.1
Electro medical	0.48	0.42	193	2.3	84.3	-36	4.7	95.5
Instruments etc.	0.41	0.55	284	3.4	131.5	68	5.3	98.1
Services	0.53	0.63	4,573	55.1	176.2	1,978	74.7	147.7
Wholesale trade	0.33	0.35	846	10.2	137.6	231	24.5	127.9
Telecommunications	0.62	0.99	1,777	21.4	**200.8**	892	18.4	125.2
IT services & software	0.67	0.63	1,950	23.5	178.1	855	31.9	190.1
Total ICT sector	0.70	0.85	8,304	100	163.5	3,226	100	133.7

Note: The specialisation indicator is the share of ICT employment of the total employment compared with the national average. A value above 1 indicates an above average employment share - i.e. the county is specialised. Specialised industries and a positive change in employment is marked in bold. The data is from November that year. Source: Based on data from Statistics Denmark.

Table 1: The structure of the ICT sector in North Jutland

A special feature of the ICT sector in North Jutland is the presence of a wireless communication cluster mainly consisting of firms working with mobile communication equipment and equipment for maritime communication and navigation. In 1999, the cluster consisted of 30 firms, which employed more than 40% of the total number of employees in the ICT sector and a large share of these was related to R&D activities (for a detailed analysis of the development of the cluster, see Dalum et al, 2005). The cluster had grown out of a few maritime communication firms from the late 1970s and had experienced high growth in the 1990s. It attracted many subsidiaries of large multinational companies. The cluster was thus an important part of the entire ICT sector and it also attracted a lot of attention at national level due to its success and international profile during the last half of 1990s.

DDN, innovation system, innovation policy, and the ICT sector

The basis for innovation policy is an analysis of the innovation system with point of departure in the existing knowledgebase, institutional context, regional industry specialisation, and how the system produces and reproduces knowledge and competences. Thus deliberate innovation policy is often focused on incremental change by following the existing trajectories.

The terms radical and incremental change are classified according to how radical they are compared to the current structure. Therefore, a programme targeted at the ICT sector in North Jutland would be incremental if it focused on cumulative improvement of the existing structure including the cluster. Radical change implies a shift of the regional development trajectory. To promote this, the focus could be on the more dispersed, but promising activities in the ICT sector The radical and incremental change could both be supported by the university since it provides a supply of qualified labour and since it has top-level research groups in knowledge bases that are not or only little present in the existing industrial structure. The radical change could then stem from the university through spinoffs or joint projects.

The DDN programme was to be an experiment, based on project-offers, and not necessarily include local ICT firms (due to competition rules). These three features are important, since the first implies a higher degree of failure, the second increases the uncertainty profile and outcome, and the third lessens the effect on the regional ICT sector, unless the non-local firms are attracted and open affiliates.

The history of DDN and the shaping of the profile

The early formation of DDN programme prior to the first project offer in June 2000 can be divided into the invitation from the government and the response from the region. The concept behind DDN was changed considerably within a period of six months.

Why North Denmark? The minister's invitation and The Digital Denmark report

At the 25 year anniversary of Aalborg University in September 1999, the Minister of Research and Information Technology invited the region of North Jutland to build an 'IT Lighthouse'. The programme was a part of the government's ICT strategy for 'The Digital Denmark'.

The strategy was further described in a report in November 1999 from the ministry "*The Digital Denmark – conversion to the network society*" on how Denmark should evolve from an information society into a network society (Dybkjær and Lindegaard, 1999). One of the policy measures to achieve the goal was the creation of two IT lighthouses: one in Copenhagen and one in North Jutland. While the programme in Copenhagen focused on creating infrastructure, the DDN programme was to be an experiment (Dybkjær and Lindegaard, 1999, p. 90-93). The rhetoric was very ambitious about creating internationally visible IT lighthouses that should be 'cornerstones' of the network society, and 'light up and show the way' for the rest of Denmark. They were inspired by international ICT growth areas, and believed that focused public policy had played an important role in the development of these. The purpose of DDN was to further strengthen and develop the strong growth in the ICT sector after the 1990s.

> "*An IT lighthouse should be established in Northern Jutland on the basis of the very positive co-operation which has already been established between enterprises, Aalborg University, Northern Jutland's Science Park (Nordjyllands Videnpark – NOVI) and central*

political decision makers in the area." (Dybkjær and Lindegaard, 1999, p.90)

The government wanted to build an IT lighthouse, but did not directly define what it was. A clear description of an IT lighthouse cannot be found in the background report for the policy programme. Although the rhetoric in the report makes parallels to Silicon Valley, Kista and Oulu it would be wrong to conclude that the intention was to create radical change by building a new Danish Silicon Valley. But it seems clear that the purpose was to support incremental change of the existing strengths in the ICT sector, i.e. the wireless communications cluster. The goal of incremental change is also supported by the argument of building on the existing network cooperation between public and private organisations.

"The purpose of a large-scale experiment in Northern Jutland, an IT lighthouse, is to promote development in an area which has already shown that it contains great IT potential, with private enterprises, Aalborg University and NOVI as driving forces. The large-scale experiment should promote IT development and IT use and, via concrete projects, kick-start life into the network society." (Dybkjær and Lindegaard, 1999, p.91)

When providing the invitation in September 1999, the Minister stressed that it was required that the public organisations, the university and private firms cooperated on designing a programme and building the IT Lighthouse.

"In a large-scale experiment, Northern Jutland could be Denmark's first IT lighthouse via the activities which have already been commenced and via a number of prioritised initiatives which should be formulated in partnership between the Government, decision-makers in Northern Jutland and the private enterprises in the area" (Dybkjær and Lindegaard, 1999, p.91)

Given that the proposal was presented at the university anniversary it was a common belief at least among the university employees that the programme would get a strong research profile based on joint research projects with private firms. The fear was that the DDN programme would be used to support many fragmented small projects like a traditional development programme for less favoured regions.

The response from the region

In September 1999, it was believed that a quick response was needed to show that North Jutland was able to fulfil the task. The county administration established a regional interim board consisting of the county mayor, the mayor of the municipality of Aalborg, the mayor of the municipality of Hjørring, the rector of Aalborg University and representatives from the Danish Trade Union Congress, the Confederation of Danish Industries and the Danish Employers' Confederation.

After six weeks, the result was a report on why North Jutland should be an ICT lighthouse, a vision of how it should be built and a roadmap for the further work. The vision for North Jutland consisted of ten points (The North Jutland County, 1999, p.36-38, www.detdigitalenordjylland.dk):

- *North Jutland should become a learning region*
- *North Jutland should have a strong and coherent educational system that is in the front in Denmark*
- *North Jutland should have high level research within IT*
- *North Jutland should have education and continuing education for the future worker*
- *North Jutland should have a strong service industry*
- *North Jutland should have leading development and sales firms within IT*
- *In North Jutland all citizens should have direct or indirect access to a computer and to the Internet*
- *In North Jutland use of e-business and e-services should be widespread among the citizens*
- *North Jutland should provide good framework conditions for private firms.*

- *North Jutland should have a public sector that is the most open in Denmark with good service accessible 24 hours a day*

Almost every 'politically correct' goal was included. The bullet points did not express any clear selection or choice. The list included both objects of radical and incremental change, and even some points that were already fulfilled (e.g. leading development and sales firms within IT). However, a new focus on improving the efficiency and quality of the public sector had been included. The effectiveness in the private sector was also stressed.

By fulfilling the 10 points, it was believed that the productivity in the private and public sector would increase. The rationale was that the technological development would not result in rationalisation and increase in productivity in itself, without a joint effort from education and organisational development. IT was not considered a goal, but a mean to build the lighthouse. To create positive synergies, it was stated that the forthcoming experiments should be large and comprehensive in order to 'make a difference'. The selected experiments should be able to reach and be important for a large proportion of the citizens of North Jutland (The North Jutland County, 1999, p.42).

It was specified that an important part of the vision was North Jutland as a learning region. There was, however, no clear definition of this concept, although the keywords were ability and will among citizens, firms and other organisations to change, renew, innovate, learn, cooperate and to build new capabilities, networks and supporting institutions (The North Jutland County, 1999)[5]. These are the principles underlying structural change, but the means were of an incremental nature. The profile of DDN had thus begun to change from having a focus on research, industrial development of the ICT sector and networks between university and firms, to become broadly user-orientated with a wider purpose of IT education, application and diffusion.

The DDN organisation was to consist of a board of directors with the responsibility to select the themes of the programme in cooperation with the ministry. It was also to appoint[6]: Project groups connected to each theme; a board of executives with responsibility for the practical implementation; project

---

[5] Dybkjær and Lindegaard (1999) do not use the term learning region.
[6] In addition, they wanted to nominate an independent participatory research group consisting of university researchers to carry out research in relation to the DDN.

groups with responsibility for selecting the winning projects; and a secretariat with responsibility for all the practical work.

The interim board of directors was almost identical in the new DDN organisation. The editors of the report[7] were to be a part of the board of executives (The North Jutland County, 1999, p.48). The board of directors included a wide selection of interest groups to secure a broad acceptance in the region, especially among the municipalities. The selection of specific actors in the two boards strongly influenced the DDN profile.

The wireless communications cluster and the university were little included in the plans for DDN[8], but the building of the lighthouse could still offer opportunities for these actors.

Building the lighthouse

The discussions of the DDN programme became intensified after the region's response in November 1999. In the report it was stated that the final profile could still be changed. As a result, various ideas of the implementation of the programme flourished. The report on DDN had described a roadmap for the building of the lighthouse. The board of directors was to decide upon four themes and the profile and then appoint four project groups to select the projects. DDN was to be organised as project offers within the four themes.

Three different profiles were competing for dominance in the large-scale experiment (see also Bruun, 2001):

1. The industry innovation orientated profile that stressed the importance of industrial development through innovation and cooperation with the university.
2. The research-orientated profile that had a point of departure in the university research projects with industry
3. The user-orientated profile that focused on extensive use of IT.

---

[7] The editors were the clerk of the county council and the university director.
[8] The phrases of 'development of the ICT sector' and networks with the university' had been toned down in the report.

The planning phase and the final programme

The board of directors was officially appointed in February 2000. Their first task was to further specify the four themes and to appoint the four projects groups. But this work had already begun in advance. During December and January, the themes were specified and enrolment of actors to the project groups and mobilisation of actors to create ideas and projects had begun.

The director of the Lighthouse Secretariat joined the board after her appointment in the spring 2000. The board thus included a wide selection of groups to secure a broad acceptance of the programme and to mobilise as many actors as possible. The selection was, however, dominated by political and organisational interests, and the interest of the ICT sector was given low priority.

The profile was, however, not definitely decided upon in mid-January. The heads of the county and the university administrations, both members of the board of executives publicly expressed opposing views. They admitted that the 'fight' could be whether the money should be used broadly for IT experiments within the population of North Jutland or more narrowly in targeted research. The head of the university administration argued that the funds should be used to increase the present high level of the ICT sector while the head of the county administration argued that the funds should only be invested in projects with a (short-run) return[9].

In January 2000, the four themes were selected[10]: IT Infrastructure, IT Industrial Development, Qualification and Education, and Digital Administration.

A project group was attached to each theme, which was to participate in the selection of winning projects from the forthcoming project call. Their first task was to create a project strategy and frame. Based on this, each group should select the best projects, and the board of directors would afterwards appoint the winners. A professor from the university was selected as chairman for the first theme. A managing director from a private firm was selected for group two, a chief executive from a municipality for theme three and a director from the

---

[9] Thorhauge, Claus "Nordjysk IT fyrtårn leder efter ideer" Computerworld 14 January 2000
[10] The names of the themes are a bit different in January, but they are covering the same areas: Infrastructure, E-business and technological framework conditions, IT in the public sector, and Qualification and Education.

county administration became chairman for theme four. The four groups consisted of up to nine members and had a strong influence on public organisations. The groups worked from April to June on the description of the four themes in the project offers.

In February 2000, the Ministry of Research and Information Technology approved the DDN programme. Although no project call had been made, the work continued on the sidelines. In mid-February, several forthcoming DDN projects appeared in the media[11]. The head of the county administration argued e.g. for a project that included a PC for all the public sector employees in North Jutland. This idea was, however, never turned into a specified proposal.

The DDN secretariat was also established in spring 2000 and a head of the secretariat was hired from the Aalborg municipality administration. She represented the broad user-orientated profile of DDN that became dominant. This appointment also clearly indicated the direction of DDN. The profile had been changed from the original idea described in the Dybkjær and Lindegaard (1999) report and in the minister's speech in September 1999. The profile was not specified to build on the existing industrial and research strength in region, but to broaden the use of IT to lift the entire region and create a learning region. The project was not to focus on a single sector but all sectors and not to concentrate on a single problem or area, but to 'cover all of them' (The Lighthouse Secretariat, 2000, p. 5).

The allocation of funds to the four themes in the first round of project offers assisted the user-orientated profile[12]:

- IT Infrastructure received € 2 million
- IT Industrial Development € 2 million
- Qualification and Education € 4 million
- Digital Administration € 2.7 million.

---

[11] Special supplement to Computerworld 28 February 2000
[12] Of the total project sum of € 23 million, € 21 million were allocated to projects, whereas the rest were to cover administration costs, participatory research and evaluation. Approximately 50% of the funds were allocated to the first project offer.

How the university was put on the sideline and the missing participation of the wireless cluster firms

In spring 2000, the Ministry of Finance decided that the national government were not to pay more than a third of the total project sum. This meant special rules for public financed organisations and organisations that wanted to use EU Objective 2 funds for the DDN projects. As a result, the university could not use regular funds or let the employees participate as a part of the two-thirds of the funding that had to be self-provided. To participate, the university had to use external funding for the projects or let the potential project partners pay the total funding. It was believed by many university people that this put an end to university participation in DDN projects and clearly influenced its profile.

The funding rules did stop many project ideas, but the university still managed to become partner in some projects through special arrangements. But DDN did not become as research-oriented as the university believed it should have been. Analysis of the timing of events and processes, however, indicate that the user-orientated profile of DDN was already determined, and that the university was put on the sideline before the ministry decided on the rules for funding. Researchers from AAU participated in 15 % of the DDN projects (The Lighthouse Secretariat, 2003). In terms of university research groups, the participation had moved away from the technical disciplines to the more 'soft' research fields.

The missing participation by the wireless communications cluster firms became evident during the project offers. They only participated in six of the total 90 DDN projects. The main participants were the service provider Sonofon and L.M. Ericsson, while other cluster firms only participated in two small projects. There were no representatives from the cluster or from the ICT sector in the regional interim board of directors who wrote the initial DDN report. Later on, a member from the cluster was included in the board of directors, but as a representative for the local Confederation of Danish Industries.

The DDN profile clearly did not encourage the cluster firms to participate. The IT infrastructure theme was focused on the fixed network and the IT industrial theme was mainly directed at e-business. Why the cluster was only sparsely involved in shaping the DDN profile is still unclear. But it could be related to the boom in the industry in 1999-2000. The main problems within the cluster were the increasing wages and the lack of qualified labour. The cluster firms had plenty of projects with a higher priority than DDN. However, before the first round of project offers, the cluster association arranged meetings to mobilise members to participate in the DDN programme. The cluster association wanted to secure that the DDN policy programme did not become a failure that could have negative reputation effects for the region.

Although only six DDN projects had participation by cluster firms, there was a group of projects that included mobile e-business and diffusion of the mobile phone platform to various industries. These areas were in the periphery of the focus of the wireless communications firms.

What determined the broad, user–oriented DDN profile

Bruun (2001) analysed the initiation and the first steps of implementation of DDN as a process. He described five determinants in shaping of the broad, user-orientated profile:

- Strong commitment from the leadership of influential public organisations
- The composition of the DDN organisation
- Formal mode of operation
- Ministry rules for funding
- Appointment of the director of the lighthouse secretariat

These five factors seem, however, not to be mutually independent. It seems that the strong commitment from the leadership of influential public organisations lead to the broad user-orientated profile. The ministry rules for funding have weakened the 'university preferred' research-orientated interpretation, but it seems as if the user-orientated profile already dominated when the ministry issued the rules. The appointment of the director of the lighthouse secretariat with a profile that supported the user-driven DDN interpretation is more a consequence and underlining of the already selected DDN profile[13].

---

[13] The director had been involved in the writing of the initial report, but it is unclear to what extent, see Bruun (2001).

A possible determinant is somehow missing in the list. The ICT sector was booming and there was a widespread fear that the public sector was lagging behind. The solution to this problem could be to diffuse ICT broadly in society and to upgrade the use of ICT in the local public administration and other public organisations. This fear combined with the strong commitment from the public sector and the exclusion of representatives from the ICT sector seem to have outlined the final DDN profile.

DDN and the shift from radical to incremental change

Many of the first round projects in autumn 2000 were 'high profiled', i.e. large projects with many participants and high ambitions. They were mainly focusing on radical change. The enrolment of many public organisations had clearly created a bulk of applications, but also other organisations felt that they had to participate due to the commercial value and to avoid that DDN became a failure. The prestige attached to DDN also attracted participants.

The DDN secretariat received 118 project-applications and 44 projects were selected as winners in the first round (The Lighthouse Secretariat, 2001). The € 11 million in support generated a total project sum of € 50 million[14]. The distribution was:

- The IT infrastructure theme received 10 applications and 4 winners were selected.
- IT industrial development received 33 applications and 12 winners were selected.
- Digital Administration received 24 applications and 7 winners were selected.
- Qualification and Education received 51 projects applications and 21 winners were selected.

The aims of the projects were very diverse and could be characterised as let a thousand flowers bloom. Among the high profile and ambitious projects were:

---

[14] The funding given to each theme varied slightly from the expected amount, the expected amounts are noted.

- The Digital County Administration and The Open Municipality on digitalising the county administration and the administrative procedures in the municipalities.
- North Jutland Netforum planning an optical fibre based infrastructure.
- TV2 Nord Digital broadcasting digital TV with interactive services among the first in Europe.
- Personal, Mobilised Broadband Services using front line technology and creating and testing the future home mobile broadband services.
- The Digital Mall was to be the electronic shopping site on the Internet preferred by citizens of North Jutland.
- E-business between private companies and the North Jutland county administration, a full-scale e-business solution.
- Digital Villages in North Denmark, an effort to maintain and develop the rural districts as vital enterprising and viable local communities and to attract new inhabitants to the villages.

Later on, many of the 'high profile' projects had to adjust their goals and change methods to complete the projects. Some of the projects shifted from radical to incremental change. The international crisis in the ICT sector also had a major influence because it fundamentally changed the beliefs on what was possible and what was not.

In the later rounds of project offers, the winning projects were more focused and specific than the first projects, i.e. more focused on incremental rather than on radical change. The themes were also more specific in the later projects offers (The Lighthouse Secretariat, 2002):

- Qualification and Education with a focus on democracy, children and young persons, and adults with weak IT competencies in the spring 2001 (€ 3.6 million).
- Digital Administration with a focus on the healthcare system in the summer 2001 (€ 3.4 million).
- IT Industrial Development with a focus on competitiveness in small and medium sized firms in the summer 2001 (€ 2.4 million).

- Qualification and Education with a focus on art, culture and IT in the network society in early 2002 (€ 0.9 million).

But although the themes in the later projects offers became more coherent and the type of projects changed, it does not change the overall picture of DDN as a very wide range of projects.

Due to the large variety in the projects, it is hard to compare the success rate of the first round projects with the other rounds to see if the incremental projects were more or less successful than the radical projects. The projects on digitalisation of the county administration or the hospital sector could potentially have a huge effect on the public sector and could, when completed, be a success factor for DDN. Also radical change projects from the first round on creating the Digital Mall, broadcasting interactive Digital TV and planning (and building) a fibre based infrastructure for the entire region could be important parts in making DDN a success. These large projects could have had a larger and more visible impact on the region than the many differing, smaller DDN projects. They clearly contained elements of radical change from the outset.

The goal of the Digital Mall was to be the electronic shopping site on the Internet preferred by citizens of North Jutland. However, it ended shortly after the take-off basically because a 'focus group' approach based on a series of interviews with potential customers clearly indicated that consumers were not willing to pay the extra costs for the new services. The county administration considered joining the project or using the e-business solution, but decided to build a separate e-business solution as a part of the Digital County Administration. A group of municipalities including the large municipality of Aalborg also decided to create separate e-business solutions as a part of DDN. If these projects had merged, it would maybe have been possible to create a commercial, sustainable digital mall, since the joined effort could have created a large volume and a lot of publicity, but cooperation, common will and vision were not established to the necessary extent.

The Digital TV project intended to transmit digital TV with interactive services among the first in Europe. Although the project progressed fairly slowly, it attracted a lot of attention from other TV stations, whereas interest from the large equipment manufactures was sparse and the project turned out to be a success in terms of technology and users. However, in late 2003, the Danish government decided upon a less ambitious plan to begin broadcasting from April 2006, which partly undermined the project.

The IT infrastructure project wanted to design local, optical fibre based network solutions, which would bring broadband to local government organisations as well as to private firms and consumers. The project could - if implemented - make the IT infrastructure in North Jutland the most advanced in Denmark and in most of Europe. This would create a visible and lasting effect on DDN. The public sector was important to boost the project. However, the North Jutland County has been very slow to react, while other Danish counties have been faster. The County of North Jutland have left the initiative to private actors and seems to have missed the opportunity of becoming a 'lead user' in this field.

DDN and the development of the ICT sector in North Jutland

DDN generated 90 winner projects with a total sum of € 90 million, which was considerable higher than the expected sum of minimum € 64 million, i.e. the government funding of the projects was on average less than one fourth (The Lighthouse Secretariat, 2003). The projects were initiated during 2000 to 2002 and have been concluded continuously.

On the positive side, the DDN programme created lots of ideas, initiated many projects and constituted a large commercial value for the region for a rather modest government support compared to the Objective 2 funds. Interviews with participants conducted during 2002 and 2003 reveal that the programme has formed networks between firms and public organisation that may contribute positively to the development perspectives for the ICT sector in North Jutland. There were some success stories of small local IT service firms who benefited from the programme, and many projects where participation was considered positive, but with an uncertain overall effect.

ICT firms participated in many of the 90 projects as project partners or suppliers of software services and hardware. The impact of DDN on the development perspectives of the ICT sector in North Jutland is blurred, since the ICT firms participated in different ways and not all of the participants were located in North Jutland. It is also important to distinguish between ICT firms that participated as suppliers of standard software and hardware and firms that developed software and services that were more specific towards the project. The latter group could experience a competence enhancement and create externalities that would affect the development perspectives more positively than the pecuniary effect on sales. The description of projects reveals that ICT firms participated in more than 40 projects, but the scope of the projects are varying and the internal competence building is not possible to assess without more thorough analysis that is beyond the scope of this chapter.

The Danish ICT sector has had a remarkable growth in employment and number of firms from 1992 to 2000. The growth in ICT stopped in 2000 when the sector went from boom to burst and employment declined[15]. Especially ICT manufacturing was hit hard in this period while ICT services performed less badly, except for wholesale trade. The crisis in the worldwide ICT sector does not appear to have hit Denmark as severely as other countries. The impressive growth in Danish ICT employment stagnated in 2000-2001 and decreased in 2002-2003. These external events influenced the results of DDN. It was presented in 1999, when the ICT sector was booming, but implemented from late 2000, when the ICT crisis had begun.

From 2000 to 2002, ICT employment in North Jutland decreased with 5.6% compared to 7.7% in Denmark. Therefore, the effect of the crisis from 2000 to 2002 appears to have been less negative in North Jutland. However, this can also be partly explained by the composition of the ICT sector in North Jutland. The major share of the region's ICT employment is within wireless communication that was hit later by the crisis. Most of the cluster firms were very R&D intensive, owned by foreign firms, or R&D subsidiaries of well-known multinational companies. The crisis affected the cluster and caused problems. Some firms downsized and some moved away from the region. Meanwhile, other local firms hired most of these engineers and new firms entered. The employment of engineers in R&D has been fairly stable, but large downsizing in manufacturing and mobile communication service has made the total

---

[15] The worldwide crisis in the ICT sector 'started' with the burst of the dotcom bubble in March 2000 when the share prices at the stock markets started dropping. During 2000-2001, the economy-wide business cycle also experienced a downturn, starting in USA and quickly spreading to Europe and the rest of the world. This reduced the end-user demand for ICT equipment and services, which added to the crisis (Fransman, 2002).

employment decline. Employment declined from 4,300 in 2002 to 2,800 in 2006. In June 2004, Flextronics decided that a major mobile phone manufacturing plant in North Jutland was to be closed down. In 2003, at its peak, it employed 1,700 persons in Pandrup, North Jutland. This turbulence somehow made the policy makers' attention turn away from the cluster and focus on other areas.

The NorCOM cluster is still a visible high-tech cluster in a peripheral region. It is still the force of the ICT sector even taking the recent turbulences into account. A look at the NorCOM history reveals that the cluster has experienced many crises in the entire cluster and in individual firms. The doom of the cluster has been foreseen many times, when prominent firms went bankrupt or when multinationals chose to close down their division in the cluster. But somehow it has proven to be very hard to extinguish.

The development perspectives for the ICT sector in North Jutland is related to the development perspective for the cluster and the other interesting technological knowledge bases that also hold well performing firms, such as biomedicine, logistics software, electro medical, etc. and a knowledge base. But these do not produce many spinoffs and lack critical mass of firms before the self-augmenting processes could potentially create a process of further growth in number of firms. (Pedersen, 2005) Specialisation by clusters creates vulnerability and lock-in effects in terms of dependency of a single technological knowledge base, but it is also a sign of strength. That is, NorCOM makes the ICT sector more vulnerable for shocks in markets and technologies, but it has also been the growth driver of the sector. It has created visibility, attracted firms and funds, and more importantly generated a large pool of highly educated qualified labour in a peripheral region. The possible lock-in could create long-term negative effects with lower innovative activity and revenues, etc., and it could raise a debate on how to destroy clusters when they have outlived their performance. However, then it should be possible to measure the point when the negative effects of the cluster were larger than the positive.

After DDN: Sustaining regional change?

The overall DDN project was evaluated by the Danish Technological Institute. The evaluation report was published in October 2004 and it was essentially positive and stressed the importance to continue the development. Radical and incremental change is an ongoing process, however, there are some in-built problems in DDN like many other programmes in relation to sustaining the processes started by the programmes, after the termination of the financial support. This creates some tension between termination of the support or continuation with a new programme until the processes are self-sustaining. Likewise Lundvall and Borrás note:

> "Many evaluations end up addressing users of the programs with questions about the efficacy of the program. Not surprisingly, such studies often end up reporting that the program was very good and that more of the same would be welcome." (Lundvall and Borrás, 2005, p. 611)

Although 'more of the same' seems to be a frequent conclusion in evaluations, it could be a fair conclusion if the goal is long-term 'radical' change. However, the continuation of DDN and sustaining process of change were not planned initially.

DDN ran from 2000 to 2003 and the last projects were finalised in the spring of 2004. When the projects ended, there were no announced plans to continue DDN as a large-scale experiment after the end of financial support from the government. The original DDN report stressed the necessity of avoiding that the experiment just faded away after the end of financial support. To avoid this it appeared necessary to collect the experiences by a continuous documentation of the results (The North Jutland County, 1999, p.48). However, from the beginning of the DDN project period in late 2000, the expectations have apparently been that the programme would end with an evaluation.

In early 2003, a group of public organisations formed a think-tank named North Jutland Innovation Forum to evaluate and create initiatives related to the future development of the region. It was, however, not evident that this forum in reality had the political momentum to carry on the positive initiatives created by DDN. However, in February 2004, it decided to form a regional digital taskforce financed by the County and Municipalities of North Jutland, to continue for one year the work on digital administration and competence building in the public

44   Background

sector that DDN had started. This period was prolonged after the evaluation of DDN in October 2004 when the Minister of Science and Technology supported the initiative with € 1.2 million. As a result, the new Centre for use of IT (CITA) was founded in 2005[16]. CITA was to have a broad profile like DDN, but focused on: digital administration, e-learning and competence building (mainly use of IT in the public sector). CITA was also to coordinate other projects, such as the € 5.6 million DEMO-net project on e-democracy and e-governance financed by the EU, working together with AAU Centre for Electronic Governance.

In December 2004, the IT infrastructure project gained support from the North Jutland County. The North Jutland Development Fund decided to allocate € 9.3 million from EU Objective 2 funds to initiate the building of a fibre-based infrastructure in the Objective 2 municipalities in North Jutland. However, the project soon faced several problems and was finally closed down in May 2005 when they found out that the Objective 2 funds could not be used for that purpose.

During the election campaign in January-February 2005, the government decided to support the North Jutland region with € 26.7 million since it had suffered from the closing-down of several large companies. The North Jutland Innovation Forum was closed down and a temporary Growth Forum was founded in May 2005 to initiate projects that could generate growth and employment in the region. The forum had 20 members of which 1 were from the ICT sector. It supported 20 projects within the following themes: the experience economy, the service, manufacturing and food sector, and high technology and growth capital. In April 2006, the temporary forum was replaced with a new Growth Forum. One of its tasks is to produce a business development strategy for four 'clusters': construction materials, food, health technology, and ICT.

Conclusion

From the outset, the original government vision of DDN appeared to have been a radical change of North Jutland towards a 'network society'. But the means

---

[16] The profile of CITA was supported by the composition of the board of directors. It consisted of the former director of the DDN secretariat, four from the administration of various municipalities, one from the university and one from the IT sector.

proposed – although they were never clearly formulated - appear to have been rather incremental in terms of building on what was already achieved in the region, which undoubtedly referred to the progress of the wireless communications cluster during the 1990s. The means were conceived as a 'localised' policy programme focusing on incremental change. Apart from all the rhetoric and 'hot air' on the transformation to a network society and a learning region, the main purpose was to build on the existing strong capabilities of the ICT sector.

In North Jutland, the wireless communication cluster was an important part of the ICT sector, but these firms were not successfully mobilised in DDN. The university was only partially integrated in the programme. It played an active role in DDN, but the technical research groups that are probably the most important for a major part of the ICT sector have not been active in to any significant extent in DDN.

The profile became broadly user-orientated as a result of a deliberate strategy among the dominant actors at the very early stage of the programme. The strong commitment from the leadership of influential public organisations and the missing representatives from private ICT firms lead to the final profile. On the other hand, the industry side could, perhaps, be blamed for not being sufficiently active in this process. The strong growth in mobile communications industry – up until 2001 - was likely to make them less interested in participation. The business opportunities were plenty at the time.

The goals of DDN were multiple and somehow lost focus. It could be characterised as let a thousand flowers bloom, which proved to be problematic since 'people who do not know where they are going usually end up somewhere else'[17]. The initial idea of localised change following the development trajectory of the ICT sector was replaced with a more chaotic framework. The goals of DDN contained a lot of radical-change-like rhetoric. The winner projects within the IT industry theme included a mix of radical as well as incremental change oriented projects in many different sectors, and at different levels. But the large

---

[17] A quote related to the lack of a clear specified goal in DDN is: Alice came to a fork in the road. "Which road do I take?" she asked. "Where do you want to go?" responded the Cheshire cat. "I don't know," Alice answered. "Then," said the cat, "it doesn't matter." (Lewis Carroll, Alice in Wonderland).

and 'high profiled' radical-change projects have not been realised at a sufficient scale. From an ICT industry perspective, DDN appears to have been too broadly formulated – the effects to have been too scattered.

The role of DDN and its impact on the development perspectives of the ICT sector could also be more broadly sketched in a user-producer interaction in a system of innovation approach. The demand side of the NorCOM cluster is global. Likewise the users of IT services are a part of a global system. The local market for wireless communication equipment is very small[18], while some of the IT service solutions still have a Danish specificity. The global market for these parts of the ICT sector puts additional requirements on the advanced users and user-producer interaction, since the pecuniary effect of the local market is small.

DDN was supposed to make the ICT environment in North Jutland stronger and better equipped to be an IT lighthouse of an international standard. The profile of the DDN programme when it was initiated was, however, much softer and broader than proposed by the Minister, mainly targeting the public sector and many widespread smaller projects. The profile became broadly user-orientated, instead of oriented towards industrial R&D and innovation and public research, which at no surprise affected the programme significantly.

It appears, on the other hand, fair to state that there has been a series of positive results from DDN in a business development context. There are several success stories of small and medium sized local IT service firms who have benefited from the programme, and many projects where the participation has been positive for the participants, but with no significant impact on the development of the ICT sector in North Jutland *per se*, at least so far. DDN has created a focus on the ICT sector in the region and has represented a certain commercial value. The programme seems to have created some contacts among firms and public organisation that may contribute to the future development perspectives for the ICT sector in North Jutland. The DDN programme was not a large financial support programme compared to the EU structural funds. However, it had a possibility to strengthen the cluster or to focus on developing other segments of the ICT sector, but became too broad and unfocused. Unluckily, it was launched at the worst possible time by coinciding with the

---

[18] Measured in sale of terminals. Some of the cluster companies have customers within the cluster.

worldwide crisis in ICT. The broadly user-orientated profile seems to have started a positive process of use of IT in the public sector in North Jutland and the experiences from DDN projects on digital administration are somehow carried on in CITA. DDN has had some positive effects, but it does not appear to have left a visible, lasting fingerprint on the development perspectives for the ICT sector in North Jutland.

References

Boschma, R. (2004). Rethinking, regional innovation policy. The making and breaking of regional history. In: G. Fuchs and P. Shapira, *Rethinking regional innovation and change: path dependency or regional breakthroughs?* Dordrecht, Kluwer International Publishers.

Bruun, H. (2001). Mobilising a Regional Lighthouse - A Study of the Digital North Denmark Programme.

Cooke, P. (2001). *Regional innovation and learning systems, clusters, and local and global value chains.* Innovation Clusters and Interregional Competition, Kiel Institute of World Economics, Kiel, Germany.

Dalum, B., C. Ø. R. Pedersen and G. Villumsen (2005). Technological Life Cycles: Lessons From A Cluster Facing Disruption. *European Urban and Regional Studies* 12(3): 229-246.

Dosi, G., C. Freeman, R. Nelson, G. Silverberg and L. Soete, Eds. (1988). *Technical Change and Economic Theory.* London, Pinter.

Dybkjær, L. and J. Lindegaard (1999). *Det digitale Danmark [The Digital Denmark].* Copenhagen, Ministry of Research and Information Technology.

Edquist, C., Ed. (1997). *Systems of Innovation: Technology, Institutions and Organisation.* London, Pinter.

Edquist, C. (1999). *Innovation Policy - A Systemic Approach.* DRUID Summer Conference, Rebild, Denmark.

Fagerberg, J. (2005). Innovation: A Guide to the Litterature. In: J. Fagerberg, D. Mowery and R. R. Nelson, *The Oxford Handbook of Innovation*. New York, Oxford University Press: 1-26.

Fransman, M. (2002). *Telecoms in the Internet Age: From Boom to Bust to ...?* Oxford, Oxford University Press.

Freeman, C. and L. Soete (1997). *The Economics of Industrial Innovation*. London, Pinter Press.

Krugman, P. (1991). *Geography and Trade*. Cambridge, Massachusetts, MIT Press.

Lorenzen, M. (2001). Localised learning and policy. Academic advise on enhancing regional competitiveness through learning. *European Planning Studies* 9.

Lundvall, B.-A., Ed. (1992). *National Systems of Innovation: Towards a Theory of Innovation and Interactive Learning*. London, Pinter Publishers.

Lundvall, B.-Å. and S. Borrás (2005). Science, Tehcnology, and Innovation Policy. In: J. Fagerberg, D. Mowery and R. R. Nelson, *The Oxford Handbook of Innovation*. New York, Oxford University Press: 599-631.

Maskell, P., H. Eskelinen, I. Hannibalsson, A. Malmberg and E. Vatne (1998). *Competitiveness, Localised Learning and Regional Development - Specialisation and Prosperity in Small Open Economies*. London, Routledge.

Ministry of Industry (1994). *Erhvervsudvikling i Nordjylland [Industrial development in North Jutland]*. Copenhagen.

Mowery, D. and R. R. Nelson (1999). *Sources of Industrial Leadership: Studies of Seven Industries*, Cambridge University Press.

Nielsen, C. V., F. B. Jensen, O. Nielsen and D. Amskov (2002). *Kandidat- og Aftagerundersøgelsen 2002 [The study of graduates and employers 2002]*. Aalborg, Aalborg University and Roskilde University Center.

Pedersen, C. Ø. R. (2005). The Development Perspectives for the ICT Sector in North Jutland. *Department of Business.Studies*. Aalborg, Aalborg University: 329.

Rogers, E. M. (1995). *Diffusion of Innovations*. New York, Free Press.

Storper, M. (1997). *The Regional World: Territorial Development in a Global Economy*. New York, The Guilford Press.

The Lighthouse Secretariat (2000). *Det Digitale Nordjylland*. Projektkonkurrence. Aalborg.

The Lighthouse Secretariat (2001). *Virksomhedsberetning 2000*. Aalborg.

The Lighthouse Secretariat (2002). *Virksomhedsberetning 2001*. Aalborg.

The Lighthouse Secretariat (2003). *Virksomhedsberetning 2002*. Aalborg.

The North Jutland County (1999). *Det Digitale Nordjylland [The Digital North Jutland]*. Aalborg.

Utterback, J. M. (1994). *Mastering the Dynamics of Innovation*. Boston, Massachusetts, Harvard Business School Press.

50 Background

Social Experiments and Participatory Research as Method

Lone Dirckinck-Holmfeld

> Interdisciplinary research with stakeholders and users challenges the research methodologies to be used. The methodologies have to provide a shared language for all participants, to establish trust, and to offer insights into the diverse perspectives of the participants. Furthermore, it challenges ways to discuss and validate contributions from each others - across different criteria for each discipline, and across different agendas of stakeholders, politicians, practitioners and researchers. Participatory research and social experiments are methodologies which have been developed to cope with this kind of complexity in regards to technology development and design projects. Based on experiences and lessons learned from the project "The Digital North Denmark (DDN), the chapter reflects on participatory research in a complex organizational setting of researchers, stakeholders and users emphasising practice-based methods where "social experiments with technology" and "dialogue research" are the key-words.

Introduction

The research taking place in relation to the Center for Digital Governance at Aalborg University and in relation to the European Network of Excellence, "Demo-Net" is interdisciplinary, and is carried out in cooperation and collaboration with stakeholders from municipalities and regions as well as with producers and users of digital tools for governance. The objects of research are complex and often interdisciplinary in nature. The research within the Aalborg-team draws especially on the following core knowledge areas: Policy and organization, technology and infrastructure, and communication and interactivity (Center for Digital Forvaltning, n.d.). Moreover, diverse research groups participate in the Center bringing various methodologies and scientific tradition together – researchers from Department of Communication, Computer Science, Policy and Governance, and Social Development and Planning.

Interdisciplinary research with stakeholders and users challenges the research methodologies to be used. These have to provide a shared language for all the participants, to establish trust, and to offer insights into the diverse perspectives of the participants. Furthermore, it challenges ways to discuss and validate contributions from each others - across different criteria for each discipline, and across different agendas of stakeholders, politicians, practitioners and researchers.

Participatory research and social experiments are methodologies which have been developed to cope with this kind of complexity. Based on experiences from a previous project "The Digital North Denmark (DDN), I will present the approach to participatory research in this large, regional project, and in a complex organizational setting of researchers, stakeholders and users. Reflections on the lessons learned will be used to provide some guidelines, which can be used in Center for Digital Governance and other complex, interdisciplinary research projects.

The chapter will give an account of the themes and methods of participatory research. The point of departure is adopted from earlier participatory research initiatives within technology and local community development, the 'Local Society Experiments' in 1986-1989 (Cronberg, Duelund, Jensen, & Qvortrup, 1991), Manicoral[1] (Nielsen, J., Dirckinck-Holmfeld, & Danielsen, 2003) and "Ansigt-til-Ansigt"[2] (Dirckinck-Holmfeld, L, Konnerup, & Petersen, 2004). The central experiences which form the basis of our approach to participatory research are associated with the concept of "social experiments with technology"

---

[1] European R&D-project on Multimedia And Network In Co-operative Research And Learning (MANICORAL). The project consisted of a group of geophysics with a natural science background, Human Computer Interaction researchers from humanities and social sciences, and a group of engineers with expertise in Computer Supported Cooperative Work systems sharing an interest in understanding the conditions for technology-mediated communication and collaboration among a group of scientists and the development of a dynamic visualization group work system to be used for shared dataanalysis.

[2] "Ansigt-til-Ansigt" (Face-to-Face) was a project carried out with the Institute for Speech Disorder, The County of North Denmark. The project consisted of a group of learning researchers and a group of teachers and managers from the Institute of Speech Disorder sharing an interest in understanding the potentials of technology enhanced learning of humans with aphasia and the developing of new training methods.

Social Experiments and Participatory Research as Method

and "dialogue research". The chapter further explores these concepts and their application in connection to the participatory research in the Digital North Denmark-project. The chapter is concluded by a discussion on how the experiences from the DDN-project can be carried on in new interdisciplinary projects and research centres such as the Center for Digital Governance.

Setting the stage

In December 1999, North Denmark was selected by the Danish government as one of two regions to explore and develop experiences with the use of information and communication technology (ICT). The arguments for selecting the region were among others the strong mobile industry and the well-established collaboration in the region between the university, the county, the municipalities and the private companies.

The overall strategy for DDN covered a wide range of priority areas. In the first call, there were four main themes and a series of focus areas:

- IT-infrastructure including enduser net, access net, transport net, and facilities for access, storage, and distribution of information
- IT-business development, e-trade and conditions for the industry with regards to e-trade, IT-development and IT-conditions
- Competence and education, including IT in teaching, IT at the labour market, IT in culture and leisure, and IT as promoter of welfare
- Digital administration, including service, authority management and efficiency, as well as citizens, democracy and information

Within these themes, 79 projects were realized. In the second phase, 11 new projects were added. All in all, the DDN project had a budget of 510 m. DDK, where 170 m. were government funding.

The project was met with huge enthusiasm in the region – among citizens, politicians, university and companies, and there was a strong commitment from all stakeholders at all levels. Many actors were engaged in the formulation and preparation of development projects, and many new connections were established among the stakeholders in the region. The motto for the DDN project was the old Mao Zedong proverb from 1956: "Letting a hundred flowers bloom" stressing the freedom to express many diverse ideas and projects (though without any point of resemblance with the Chinese cultural revolution ☺) (Hundred Flowers Campaign 2007).

From the beginning, Aalborg University was thought to have a very central role in DDN. But due to a fixation of the government funding, the university was not able to participate in the originally planned extent. Some of the more technically oriented departments were thus never seriously engaged in the DDN, while a series of other technical environments were involved as a sort of suppliers to the project – according to the device "if there is a will, there is a way".

Only a few number of projects were headed by researchers from the university.

The participatory research group was established as part of the overall DDN project. The group was co-financed by DDN and the university, and had an autonome relation to DDN. The aim of the participatory research group was to follow the projects and to draw and generalize experiences within and across projects. Moreover, the participatory group served as a critical sparring partner to the steering committee and the project group for DDN.

The participatory research group[3] was established as a cross-faculty team of researchers from various departments at Aalborg University from Humanities, Social Science and Natural Science and Engineering and consisted of six senior researchers and six doctoral students. The cross-faculty composition made it possible to match the multi-facetted experiments of the projects as well as it made it possible to study the "problem areas of DDN" from various complementary perspectives: technology, economy, planning, democratization and learning.

The participatory research group was not established without "striking a blow". As in many other governmental projects there was funding for evaluation, but not for participatory research and transversal research activities. However, after persistent negotiation among the steering committee and the university, the participatory research group was established. DDN therefore became an interesting alternative to most governmental projects making it possible for a group of researchers to follow and participate in the project. The situation was

---

[3] For elaboration, see the webpage of the participatory research: (DDN, n.d.) www.hum.auc.dk/ddn

new for the Steering Committee for DDN and for the group of researchers, but still a unique opportunity to get deeper insight into the research area with point of departure in the different projects, and the collaboration with stakeholders, users, fiery souls, etc.

For more information about DDN and the political process, I refer to the analysis by Østergaard (this book).

The method of participatory research

As argued in the article "Dialogue Design - With Mutual Learning as Guiding Principle" written by Nielsen, Dirckinck-Holmfeld and Danielsen (2003), the basic approach in *Participatory Research* appeared from a focus on, and belief in, a dialogue between experts and laymen at socalled dialogue conferences. The laymen saw experts as resources. Through questions to and discussions with expert panels, the laymen would acquire sufficient understanding and knowledge to unfold their own recommendations to local politicians, administrators, governments, etc. concerning a given policy. The slogan was: This is much too complicated to hand over to experts. Future workshops (Jungk & Müllert, 1984) and scenario workshops were among the techniques used, and the laymen group was composed to represent the population of a given community: officials, politicians, citizens, school children, people from supply companies, entrepreneur enterprises and the financial sector, etc.

The conception of the process was dialogue understood both as the fundamental tool, and as the process through which mutual understanding could be reached. The role of the researcher was to act as midwife for the process, to help with co-ordination, to set up dialogue workshops and communicative ethic rules so that the participants could discuss and negotiate between them. S/he also had to act as a critical partner (expert) in the project but without taking control.

Participatory research as a method is also embedded in *proactive technology assessment* - not as a traditional product evaluation but as a dynamic process assessment taking place during the course of a project (Remmen, 1991). This implies that the researcher is in a continuous dialogue with the acting participants, and it also includes a continuous presentation and discussion of findings to ensure that the participants are able to influence and guide the process. The locus of control and of influence is in the hands of the acting participants. In Denmark, the production of windmills can be seen as a very concrete example of proactive technology assessment. It has become a profitable business and has developed a stronghold position on the world market.

Within participatory research, we can talk about a continuum of engagement (see later). The dialogue researcher who does not participate in the experimental work but observes processes and reports the observations to the actors - as opposed to the action researcher who takes action together with the other participants. One could say that the role of the dialogue researcher is that of a scribe keeping record, and that of a storyteller recounting the ongoing process (Nielsen, J. et al., 2003). This is the very essence of Participatory Research. The methodology was, however, also a deliberate attempt to mark a distance to the action research from the 70'ies, which was criticized for being too little research and too much action (Nielsen, K. A., 1996). Setting up fora for dialogues and acting as negotiator for the different interests within a project became a task for the researcher. In this work, the ethical principles of discourse, *Communicative Actions* as formulated by the German philosopher, Jürgen Habermas, became the epistemological inspiration for the approach (Duelund, 1991).

Participatory research is not a very well defined method, however it is centered around approaches putting democratic dialogues in the center of analysis, development and designs. In that sense, participatory research is an umbrella for approaches dealing with "participation" across boundaries between laymen and experts (vertical boundaries) as well as boundaries between interdisciplinary expert groups (horisontal boundaries).

With respect to the DDN project, participatory research was integrated with a methodological approach to "social experiments with technology", which grew out of some of the first projects in Denmark dealing with technological development, the socalled 'Local Society Experiments in 1986-1989 (Cronberg et al., 1991). This approach has an overall understanding of 1. Technology development as "social experiments" and 2. The method of participatory research as dialogue research.

Social experiments with technology

In the anthology "Danish Experiments - Social Constructions of Technology", (Jæger & Qvortrup, 1991) present a definition of "social experiments":

Social Experiments and Participatory Research as Method 57

> "Social experiments with information technology are specific forms of implementation of IT:
> - in which the primary aim is to establish new social organisation using information technology;
> - in which the activities and resulting socio-technical products can be used as models for a more widespread - though necessarily contextually-modified - implementation of similar IT-systems;
> - and in which, to this latter end, independent researchers describe and evaluate the implementation process concerned and its results."
> (ibid. p. 37-38)

In the above mentioned publication, three hypotheses on social experiments are presented:

> "1. Social experiments are processes in which society as a whole can promote socially beneficial ways of exploiting new information technologies.
> 2. Social experimentation is a method for production, evaluation, and refinement of socially advanced information systems.
> 3. Social experimentation is not primarily a forecasting instrument. It is rather a way to influence the future by developing new and socially advanced IT products and services through demonstrating new forms of social organizations through IT and by generating social awareness and societal learning processes." (ibid. p. 40)

This definition of social experiments shows very well the type of work that DDN involves as a large scale project experimenting with the use of ICT for creation and development of the network society. The social experiements do not primarily concern the development of high-tech tools, but are rather a way to influence the future by developing and integrating socially advanced ICT-products and services.

However, looking back at the DDN project, I will reflect on a discussion of "excellence and IT-high-tech development/business development" versus "main stream", which remained very distinct through the project.

The different perspectives trace back to the Digital Denmark initiative, which were the forerunner and main foundation for DDN. One result of the Digital Denmark was to establish a big-scale social experiment in a region with focus on strengthening IT-growth areas (within production and business) at the same time as disseminating the use of ICT – directed towards the citizens, the education sector, the public administration, the business sector, and the infrastructure (Dybkjær & Lindegaard, 1999). This double strategy has followed the DDN throughout the entire period and, in some instances, it has been applied as a discussion of "excellence" versus "mainstream". Additionally, the strategy has been criticized for a lack of effort in creating "new knowledge and new products" and just disseminating "old knowledge" (Danholm & Mølsted, 2003; Mølsted, Henning & Danholm, 2003; Mølsted, H & Pedersen, 2002a, 2002b).

This discussion is fundamental and also very actual regarding research on ICT. In many ICT high-tech research and development programs, it seems as if the development of ICT is disconnected from the *use*.

The approach of "social experiments with technology" and projects contributing with experiences on the social construction of technology bridge the above mentioned positions. The approach "social experiments with technology" considers appropriation of technology as both a technological and a social adaptation why it is not only a matter of disseminating "old knowledge". Viewing projects as "social experiments" contributes with substantial insights into technological as well as social processes at play in the integration of ICT, insights which feed-back to the design of new products and services.

Within the approach of "social experiments with technology", the application and development aspects are complementary. The application aspect focuses primarily on integration of ICT into the work practices, and the enhancements of capabilities, however it also produces insight into technological design, and can therefore assist in the development of new services and tools, which correspond to the social needs.

From the beginning, the participatory research group was confronted with this controversy between *high-tech development* and *use*. Both perspectives were represented in the research team. The controversy was accepted – and from the participatory research point of view, DDN was roomy enough to handle both perspectives.

Working with the aspect of use in connection with social experiments is thus not only a "dissemination" strategy but should rather be viewed as a productive foundation for exploiting the potentials of technology, for developing human capabilities in the social organization where technological competences goes hand in hand with the preparation of the ground for new practices – all together making a basis for design of new services and new technologies.

Participatory research and social experiments

According to Jæger and Qvortrup's definition, participatory research is an integrated element in social experiments. Participatory research contributions must be found in the description and in the evaluation of the implementation processes and in their results. Additionally, participatory research plays a vital role in relation to the conceptualization of the experiences.

The three modes of participatory research

Research on social practices is always based on intervention. Even the "detached" researcher intervenes when s/he makes an interview, presents a questionnaire, etc., and when the result is finished releases the findings in a scientific paper. In principle, participatory research is about being aware of how you as a researcher intervene in the social practice, of being concise, and of developing, tools which are in agreement with the guiding principles of dialogues.

The participatory research group related to DDN used the following approaches depending on the research object and the relations to the involved actors:

Sideline research where researchers analyze, evaluate and generalize project experiences and results in relation to the overall goal of DDN without direct involvement in the projects.

Dialogue research, where researchers are in dialogue with the projects and relate to these as consultant partners in the development of the individual project. Furthermore, the dialogue researcher facilitates the conceptualization and generalization of the experiences and results of the project in close collaboration with the project partners, however with the project partners as the "owners" of the problem area, and the researchers as the experts on research design.

> *"The researcher's criteria for truth are not reduced to the effects of the actions but also largely rest on intellectual reflection and critique of the findings, which the theories produce as facts. It is indeed in the conceptualization that the dependance of the specific objects are maintained and therefore, it is in the conceptualization that the social dimension is thematized with a substantial departure in the research object." (Nielsen, K. A., 1996)*

Finally, they engaged in action research/technology application where the researchers are directly involved in the project and actively contribute to the technology development and implementation. The action researcher uses his/her knowledge to facilitate the design of the social experiment, and uses his/her insights to argue for and document the results of the intervention.

The scientific criteria can either be pragmatic criteria on what works or critical theoretical criteria using the intervention to reflect upon the possible conditions to which the action may lead. The action researcher in the last version is an expert whose expertise is used within a use domain to incrementally or radically change the use domain (Følgeforskningsindsatsen, 2001).

The different modes of participatory research have all been applied in relation to DDN. The overall approach within the participatory research group has been a kind of critical research, where the focus has been on the critical conceptualization of concepts, relations and findings. Aagaard (1996) formulates: *"The researcher's criteria for truth are not reduced to the effects of the actions, but also largely rest on intellectual reflection and critique of the findings, which the theories produce as facts* (p. 347, my translation), or in more general terms critical research is about developing the discourse and the language about a problem area, and hereby contribute to a more complex and differentiated view.

The participatory research has been carried out using all three modalities and variants hereof. It has varied from research theme and research team depending on the problem area and the tradition of the research teams. In general, the participatory research group has wanted to closely follow and interact with the projects, but at the same time, to maintain a certain distance to the projects so that the participatory research teams could carry out the necessary conceptual development and generalization. Saying so in the division of work between practitioners and researchers, the researchers have certain tools and ways of working which can be used to frame the experiences of the projects and to develop theories based on the projects.

Within this scope, some of the research projects can be characterized as "sideline research" where the DDN-experiments have primarily functioned as cases for the researchers while other research projects have functioned more collaboratively – or as direct action research. Examples of "sideline research" are provided e.g. in the articles on "implementation" and "digital competence, where the projects have been used as cases to gain insight into specific problem areas, and the research has contributed to the conceptualisation of the findings (Bygholm & Boisen, 2004; Dirckinck-Holmfeld, L., Kanstrup, & Buus, 2004). Other projects, e.g. the project "Face-to-face" on aphasia (Dirckinck-Holmfeld, L et al., 2004) have been using a dialogue research approach, where the researchers have contributed as collaborative partners and critical facilitators. On basis of the project, which was carried out by the Institute for Speech Disorder, a number of dialogue sessions were established on data collected by the participants and the researchers. These shared data sessions provided specific and concrete insights into the application of ICT in the training of aphasia, and were used to discuss the strategies and solutions proposed by the Institute. However, the research teams and the practitioners together identified additional problem areas of shared interest, and started to conceptualise these issues. The dialogue research is in that sense a kind of mutual and collaborative learning process where two activity systems – the research system and the practitioners' system are brought into systematic interaction. In the project with the Institute of Speech Disorder, this process went very well, and both partners found the process beneficial, as well as it produced new insights into the training of participants with aphasia.

The article on IT Infrastructure and Broadband in North Jutland is the most direct expression of an action research approach (Madsen & Knudsen, 2004). In this project, the researchers were the main actors for developing strategies for the

North Denmark region in building up the necessary networked infrastructure for high bandwidth services. Furthermore, the team strongly contributed to the establishment of a political as well as a broader common awareness of the strengths and challenges related to networking infrastructures.

Common to all the projects was the relatively close relation to the project promoters and participants. This constitutes a series of challenges to the role of the 'independent' researcher. On the one hand to keep a distance for reflection, and on the other hand to relate to the project partners in a trustworthy manner. With respect to the concrete project-promoters and actors involved in DDN, the researchers are parts of a mutually obligated relation which evidently must be reflected in the research methodology. The participatory researchers should not be mixed up with evaluators as someone controlling the projects. On the other hand there is an expectation that the researchers contribute with conceptual insights which are productive to the projects.

In participatory research, partners and projects have to get something back from the researchers. The more involved the researchers are with the projects the more the project participants expect to get back.

The philosophical and methodological foundations of participatory research

Participatory research and social experiments of technology take point of departure in the critique of traditional technology assessment and development, which rests on a rationalistic and techno-centered view (Remmen, 1991). Instead, social and cultural dimensions must be included in the construction and development, and the methods used incorporate how to deal with these dimensions. This socio-cultural understanding of the technology development points towards proces-oriented and participatory (user-centered) design and methodological principles which build on active involvement of the different actors (designers, programmers, management and different usergroups).

In his doctoral thesis, Nielsen (1996) describes that we, in the late 80ies, see a shift in action research. The action research in the 70'ies was in Denmark characterised by the "overidentity" among researchers and participants, and in the 80ies this approach is replaced by – what he calls, the researchers' normative identification with the methods and procedures (ibid p. 349). The objectives of action researchers stay open as a broad interest in participation in the transformation of work practices. However the specific nature of the work practices is compared to the action research from the 70'ies conceived as the matter of the participants – and not the researcher. The researchers' direct engagement in the formulation of the goals is replaced by the researchers' identification with methodologies and procedures for participation.

On the basis of the "Local Community Projects", particularly Duelund (1991) and Storgaard (1991) developed a foundation for dialogue research. Duelund describes the origin of dialogue research as follows:

> *"Dialogue research as formulated on the basis of the "Local Community Projects" was introduced as a pragmatic method for solving the clash of interest which existed between researchers and projects." (Duelund, 1991)*

The philosophical basis for dialogue research draws on a dialogue theory as formulated by Giddens, Habermas, Galtung a.o and builds on the fundamental assumption of civilian history that we ideally endeavour a free dialogue. On the big world scene, it apparently seems difficult at present where physical execution of power in wars and acts of terror seem to have become the new language.

In this relation, a basic dialogue approach must therefore be considered radical – and some would maybe even say – naive. In some sense, this also applies in a technology development perspective because of the always non-hegemonuous situation. If practitioners and researchers engage in dialogue, they will speak different languages because they refer to different practices, just as the confidence with using language as a dialogue tool can be very different.

As we, nonetheless, choose dialogue research as a starting point – this choice is based on the fact that dialogue research and Habermas' discourse ethical principles (Habermas, 1981) are both connected to the same ideal – a search for truth. In relation to technology development which we understand as socially constructed and therefore demands cross-disciplinary cooperation, we must apply democratic methods which make us capable of entering dialogue with each other on this development.

But, we also know from analyses and theoretical discussions that serious difficulties exist in relation to establishing a non-hegemonous dialogue and the tools we develop must attempt to take this into consideration. In the article "Dialogue Design" (Nielsen et al., 2003), we write that researchers or project managers must design workshops and frames for dialogue. Inspired by the communicative planning research (Pløger, 1998) as well as a further development of the method on dialogue design (Nielsen, Danielsen), we are able to set up a series of principles for such workshops, participant roles and communication forms, such as:

- The fundamental tool in participatory research is the dialogue and a basic perspective of mutual learning
- Participatory research is fundamentally a mutual learning process between equal professional groups who have distinctly different tasks to perform and different roles in the project
- Communication, learning processes and decisions take place within a field of many different life worlds and practices. This complexity of cultural, scientific and methodological differences should be thematically approached during the research process
- Dialogue is not only about finding the "common denominator". The process must be critical of the system and self-critical in relation to own practice
- The communicative process demands that fora for dialogue and mutual learning processes are constructed, and multiple communicative codes are ensured enough space.
- Through a deep understanding of different discursive communities trying to capture the "ways of reasoning" behind the competing views – without devaluing or excluding a priori. This implies insight into the task domain and communicative legitimacy to reconstruct and to present the interests of the different partners, and finally to be able to mediate the negotiation process between conflicting interests

In this perspective, participatory research has been selected as an overall approach due to four reasons: 1. Fundamental desires to promote the societal development through dialogue, 2. The belief that the dialogue approach may contribute to a multi-facetted and democratic development of the technology, 3. The close connection between dialogue and learning as different actors participating in "true" dialogue challenge each others' perspectives and thereby promote learning, 4. The belief that the dialogue approach may contribute to development of new products and services which correspond to the needs of the social systems.

We are also aware that the dialogue processes are always subject to a series of different conditions and perspectives, which should be taken into consideration in the research design and preparation of the cooperation between researchers, practitioners, politicians, and other stake holders.

Conclusion

The DDN project has been a big-scale social experiment with information technology on using and developing ICT for establishing a networked, learning region. The participatory research group did not assess whether DDN actually succeeded in transforming the North Denmark into a networked, learning region. To be modest, the participant researchers looked more into how ICT were appropriated and how participants, organisations and the region were learning; how specific forms of implementation of ICT were enacted and how the socio-technical products and services were realised. The participatory research approach seemed appropriate for bringing different perspectives together in the process of ICT development and appropriation:

First of all, it provided an opportunity to connect research to some of the issues and themes of the *projects* and thereby also to reflect, conceptualise and generalise the project findings. Hereby, the participatory research contributed with a sort of meta aspect on the individual projects as well as assembled researchers, project promoters and partners across traditional boundaries. Furthermore, it should be mentioned that the cross disciplinary research approach also ensured that both social and technical aspects and perspectives were dealt with (see the final book from the project (Dirckinck-Holmfeld, L., Dalum, Boisen, & Ulrich, 2004).

Secondly, the participatory research initiative has contributed to the systematisation of experiences within the individual themes as well as relating these to more principal research and development questions.

However, *The political level* has been target of rudimentary thematization. From the point of view of participatory research, focus has been on the research in relations to the projects. This prioritisation is also evident in the project description (Følgeforskningsindsatsen, 2001). However, since this was indeed a participatory research initiative, we have later realised that we should have assigned higher priority to continuous dialogue with the political system and other stakeholders in the region. The dialogues with the political system have taken place within some of the themes – particularly the "industrial development of the ICT-sector" and the "IT-infrastructure" but they were not actually thematised from the beginning as an essential part of the participatory research. On those grounds, there has also been a lack of explicit channels for the dialogues which ideally should have taken place between the participatory research and the political system.

In the last period of the project, this was thematised and handled more explicitly, and it is our understanding that the participatory research has created an essential basis for these dialogues as *trust* has been established between the research system and the political system and stakeholders from the region, and a fundamental recognition has arrived that these systems may mutually benefit from each other despite differences in objectives and functions. On this basis, we also find that the primary prerequisites for a continued research effort have been established on the political level.

Participatory research as dialogue research is about dialogues on several levels; on the individual project level, on the transversal thematic level and on the political and stakeholder level, with the use of different methods adapted to these levels. In actual terms, the participatory research has worked on all three levels, however, the first level got most attention. Taking the experiences from DDN seriously, the main lessons to be learned for this kind of projects would be to focus on all three levels at the same time: projects, transversal themes and politicians and stakeholders, and to apply the relevant dialogue methods for each level.

Acknowledgements

My thoughts on the method of the participatory research rest primarily on discussions in the DDN-participatory research group at Aalborg University. But the foundations of the article have developed over several years and throughout a series of projects of which a long lasting cooperation with Janni Nielsen and Oluf Danielsen deserves particular mentioning. From this cooperation, the method of "dialogue design" was developed which a.o. draws on the concept of dialogue research. Furthermore, I would like to express my thanks to my good colleagues from the E-Learning Lab, Aalborg University. We have engaged in a continued discussion on theory and method in relation to participatory research. My special thanks goes to the editors for constructive and interesting comments to an earlier version of this article.

References

Bygholm, A., & Boisen, E. (2004). Implementering og 'Digital kompetence' (Implementation and 'Digital Competence'. In: Dirckinck-Holmfeld, L. & Dalum, B. & Boisen, E. & Ulrich, J. (Eds.), *Det Digitale Nordjylland - Udvikling til netværkssamfundet?* Aalborg: Aalborg University Press.

Center for Digital Forvaltning (n.d.). http://www.egov.aau.dk/. Retrieved 07.12., 2006, from the World Wide Web.

Cronberg, T., Duelund, P., Jensen, O. M., & Qvortrup, L. (1991). *Danish Experiments - Social Constructions of Technology*. Copenhagen: Copenhagen Business School.

Danholm, K., & Mølsted, H. (2003). Statsstøttet IT-projekt er slået fejl (State-supported IT-project failed). *Ingeniøren (The Engineer)* *http://www.ing.dk/apps/pbcs.dll/forside*.

DDN, Participatory Research.-. (n.d.). *http://www.kommunikation.aau.dk/ddn/index_eng.htm*. Retrieved 07.12, 2006, from the World Wide Web:

Dirckinck-Holmfeld, L., Dalum, B., Boisen, E., & Ulrich, J. (Eds.). (2004). *Det Digitale Nordjylland - IKT og omstilling til netværkssamfundet?* Aalborg: Aalborg University Press.

Dirckinck-Holmfeld, L., Kanstrup, A. M., & Buus, L. (2004). Nye læreprocesser og små fyrtårne. In Dirckinck-Holmfeld, L. & Dalum, B. & Boisen, E. & Ulrich,

J. (Eds.), *Det Digitale Nordjylland - Udvikling til netværkssamfundet?* Aalborg: Aalborg University Press.

Dirckinck-Holmfeld, L., Konnerup, U., & Petersen, K. (2004). *Face-to-Face - Training of Participants with Aphasia through Distance Learning.* Paper presented at the ICT and learning in regions - Concluding conference for the Digital North Denmark, Aalborg Congress Center.

Duelund, P. (1991). Dialoque Research - Theories and Methods. In Cronberg, T. & Duelund, P. & Jensen, O. M. & Qvortrup, L. (Eds.), *Danish Experiments - Social Constructions of Technology.* Copenhagen: Institute of organisation and Industrial Sociology. Copenhagen Business School.

Dybkjær, L., & Lindegaard, J. (1999). *Det digitale Danmark [The Digital Denmark].* Copenhagen: Ministry of Research and Information Technology.

Følgeforskningsindsatsen. (2001). *Følgeforskning i forhold til Det Digitale Nordjylland.* Aalborg: Aalborg University.

Habermas, J. (1981). *Teorien om den kommunikative handlen* (Cederstrøm, J., Trans.). Aalborg: Aalborg Universitetsforlag og Institut for pædagogik og uddannelsesforskning, Danmarks Lærerhøjskole.

Hundred Flowers Campaign (2007). In Encyclopeadia Britannica Online: http://www.britannica.com/eb/article-9041531/

Jungk, R., & Müllert, N. R. (1984). *Håndbog i fremtidsværksteder [Future Workshops]* (Nielsen, B. S., Trans.). Copenhagen: Politisk Revy.

Jæger, B., & Qvortrup, L. (1991). Community Teleservice Centres - Participatory Technology Implementation (Risberg, M., Trans.). In Cronberg, T. & Duelund, P. & Jensen, O. M. & Qvortrup, L. (Eds.), *Danish Experiments - Social Constructions of Technology* (pp. 27-43). Copenhagen: Institute of Organisation and Industrial Sociology. Copenhagen Business School.

Madsen, O. B., & Knudsen, T. P. (2004). IT Infrastruktur og Bredbånd. In Dirckinck-Holmfeld, L. & Dalum, B. & Boisen, E. & Ulrich, J. (Eds.), *Det Digitale Nordjylland - Udvikling til netværkssamfundet?* Aalborg: Aalborg University Press.

Mølsted, H., & Danholm, K. (2003). Digitalforvaltning er alt for slap - Manglende målsætninger, it-strategi og fastlåst struktur hæmmer potentialet i den digitale forvaltning. *Ingeniøren (The Engineer)* http://www.ing.dk/apps/pbcs.dll/forside.

Mølsted, H., & Pedersen, M. B. (2002a). Gamle ideer får millionstøtte (Grants to old ideas). *Ingeniøren (The Engineer)* http://www.ing.dk/apps/pbcs.dll/forside.

Mølsted, H., & Pedersen, M. B. (2002b). Aalborg-dekan: IT-fyrtårn spild af penge (Aalborg-dean: IT-lighthouse a waste of money). *Ingeniøren (The Engineer)* http://www.ing.dk/apps/pbcs.dll/forside.

Nielsen, J., Dirckinck-Holmfeld, L., & Danielsen, O. (2003). Dialogue Design - With Mutual Learning as Guiding Principle. *International Journal of Human-Computer Interaction, Vol.15*(No.1), 21 - 41.

Nielsen, K. A. (1996). *Arbejdets sociale orientering [The Social Orientation of Work]*. Forlaget Sociologi.

Pløger, J. (1998). *Kommunikativ Planlegging - Mellom kommunikasjon og retorikk*. Blindern: Norsk institutt for by- og regionsforskning.

Remmen, A. (1991). Constructive Technology Assessment. In Cronberg, T. & Duelund, P. & Jensen, O. M. & Qvortrup, L. (Eds.), *Danish Experiments - Social Constructions of Technology*. Copenhagen: New Social Science Monographs.

Storgaard, K. (1991). Dialogue Research. In Cronberg, T. & Duelund, P. & Jensen, O. M. & Qvortrup, L. (Eds.), *Danish Experiments - Social Construction of Technology*. Copenhagen: New Social Science Monographs.

Part Two
Technology & Infrastructure

Technology and Government: Extending the Double Dance of Agency

Jeremy Rose

> Central to the eGovernment field, but rather little debated in its literature, is the relationship between information technology and government. How does information technology affect government; how does government affect information technology? How can we theorise and describe this two-way relationship? The problem is not new in the information systems field, where the relationship between technology and organisations has long been discussed, with attention often focused on finding a middle way between the extremes of technological and social determinism. One such contribution is the Double Dance of Agency, which reformulates the discussion as a theoretical answer to 'the problem of agency' (where does agency lie? With humans, with machines, or with both?). The Double Dance of Agency theorises both the different character of human and machine agency, and the emergent properties of their interplay. However, this formulation was devised in the context of private sector organisations and large-scale computer systems, primarily Enterprise Resource Planning (ERP) systems. The paper investigates whether the model can also contribute to the theorising of the relationship of government and technology, using a simple model of eGovernment practice. It discusses its strengths and weaknesses in relation to the eGovernment field, sketches the double dance of technology and government, and develops a research agenda to help strengthen the model for use in the theorising of eGovernment.

Introduction

The title 'eGovernment,' like its predecessor eCommerce, suggests a juxtaposition of two factors. The 'e' (standing for 'electronic') represents the technological factor, comprising computer systems and computer network infrastructures (with an association, via the more developed eCommerce field, to the Internet). 'Government' can represent many things, but is here taken as a practice. The practice factor thus comprises a multi-faceted system of human activity (with attendant structures and resources) representing the way we manage formal political organisation and administration of our societies, at the local, national and international levels. Taken together, 'eGovernment,' depicts a relationship between the two factors: the technology factor and the practice factor. Related subject areas (eAdministration, eGovernance, eParticipation, eDemocracy) duplicate the same juxtaposition: technology and social practice. Researchers in these areas are expected to consider both aspects; thus a contribution with no consideration of technology does not belong in the eGovernment field, and neither does one which ignores the relevant social practice. Therefore, it can be argued that the central theoretical task in the eGovernment field is to understand the relationship between technology and the social practice of government. That task underpins many of the other research objectives that can be seen in literature, technology developments, case studies, comparative statistical analyses, best practice accounts and in normative advice to politicians and civil servants.

EGovernment is a relatively new field, and one which is currently under-theorized Grönlund (2004). A common practice in immature, theoretically weak fields is to borrow and adapt theories from better established disciplines, and the purpose of this paper is to investigate whether one such theory, the 'double dance of agency' (Rose and Jones 2005), is a suitable candidate theory for helping to explain one facet of the relationship between technology and government. This contribution is located in the information systems field (a close relation of the eGovernment field) and seeks to explain a much-discussed problem in that field, the relationship between technology and organisation. In crude terms, the problem is a discussion between those who think that human actors control technologies (social determinism), those who think that technology determines human evolution (technological determinism) and those (the majority) who take a middle position. This discussion can be reformulated as 'the problem of agency' (Rose, Jones et al. 2005): is it only humans that act, and thus cause consequences, or can machines also act in a way which influences organisational evolution. If machines can also act, then how can this dual agency be expressed, theoretically. The 'double dance of agency' model provides one theoretical answer to this problem. The dance metaphor symbolises the ordered, but not entirely predictable interaction of the two forms of agency (like a couple on a dance floor); thus the interacting relationship between technologies and humans in shaping organisational outcomes. The model finds its theoretical inspiration in social theories (particularly structuration theory), and social theories of technology (particularly actor network theory). This explains why Government is taken to be a social practice for the purposes of this paper. The model's empirical background lies in studies of the implementation of Enterprise Resource Planning (ERP) systems in organisations – in effect the introduction of large administrative computer systems into complex organisations.

In adapting a theory from one discipline area to another, care needs to be taken to investigate the differences between the context in which the theory was developed, and the new context in which it will be applied. The theory was developed on the basis of the implementation of SAP (a leading enterprise resource planning system) in large commercial organisations, and against the theoretical background of discussions of technological and social determinism and developments of structuration theory and actor network theory (themselves theories imported into IS from other disciplines). ERP systems are becoming established in Government practice (Sivakumar 2002; Perng and Chang 2004), but so are customer relationship management systems, document handling systems, geographic information systems and other technologies. The diffusion of ERP technologies to the government area possibly lags ten years behind the private sector, and the vast bulk of the extensive ERP literature has the commercial sector as its empirical background. Discussions of the relationship between technology and organisations are not new in the eGovernment literature (see for instance Boudreau and Robey (2005)), but neither are they extensive. Structuration theory has been applied in the government arena (Walsham and Sahay 1999; Devadoss, Pan et al. 2003) but again not widely, whereas more recent developments with actor network theory have yet to reach this far. Government is made up of different kinds of organisations, but often in forms and relationships which differ from the private sector, and which are heavily influenced by formal politics. The primary external relationship that government agencies maintain is with citizens (voters, clients) not with paying customers.

It follows that there are a number of issues that should be investigated when considering the double dance of agency in the eGovernment context, which include:

- Is the practice of government comparable with the practice of business, or does it differ in fundamental ways which might invalidate the model?
- Is a government institution comparable to a commercial organisation?
- If DDoA's principal unit of analysis is an organisation; can this be extended to an interrelated complex of government institutions?
- Are ERP systems representative of the types of systems used in eGovernment?
- Are internet based information systems significantly different from pre-internet systems?

The paper investigates these questions, and formulates other relevant questions in the course of the analysis. It sketches the history of the double dance of agency model, and introduces the model itself. It presents a simple model of eGovernment practice as a structuring device for the investigation into the suitability of the model for the eGovernment field, and summarizes the major conclusions.

The Double Dance of Agency

The following description of the Double Dance of Agency (DDoA) model is derived from Rose, Jones and Truex (2005) and Rose and Jones (2005).

The problem of agency

A long-standing debate in the IS literature concerns the relationship between technology and organisation. Does technology cause effects in organisations, or is it humans that determine how technology is used? Many socio-theoretic accounts of a middle way between the extremes of technological and social determinism have been suggested; in recent years the more convincing explanations have been based on Giddens' structuration theory and, more recently, on actor network theory. The two theories, however, may be seen to adopt rather different, and potentially incompatible, views of agency. Thus, structuration theory sees agency as a uniquely human property, whereas the principle of general symmetry in actor network theory implies that machines may also be actors. This rather fundamental disagreement may be characterized as the problem of agency (Rose and Jones 2005). At the empirical level the problem of agency can be studied through ERP systems. These systems, though built and implemented by people, are thought to be wide-ranging in their effects on organizations, and offer good opportunities for the study of the interplay of human and machine agency. However these empirical stories reflect the same theoretical confusion: in some accounts the managers are the principal actors, whereas other accounts focus on the effects of the ERP system in enabling and constraining the work of the organisation. Since, it is argued, neither structuration theory nor actor network theory offers a particularly convincing account of the interaction of humans and machines, and their different accounts of agency make them hard to integrate in any meaningful way, it makes sense to try to develop a new theory of agency. This theory should specify and reconcile the different contributions of humans and machines in the evolution of organisations.

The model

The model focuses on three features of a socio-theoretical model of the interaction of machine and human agency, derived from the theoretical analysis of structuration theory and ANT, and from the empirical analysis of ERP system implementations. Structuration theory demonstrates that it is meaningless to study agency without studying the situated context in which it is exercised. Following Knights and Murray (Knights and Murray 1994), we call this context the *conditions* under which agency is exercised. Knights and Murray define 'conditions of possibility' as 'conditions that make certain course of action feasible while ruling out others.' From actor network theory we learn that a theory of human and machine agency should be able to account for the *process* of the interaction between machines and humans over time. How is it that the two forms of agency combine and influence each other over time to produce particular outcomes? From the comparison of the two theories we learn that human and machine agency is not the same, and we focus attention on this difference by theorizing the different *properties* of human and machine agency.

Properties, process and conditions are related in the double dance of agency model. Each of these will now be considered in more detail.

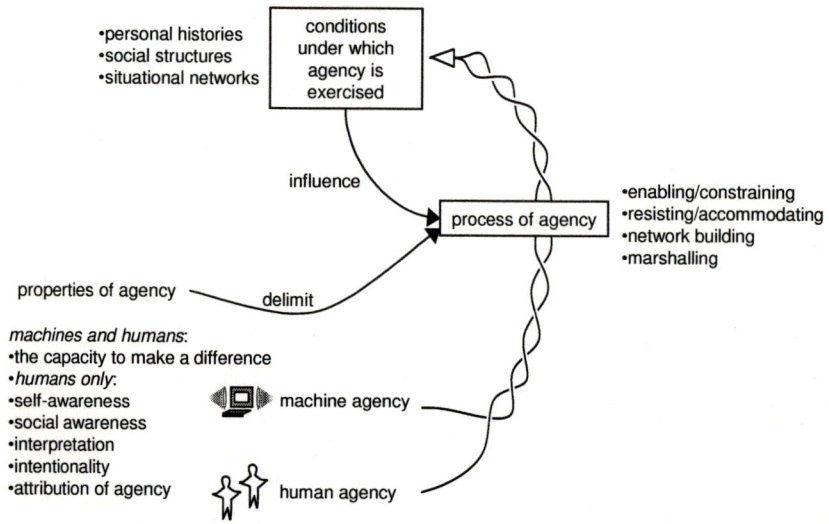

Figure 2: The double dance of agency (Rose and Jones 2005)

Properties

Stipulating the properties of agency helps us to distinguish the nature of human agency from that of machine agency. Agency is defined, following Giddens (1984) as 'the capacity to make a difference,' i.e. to act in a way which produces outcomes. From this perspective, both machines and humans can therefore be said to exercise agency. Indeed, the outcomes produced by machines may often be more evident than those produced by humans – compare the destructive power and of an unarmed human and a nuclear missile. When machines act they can be seen as tools (where they act directly under the control of humans to amplify their capacity to make a difference), as proxies (where they replace humans and act in their stead) or as automata (where they take over some (usually minor) part of human decision making as well as the power to act). Modern organisational computer systems can serve all three functions. However, human agency can be seen to have a number of distinctive properties that differentiate it from machine agency. Thus most humans are normally aware, both of themselves and of their social context. Of course machines can monitor their own internal state and may be capable of identifying, and to a certain extent accounting for, the behaviour of other agents, but they do not have the capacity to reflexively evaluate their own or others' purposes and actions in an autonomous fashion. *Self-awareness* relates to individuals' understanding of their personal history, whereas *social awareness* relates to individuals understanding of their social context (represented as structure by Giddens). Awareness, as Rose and Truex (2003) point out, is mediated by *interpretation*. Conditions and actions do not present un-ambiguous and universally agreed meanings, but are interpreted through internal personal discourses, and also through social discourse. Machine actions are normally subject to interpretation by humans, whereas a machine does not have the ability to interpret the actions of a human, though it may register them, and provide rule-based or 'learned' responses to them. A consequence of this process of interpretation is that humans also engage in agency *attribution*. That is, they seek to understand phenomena in terms of the outcomes of agency acts. Thus they attribute agency, causes and outcomes to particular actors, and may act on the basis of those attributions. As Collins & Kusch (1998) argue, however, such attribution may often be erroneous in the case of machine agency. More significantly, however, in terms of the analysis of human and machine agency, humans may also act on the consequences of that mistaken attribution.

Another important property of human agency in this context is *intentionality*, or volition – humans can direct their agency towards certain outcomes (though these may not be achieved in the manner intended, or at all). While the autonomy of human intentionality may be debated (many authors argue that human agency is heavily socially conditioned) and it must also be recognized that humans can also act in a routinized (situated) and non-intentional fashion, most current machines can only carry out tasks that have been directed at some level by humans. Thus, machines generally do not have the capability to decide which actions to take outside those parameters established by their designers.

Examining these properties of agency helps us to understand the different nature of the agencies of machines and humans. Whereas both humans and machines act in a way which causes consequences, only humans display self awareness, social awareness, interpretation, attribution of cause and effect, and intentionality.

Process

The study of machine agency also involves the study of the intentions of their human designers and the conditions under which the machines are used, and the study of human agency partly involves the study of human awareness and the way that this helps form the intention to act. However these 'properties' of human and machine agency do not determine particular outcomes; rather outcomes are an emergent product of a process of interaction of the two types of agency. An IS researcher encounters not separate technical and social components, but an ensemble (Orlikowski and Iacono 2001) in which the two are inextricably inter-related. It is this mutual interplay over time that the 'double dance of agency' metaphor seeks to capture.

A traditional way of understanding the effect of machine agency on human agency is as *enabling* and *constraining*. The fact that a machine is designed in a certain way, and operates in a particular set of conditions, implies that certain human courses of action are made more feasible, and others less feasible (or so overwhelmingly difficult that they seem impossible). 'Technology influences human agency by ......inviting specific courses of action' (Kallinikos 2002). In this perspective, machine agency is little more than the setting for human agency, part of the situation to which a person responds in acting. Humans may also be active in *network building*: that is in establishing functional co-operations with the machines that they work with in the light of the way that the machines enable and constrain their actions. This may partly involve changing the machines to better suit their purpose where this is possible. Because of the mutually interactive nature of situational machine agency and human network building, it is not necessarily easy to predict the outcomes of such a process.

In the organisational context, the choice of one technology over another may have a relatively strong influence on the actions of individuals, and the trajectory of the organisational group. Humans (for example managers) may explicitly seek to use this aspect of machine agency to reinforce their own intentions (for instance to reinforce a particular organisational strategy); Jones (1998) describes this directive use of machine agency as '*marshalling*' ('to marshal: to arrange in proper order, to cause to assemble, to usher'; Oxford English Dictionary). This should not be taken to mean that humans necessarily have control over the outcomes of marshalling. As Pickering (1995) argues, machines may '*accommodate*' some human intentions, but '*resist*' others. This is not to attribute anthropomorphic properties to machines, but to recognize that some human intentions fit more easily than others with the design trajectories of the machines and their influence displayed in organisational implementations. Humans for their part may also resist or accommodate machine agency, recognize these traits in others, and focus them towards their own intentions.

The variability of outcomes in relation to intentions and of resistance and accommodation will tend to make the process of interaction unpredictable. Humans thus rely on improvisation and bricolage to cope with the unexpected. Moreover, initial deviations from the original pattern may become amplified over time leading to significantly variant outcomes from apparently similar initial starting conditions. In emphasizing the emergent and unpredictable character of the process of interaction of machine and human agency, however, there is a danger of overlooking the stabilities. As Actor Network Theory describes, humans and machines can become enrolled in relatively stable networks (configurations of practice), some of which may even become sufficiently stabilized to be black boxed, such that the opportunities for agency in transforming them are no longer perceived to be necessary. For example, an established routine for carrying out a task may not change, despite the introduction of an information system that provides the opportunity for its radical redesign. As this illustrates, human capabilities of attribution and perception are important features shaping the way in which the process of interaction between human and machine agency works out.

The double dance of agency may be seen both in the design and development of the machine, as developers struggle to configure material artefacts (usually with the help of other machines) to achieve their objectives. It may also be seen in the use of the machine, as humans struggle to appropriate the artefacts produced by the development process to their particular needs (which may be a poor match for those intended by the designer). As Akrich (1997) argues, while designers may seek to 'inscribe' in the technical contents of the artefact they create their vision of (or prediction about) the world into which it is to be inserted, it is in users' encounters with the artefact that these visions are de-scripted and are realized (or not).

In as much as human and machine agency is mangled and conflated, it becomes an emergent process in which outcomes are seldom entirely the result of one form of agency, and seldom easily predictable. The process of the double dance of human and machine agency can thus be theoretically described as *enablement* and *constraint*, as *network building*, as *marshalling* and as *accommodation* and *resistance*. These processes lead to outcomes, where each set of emergent outcomes becomes the conditions under which the next actions are taken.

Conditions

The process of interaction between human and machine agency does not operate within a vacuum. Rather, it takes place within conditions (Knights and Murray 1994) that pre-exist the particular instance of interaction and may influence it. Individuals thus encounter their own and the machines' agency in the context of a personal identity that has a history and may also be seen as pursuing a particular trajectory into the future (Giddens, 1992). That *personal history* (here, we refer primarily to previous experience of the interaction of machine and human agency) may be a major factor in the interpretation of acts and conditions and may be an important component of individuals' self-awareness via personal reflexivity. As has already been noted, however, humans are not only self-aware, they are also socially aware. Social awareness makes possible the existence of broader *social structures* that are both the medium and outcome of human action (Giddens, 1984). Social structures (which also relate to technological artefacts: cf. Orlikowski's technological structures) influence actors' understandings of which human acts of agency are considered legitimate and of how machine and human agency is later interpreted. Communicated understandings of acts of agency (whether machine or human) feed back into social structures and have the power to reproduce or to transform them.

The situated character (Suchman 1987) of the process of interaction of human and machine agency has two important implications for the model. It suggests that the outcomes of the operation of agency need to be considered in terms of the particular circumstances of their interaction. These circumstances may be both social (a generally perceived problem with legacy systems) and material (the physical inability of legacy systems to communicate with each other). We use the term *situational network* to describe the particular socio-technical circumstances in which human and machine agency take place. As Pickering (1995) points out, however, it also has a further, more subtle implication for the role of human intentionality in the 'double dance of agency'. Thus, while human goals may orient action, they do not control it, and may themselves be transformed in practice through their encounters with machine agency. As Suchman (1987, ix) argues 'plans are best viewed as a weak resource for what is primarily *ad hoc* activity'.

Therefore, the conditions under which humans and machines act may be theorised as p*ersonal histories, social structures* and *situational networks*. Conditions are emergent: that is, though they influence the process of agency, they are also in part its outcome.

The double dance metaphor

The model of human and machine agency developed here proposes, therefore, that human and machine agency have different properties, but that the outcomes of their operation are emergent from the process of their interaction (rather than being determined by either); and that these interactions take place under conditions that shape outcomes, but may also be transformed by them. The separation of the three features is therefore largely an analytical convenience, since they are mutually interrelated (for example, properties influence process, process shapes expression of properties, conditions affect process and so on).

The practice of electronic government

Grönlund and Horan (2005) identify three spheres and associated relationships for eGovernment (Figure 3). This model acts as a simplifying device for understanding the complexity of stakeholder groups, relationships and discourse in the eGovernment. Practice in eGovernment is also complex, a recent taxonomy of relevant research areas included e-democracy, e-voting, e-hearing, e-consultation, e-deliberation, e-rulemaking, e-inclusion, e-governance, e-collaboration, e-community decision making, e-accessibility and mobile government (Rose 2006).

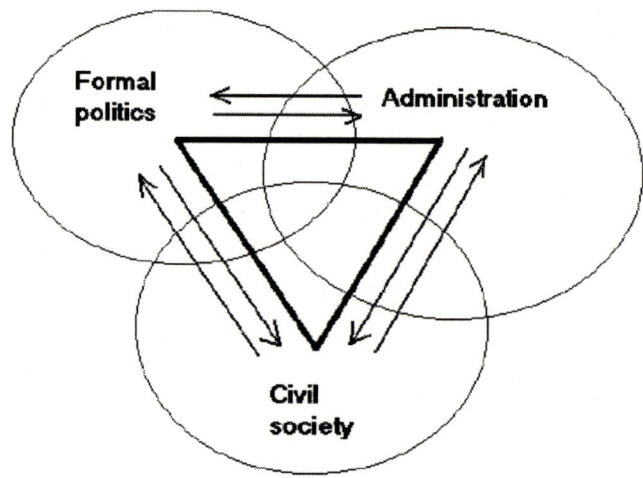

Figure 3: Basic spheres and relationships in a democratic government system
(Grönlund and Horan 2005)

This paper therefore develops a simplified model of eGovernment practice to help structure the later discussion

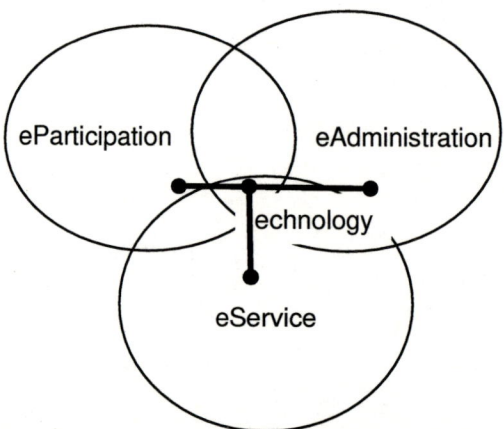

Figure 4: Basic practices in electronic government

The model reflects the stakeholders and relationships described in Grönlund's model, but focuses on three central practices of eGovernment defined as follows:

- eAdministration is the use of computer and networking technologies to support, develop and rationalise the internal process of government institutions, with a focus on efficiency and cost saving.
- eService is the use of computer and networking technologies to support and improve the delivery of government service to the public, with a focus on service quality and cost saving.
- eParticipation is the use of computer and networking technologies to support and develop the political process, with a focus on supporting and improving citizen involvement.

eAdministration reflects Grönlund's administrative sphere, targeting primarily the complexity of governmental practice distributed between many related government institutions, and the role that IT can have in helping to manage and order that complexity. However many administrative tasks (for example updating citizen registers) also involve contact with the citizen sphere. A particular interest and focus in eAdministration is the integration of administrative processes across government institutions (Layne and Lee 2001). eService reflects a primary relationship between the administration and civil society spheres, where citizens are the clients or customers of government, receiving the services to which they are entitled (and also fulfilling their obligations towards government). Services can be automated and extended through IT, and particularly though the internet which can relieve the burdens of time and space involved in face-to-face contact between citizens and government officials. The practice of eParticipation concerns the intersection of civil society with the formal political sphere, where modern communication technologies offer the potential for far greater involvement of citizens in political deliberation and decision making, and consequent evolution of democratic forms (Hoff, Löfgren et al. 2003; Rose and Sæbø 2005). Taken together, the three practices cover and subsume many of the more local practices, and, it is argued, can act as a framework for discussing the practice of eGovernment. Where administration, service and participation describe the practice of government, the 'e' (technology) element refers to the technologies that enable these practices. eGovernment technologies have two distinguishable roles (with much overlap): data-handling, and communication. In the first role, computer systems manipulate and store data (primarily for administrative purposes); in the second they function as communication media. The promise of eGovernment lies not in the technologies themselves (the computer and the telephone have been around for a long time), but in the seamless integration of the two roles. Thus, relevant eGovernment technologies include communication infrastructures underpinning mobile and web systems, and systems such as web-interfaced administration systems (e.g. ERP and CRM systems), portals enabling web services, web-based discussion, decision support and voting systems.

	eAdministration	eService	eParticipation
Technology as data-handling			
Technology as communication media			

Figure 5: Three dimensions of eGovernment practice, two technology views

Taken together, the three dimensions of eGovernment practice and the two technology perspectives (Figure 5) provide structure for the following discussion.

Government and Technology

Having described the double dance of agency model, and established a framework for consideration of eGovernment practice, this section considers whether, and how, DDoA should be adapted for use in the eGovernment field.

eAdministration

In principle, administration, service delivery and participation can all be described in terms of social practice, which can also be technologically mediated. In eGovernment, however, these practices are located in a particular kind of organisation: the government institution. Are there significant differences between commercial sector companies and public agencies which would invalidate the DDoA, or make changes necessary? The organisation and management literature features a somewhat inconclusive debate on this subject. Public agencies are argued to be different in regard to features such as:

- complexity through stakeholder variety and multiple conflicting goals
- permeability and openness
- instability due to changing political priorities
- absence of competitive pressure
- increased bureaucracy and red tape
- lower managerial autonomy
- different management ethos focused more on public service and less on material reward
- lower organizational commitment from staff because of weak linkage between performance and reward.

Boyne (2002) examined 34 surveys considering these propositions and found support for only three of them; greater bureaucracy, a stronger desire to promote public welfare and lower organisational commitment. Scott and Falcone (1998) identified three trends in the literature concerning public and private organisations: the generic approach (which assumes that organisations share generic features across the division), the core approach (which postulates fundamental core distinctions) and the dimensional approach (which suggests that organisations differ across several dimensions of 'publicness,' independent of their real ownership). They found rather little support for the generic approach, and more support for the core and dimensional approaches. However Boyne concluded that the 'available evidence does not provide clear support for the view that public and private organisations are fundamentally dissimilar in all important respects.' It would therefore seem inappropriate to dismiss the use of the DDoA to theorize eGovernment phenomena solely on the ground that it was devised in connection with commercial organisations. Few of the concepts employed in the model describe in any detailed way the aspects of organization and management theory discussed in the public/private literature; this is perhaps a weakness of the model in the context of commercial organisations. However it does mean that the more generalised sociological concepts can transfer across different types of organization. Nevertheless, a lack of specificity in relation to organisation and management concepts in eGovernment in the DDoA should be noted.

The unit of analysis in previous work on the DDoA has been the organisation, responding as it does to a particular framing of a problem in the relationship of technology and organisations located primarily in the IS literature. eGovernment cannot primarily be described as an organisational discipline; it encompasses government organisations, but its unit of analysis can be local, regional, national or international. Moreover it is relatively seldom that eGovernment studies focus on a single government organisation (though they can do); more often the focus is upon networks of organisations coupled in practice. For instance Layne and Lee (2001) focus on the integration of government organisations, a common eGovernment aspiration is the one-stop shop (Gopal, Krishnan et al. 2002) - a web portal providing integrated information and services across government departments), a prevailing technical issue is interoperability (Atherton 2002) - connectivity between information systems of different types in different locations. Again, the generality of the DDoA model might save it in respect to this plurality of units of analysis. The concept of social practice is not organisation-specific and can be located, like Wenger's communities of practice (Wenger 1998), in an organisation, in part of an organisation or across organisations. Though not designed as a contribution to different literature about the relationship of technology and society (see for example Hill (1988)), it could also describe the relationship of a particular practice and of a particular technology at the societal level. Moreover, the model includes elements of situational networks and network building which can apply to both micro and macro phenomena. An interpretation of the model could also be that macro phenomena are the result of many micro interactions of technology and people, in the same way that Giddens argues that society at the macro level is 'constituted' by many processes of structuration at the micro level (Giddens 1984).

DDoA is the result of investigations into ERP systems and it could be argued that, since eGovernment has partly focused on a variety of primarily net-based systems, this understanding cannot be transferred. However, eAdministration within eGovernment is increasingly based on large scale standard administrative systems. This is because of the integration problem: many individual bespoke systems constitute an integration nightmare. As an example, KommuneData (the company developing most of the regional government information systems in Denmark) has recently made an agreement with SAP (the leading supplier of ERP and CRM systems) which means that all its administrative systems will be transferred to a SAP backbone within the next ten years. Large administrative systems are therefore extremely relevant to eAdministration (moreover, the underlying technologies are more or less the same as those used in the commercial sector), and it should be expected that the evolution of administrative practice and its associated technologies will go hand in hand, as the model describes.

eService

The delivery of service can be studied as a social practice in the same way that other aspects of eGovernment can. However government is characterised by a different relationship with its citizens and clients, than the commercial sector has with its customers. A commercial enterprise has profit as its primary goal, and transactions with its customers are primarily financial in nature. A customer pays for goods or services, and accepts the profit seeking behaviour of a company as part of the relationship. When a government agency delivers service to its clients (whether this is healthcare, social benefits, land administration or a host of other activities), the transaction may be financial in nature, but will normally be characterised by a mutual relationship of a different nature. Government accepts the responsibility of public service, that is, a duty to act in the interests of its clients, whereas the client accepts that government has to balance the rights and obligations of individuals with those of society as a whole.

The critical, technological factor in the development of eServices is the global establishment of the Internet. Internet access shared by wide segments of a country's population enables the development of net-based electronic services – potentially any service which can be digitalised (which includes nearly all information services). Electronic services carry potential for both extensions of service and efficiency improvements. Extensions of service occur through increased range and availability of service, together with the potential for better information and transparency. Efficiency savings occur primarily because electronic transactions are much cheaper than paper transactions, and because

Government clients can be persuaded to take over much of the data-entry, such as filling in an on-line tax form. Nevertheless, achieving service extension and efficiency saving usually require both considerable investment in infrastructure and computer systems, and organisational re-organisation (so-called business process re-engineering). Though the development of the internet background has been promoted by governments, it is equally driven by commercial interests and by consumer demand. In this way it can better be described as a societal technology trajectory than a government technology. The current rapid development of mobile telephone networks shares the same characteristics. Thus the provision of eServices can just as easily be investigated as a response to a societal technology development, driven by consumers who are used to having their services delivered electronically, as it can be regarded as a government-sponsored initiative. Though the DDoA model considers technology conditions, and the emergent evolution of these conditions, as part of the internal situation in which organisational agency is exercised, it invites no specific consideration of the wider technology trajectories important for understanding these aspects of eGovernment.

eParticipation

eParticipation considers the extension of the political process by technological means. Technology can support some of the mechanisms by which that process is enacted, for instance petitioning, lobbying and voting. In its role as communication media, technology can also underpin the deliberative aspect of political debate, argument and opinion-formation. Technology can be an important instrument for politicians wanting to establish consensus behind their policies, and for social movements wanting to influence the developmental direction of their communities. However eParticipation is in some respects the poor relation of this eGovernment triangle, in that it has few obvious benefits for the administrations that should introduce it (Flak and Rose 2005). Moreover, it is even more clearly the product of a wider development in society. On-line chat, SMS, internet campaigning, blogging, e-newspapers, internet pressure groups and petitioning are an unstoppable and irreversible development in modern democracies. As an example, a Danish politician is said to have exploited the chain SMS technique to generate anti-Muslim sentiment during the recent

Mohammed cartoon crisis. However, she could hardly be said to have anything to do with developing the technique, let alone the background technologies or infrastructure – she simply recognized and borrowed a phenomenon familiar in youth culture and marketing. Government-sponsored eParticipation is thus more likely to gain ground as a result of societal technological development (technology push) and citizen pressure, than political action. As mentioned above, the DDoA is poorly focused on societal technology trajectories, but it also lacks reference to any formal political process. Of course the negotiation of differing interests is part of any social practice, but DDoA contains only passing references to these, and none to any known formal political theory. The model is better furnished with sense-making and meaning attribution concepts, but its technology frame is rather locked in the data-handling view (for which ERP systems are a classic example), and poorly equipped to explain the communication media perspective. According to DDoA, computer systems rather mechanistically exert agency in an organisation by enabling and constraining organisational process. Their role in supporting and affecting sense-making, deliberation or meaning attribution is not so much considered.

A further phenomenon that DDoA is poorly equipped to explain is the development of democratic or societal structure in conjunction with technology. Cyber-democracy (a potential form of distributed democracy enabled by the internet) is a point of discussion amongst technology-oriented, political scientists (Bellamy 2000), whereas Castells (2001), taking a soft technological determinist perspective, describes a network society in which the shape of society itself is inherently bound to, and shaped by the galaxy of computers connected by the Internet. To paraphrase Marx: the plough gives you agrarian society, the steam engine gives you industrial society and the Internet gives you the network society. Though the thrust of the argument of DDoA is not impossibly far from Castells' position, it considers none of the features of society (such as economic forms, social movements, urbanisation) that carry his argument. Both democratic forms and social structure are related to social practice; in the structuration theory influenced way that DDoA relates agency to conditions, but both the substance of these arguments (social structure, democracy) and the scale (society) are missing.

The double dance of technology and government

Having reviewed some strengths and weaknesses of DDoA in relation to eAdministration, eService and eParticipation, the next section serves two functions. It firstly presents some sketches for the relationship between technology and government based on the double dance of agency model, and secondly develops a research agenda based on the preceding analysis.

In as much as the DDoA theorises the relationship between the agency of machines (computer systems) and humans in social practice, then, in principle, it can be transferred to describe the emergent relationship of computer based technology with the social practice called government. In one rather limited eGovernment research application area, the implementation of large administrative computer systems in a government agency, the model is in familiar and safe territory. Thus it can be used to analyse conditions under which the implementation takes place: the set of existing computing arrangements and administrative practices, personal and shared experiences of work practice and other implementations. Civil servants and consultants make the decisions and implement the new hardware and software, but the system has already a work model inscribed in it, and thus has an influence on developing practice. Over time, the system resists some of the managers' and clerical workers intentions and accommodates others, with some actors using it to further their own plans and strategies; the new technologically enabled practice emerges as a product both of the system's inherent character and the intentional situated actions of the actors involved with it. Experience of the implementation is interpreted by the human actors, and the emergent understandings and arrangements help to form the practice situation which forms the set of conditions under which the next technology implementation takes place. Although a government agency is a specialised form of organisation, and a large administrative computer system is not necessarily an ERP system, the differences are minor and can easily be accommodated in the analysis.

However, this research application is rather narrowly located in the broader frame of eGovernment research, since it is combines a focus on eAdministration with a data-handling perspective of computing technology (Figure 6). It is also focused at an organisational level of analysis.

Technology and Government

	eAdministration	eService	eParticipation
Technology as data-handling	X		
Technology as communication media			

Figure 6: Immediate application of DDoA in eGovernment

Even this narrow application ignores the role of technology in integrating the practice of diverse government agencies – a rather central theme of eGovernment.

Broader accounts of the relationship between technology and government are at

1. the practice level: administration, service, participation
2. the societal level: the relationship between societal practice in the development and use of technologies and government's practice.

At the first level, DDoA serves to suggest a picture of eGovernment practice which is neither the outcome of politicians', administrators' or citizens' actions, nor is determined by the trajectory of technology development. Instead it is the emergent outcome of both forms of agency. Moreover, every practice is situated in a pre-existing set of social and technological conditions, and the outcome of eGovernment initiatives helps to shape the conditions under which later initiatives take place. The situated and emergent nature of these interactions make the management of such projects difficult, and the outcomes hard to predict. At the second level, DDoA could suggest a parallel account of human/technology interaction, where developments in eGovernment are partly mirrored, and partly shaped by wider developments in society. However, neither of these accounts are, at present, particularly well-developed.

As a result of the preceding analysis, a research agenda for the development of DDoA in the eGovernment field could be suggested as follows:

- Technology: the communication media perspective of technology is absent from the model and could be better developed and included.
- Technology: the role of technology as infrastructure is also undeveloped; in particular the model should be capable of saying something more specific about the Internet's role in enabling interactions between different functions and agencies of government, and between citizens, administrators and politicians.
- Technology: the role of wider technology trajectories in society in influencing eGovernment practice should be explored.
- Technology: the role of technology push versus government pull should be investigated (does technology respond to government requirements, or does government respond to the trajectory of technology in the wider society?).
- eAdministration: concepts related to public administration, management and organisation forms are lacking and could be developed in a more specific way.
- eService: concepts relating to the relation of government to citizens are lacking and could be developed in a more specific way.
- eParticipation: both the 1) explicit political and 2) evolution of society dimensions are missing and need to be developed.

In addition, there is a substantial question of scale to address when theorizing should cross various levels of analysis; for example, individual, organisational, governmental, societal. The mutually emergent relationship between micro and macro socio-technical phenomena should be explicitly addressed, as should the connections between the individual and their computer, organisational computing, multiple networked organisations and online society.

Conclusions

This paper addressed a central theoretical problem in eGovernment: the relationship between technology and government. It contributed to the discussion by taking an existing model from the Information Systems field (the Double Dance of Agency) and considering its relevance and applicability in the eGovernment field. DDoA is a contribution to the literature about the relationship of organisations and computing systems, based on re-framing of a classical discussion of social and technological determinism as 'the problem of agency.' The problem of agency is equally relevant in the eGovernment field; it invites consideration (for instance) of whether eGovernment outcomes are principally influenced by the technology available or the people designing, implementing and using it. If both have an influence, then what is the character and nature of the different kinds of influence, and how do they combine? Are these influences generic, or situationally located? The paper framed the discussion by considering three eGovernment social practices: eAdministration, eService and eParticipation, and two perspectives of technology: a data-handling perspective and a communications media.

The consequent discussion isolated many areas of interest in the eGovernment field which were not explicitly addressed by DDoA, for instance: the communications media perspective of technology, the role of technology as infrastructure, the role of wider technology trajectories, concepts related to public administration, management and organisation forms, the relation of government to citizens, formal politics and the evolution of society, as well as the question of scaling across levels of analysis. Nevertheless, it was concluded that the model could make an immediate contribution to eGovernment research application area: the implementation of large scale administrative systems in government agencies.

However, the real contribution of the model in the wider eGovernment debate might be to focus attention on the similarities and differences between human government actors and computer systems, the different roles they play in producing eGovernment outcomes in different situations and under different conditions, and the emergent and inter-dependant character of those roles. This debate would seem rather central to the evolution of the field.

Acknowledgements

Duane Truex and Mathew Jones, without whom this project would have been impossible.

This work was supported in part by Demo-Net: the European Network of Excellence in eParticipation funded under the European 6th Framework research programme.

References

Akrich, M. (1997). The de-scription of technical objects. In: W. E. Bijker and J. Law, *Shaping Technology, Building Society*. London, MIT Press: 205-224.

Atherton, L. (2002). SeamlessUK--building bridges between information islands. *New Library World* 103(11/12): 467.

Bellamy, C. (2000). Modelling electronic democracy, Towards democratic discourses for an information age. In: J. Hoff, Horrocks, I., Tops, P., *Democratic governance and new technology, technologically mediated innovations in political practice in Western Europe*. London, Routledge.

Boudreau, M. C. and D. Robey (2005). Enacting integrated information technology: A human agency perspective. 16(1): 3-18.

Boyne, G. A. (2002). Private and public management: what the difference?. *Journal of Management Studies* 39(1): 97-122.

Castells, M. (2001). *The Internet Galaxy - Reflections on the Internet, Business and Society*. Oxford, Oxford University Press.

Collins, H. and M. Kusch (1998). *The Shape of Actions: What Humans and Machines Can Do*. Massachusetts, The MIT Press.

Devadoss, P. R., S. L. Pan, et al. (2003). Structurational analysis of e-government initiatives: a case study of SCO. *Decision Support Systems* 34(3): 253-269.

Flak, L. and J. Rose (2005). Stakeholder Governance: Adapting Stakeholder Theory to the E-Government Field. *Communications of the ACM* 16(article 31, October): 642-664.

Giddens, A. (1984). *The Constitution of Society*. Cambridge, Polity Press.

Gopal, A., M. S. Krishnan, et al. (2002). Measurement Programs in Software Development: Determinants of Success. *IEEE Transactions on Software Engineering* 28(9): 863-875.

Grönlund, A. (2004). State of the art in e-Gov research - A survey. *Electronic Government, Proceedings, Lecture Notes in Computer Science* 3183: 178-185.

Grönlund, Å. and T. A. Horan (2005). Introducing e-Gov: History, Definitions, and Issues. *Communications of the Association for Information Systems* 15(713-729).

Hill, S. (1988). *The Tragedy of Technology.* London, Pluto Press.

Hoff, J., K. Löfgren, et al. (2003). The state we are in: E-democracy in Denmark. *Information Polity: The International Journal of Government & Democracy in the Information Age* 8(1/2): 49-66.

Kallinikos, J. (2002). *Reopening the black box of technology: artifacts and human agency.* Twenty-Third International Conference on Information Systems, Barcelona.

Knights, D. and F. Murray (1994). *Managers Divided: Organisation Politics and Information Technology Management.* Chichester, Wiley.

Layne, K. and J. W. Lee (2001). Developing fully functional E-government: A four stage model. *Government Information Quarterly* 18(2): 122-136.

Orlikowski, W. I. and C. S. Iacono (2001). Research Commentary: Desperately Seeking the "IT" in IT Research - A Call to Theorizing the IT Artifact. *Information Systems Research* 12(2): 121-134.

Perng, Y. H. and C. L. Chang (2004). Data mining for government construction procurement. *Building Research and Information* 32(4): 329-338.

Rose, J. (2006). *Framing eParticipation.* Understanding eParticipation workshop, dgo (7th Annual Conference on Digital Government Research), San Diego, Digital Government Research Centre.

Rose, J. and M. Jones (2005). The Double Dance of Agency: a socio-theoretic account of how machines and humans interact. *Systems, Signs and Actions:* 19-37.

Rose, J., M. Jones, et al. (2003). *The Problem of Agency; How Humans Act, How Machines Act.* ALOIS Workshop: Action in Language, Organisations and Information Systems, Linköping, Sweden, Linköping University.

Rose, J., M. Jones, et al. (2005). Socio-theoretic Accounts of IS: the Problem of Agency. *Scandinavian Journal of Information Systems* 17(1): 133-152.

Rose, J. and Ø. Sæbø (2005). Democracy Squared: designing on-line political communities to accommodate conflicting interests. *Scandinavian Journal of Information Systems, E-government special issue* 17(2): 133–168.

Scott, P. G. and S. Falcone (1998). Comparing public and private organizations. *American Review of Public Administration* 28(2): 126-145.

Sivakumar, D. (2002). Social interventions for e-governance, decentralised democracy, Panchayati Raj and sustainable development: Challenges and opportunities. *Indian Journal of Social Work* 63(3): 436-444.

Suchman, L. A. (1987). *Plans and Situated Actions: The Problem of Human-Machine Communication.* New York, Cambridge University Press.

Walsham, G. and S. Sahay (1999). GIS for District-Level Administration in India: Problems and Opportunities. *MIS Quarterly* 23(1): 39-66.

Wenger, E. (1998). *Communities of practice: learning, meaning, and identity.* Cambridge, U.K.; New York, N.Y, Cambridge University Press.

The Evolution of the Danish ICT Infrastructure Since 2000

Ole Brun Madsen

> ICT infrastructure was one of the four main areas in the Digital North Denmark project, DDN, and selected as one of the topics for the associated participatory research projects. It was proposed by Aalborg University, AAU, taking the lack of evolution of the regional infrastructure into account. This included a foreseen very fast growth in capacity demands from ICT based services such as e-government and the democratic aspects of preventing a major part of the population from potential participation.
> ICT infrastructure was a new research field at university level. The participation in DDN was an opportunity to create a framework for fast dissemination of new research results from AAU in a project dealing with the planning of the next generation ICT Infrastructure with access to the results from a large scale investigation on the needs and possibilities in a modern ICT based society and in this context an improved insight in the requirements for the next generation ICT infrastructure.
> This contribution describes part of the history and results achieved during the DDN period and the potential impact on the state of the art with respect to the national ICT infrastructure and the research field.

Introduction

A state of the art Information and Communication Technology (ICT) infrastructure plays a key role in the evolution of the global ICT based society.

The term *infrastructure* is used as a synonym for the organisation of elements forming the network structure.

ICT infrastructure is especially important in relation to e-government because of the democratic issues related to this technological area (cf. Torpe's and Nielsen's papers in this book). Providing e-services to citizens requires not only good design of such services (as dealt with by Christiansen in this book) but also an infrastructure which can deliver such services to all citizens. This paper introduces issues related to infrastructure and provides an insight into the area in order to clarify that infrastructure is not something which is just there but rather brings with it several considerations of relevance to both research and practice.

The ICT infrastructure has evolved from a set of more or less vertically integrated networks dedicated to specific applications and service types, towards an interworking set of horizontally integrated and converging infrastructure platforms, common for literally all services.

The complete digitalisation of video, audio and picture services makes this evolution possible and forms the base for further integration and convergence. Sharing the physical transmission facilities for both wired and wireless technology has turned the basic infrastructure into an autonomous communication level providing the common base for the implementation of the logical infrastructures on the switching and the application l (Figure 7).

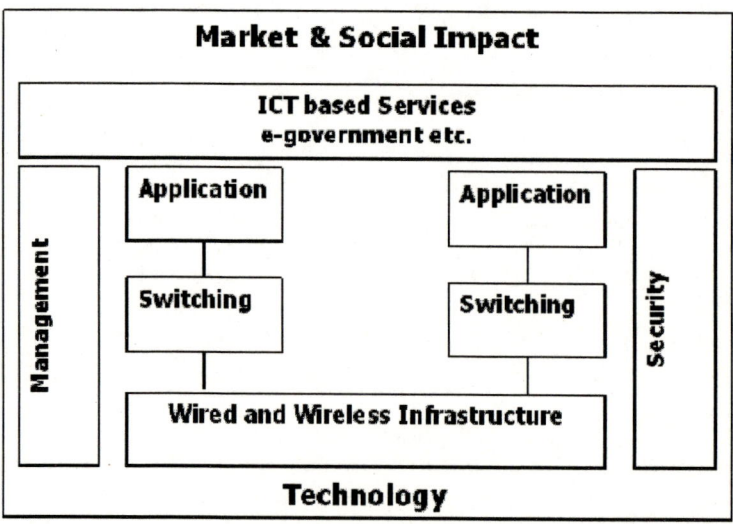

Figure 7: ICT Infrastructure

One of the benefits has been a constant drop in the price/performance ratio for the infrastructure services, but also an increase in the complexity of the requirements due to the coexistence of an increasing variety of different transmission demands ranging from best effort type of services to services with strong demands for real time behavior, reliability, fault tolerance, etc. on the same platform. These types of demands were previously solved service by service, each with full control over the transmission facilities involved.

On the other hand, it also opens the potential of bringing new data and telemetric services with strong Quality of Service (QoS) requirements into the Wide Area Networks (WAN's). This kind of services were previously limited to the Local Area Networks (LAN's) due to the relatively high costs for dedicated leased-line based WAN infrastructures, in particular if redundancy was required in order to obtain sufficient reliability.

The absence of new design principles, allowing for smooth and cost efficient scalability without loss of control over the structurally based properties may prevent or seriously delay the introduction of such new services.

The implementation of an up-to-date global ICT infrastructure is a long term irreversible investment. The implementation is time consuming and with the fast evolution in the demand for capacity, coverage and quality extreme care has to be taken into account in the planning process in order to prevent serious delays in meeting the requirements.

The infrastructure concept

The infrastructure concept is used in many contexts and on several abstraction levels covering a commonly shared, underlying system for one or more application or service areas. Exactly the presence or planned presence of one or more applications is a precondition for the infrastructure concept.

In many cases, the infrastructure is identified as a set of shared elements forming a reasonable self-contained subsystem in a system expanding with more parallel technical or organizational applications.

The definition will usually take offset in rational technical or organizational considerations. For larger infrastructures, political considerations can play a major role in order to ensure general interests like national security, promoting fair competition on the application or service level, equal conditions for service access for the population at large including the private, the public and the industrial market, etc.

An infrastructure is not a goal in itself, but plays an important role as the common founding element for the evolution of services and applications.

Biased ownership and control over an underlying infrastructure in combination with service provisioning can easily lead to near-monopoly situations in a market otherwise intended for competitive services.

In practice it is not possible or economically feasible to establish parallel infrastructures for the same class of services or applications.

An ICT infrastructure has many similarities with other infrastructures like the road network where bridges, tunnels, traffic lights, etc. are serving as a common platform for a variety of active transport systems such as private cars, trucks, busses. No one would ever dream of establishing competing parallel highways.

Technical elements in the ICT infrastructure

The ICT infrastructure covers medias like cables, radiofrequencies and parts of the technology associated with the transport and distribution of information. In a broader sense, the ICT infrastructure also includes the ducts, facilities for housing of equipment, power supply, cooling systems, masts for antennas, etc.

The scope for the ICT infrastructure is floating as parts of the switching systems and application service systems may be included. An ICT network architecture is illustrated in (Figure 8) where the basic ICT infrastructure covers the three lower levels.

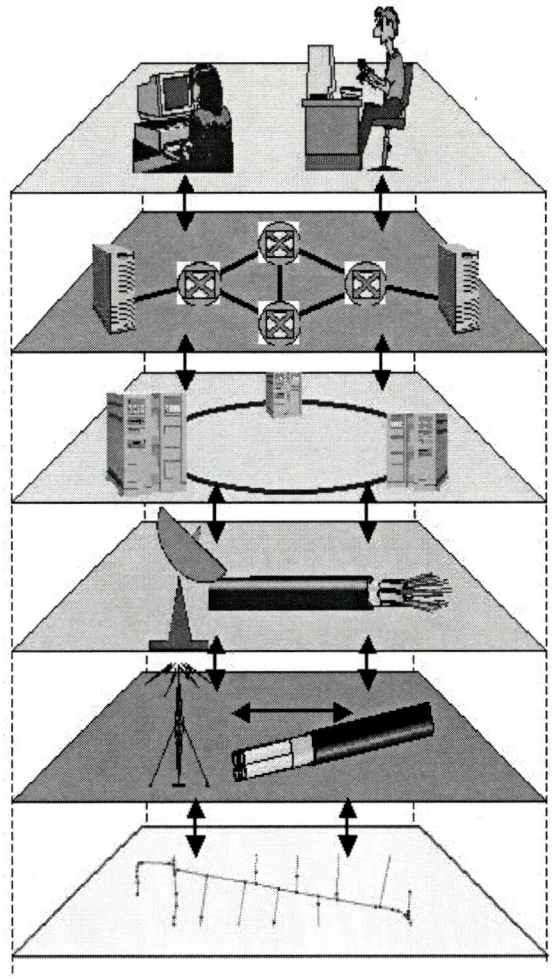

Application level, end-users
End-user equipment, program databases etc.

IP level, switching
IP operator networks. Services for end-users.

Transmission level, connectivi
More logical connections over one physical connection.

Cable and Antenna level
Cables, blank fibres, antennas, etc.

Ducts and mast level
Ducts for cables, masts for antennas, etc.

Trace level
Trace's for ducts, cables, area for housing and masts, etc.

Figure 8: ICT network architecture

The main function of an ICT infrastructure is to establish the potential for basic connectivity for exchange of information between any two network termination points, based on wired and wireless technology.

The infrastructure can in general be divided in three general network components:

- *The Connection Networks*
- *The Distribution Networks*
- *The Main Networks*

A Connection Network connects the end users to a Distribution Network and provides the local wide area coverage. Until now, the transmission in the Connection Networks has in general been based on either twisted pair access lines (telephony and data), coax (cable-TV) systems or wireless access systems (mobile telephony). The next generation Connection Networks will be based on fibre optical cables. The wireless evolution over the past decade has provided almost all end users with a potential secondary connection network and thereby potential dual access for voice communication and limited data communication.

The Distribution Networks provide the local wide area connectivity and distribution structure for a group of Connection Networks, to and from the Main Networks. The coverage is typically corresponding to a municipality or a region. The dominating technology is fibre optical cables.

The Main Networks interconnect the Distribution Networks, providing the global world wide area connectivity. The MNs are organised in hierarchical levels, like regions, countries, continents. The technology is fibre optical cables.

The Danish ICT infrastructure in 2000

In 2000 the Danish ICT infrastructure was established with a Main Network and a set of Distribution Networks based on fibre optical cables covering approx. 2000 distribution points with access for the Connection Networks.

The liberalisation of the telecommunication in the previous decade has led to parallel implementation of multiple Main Networks and a limited set of Distribution Networks primarily in connection with implementations of global infrastructure by larger international carriers.

The general opinion was that there was an extremely high, unexploited capacity in the Main Networks compared to the actual needs generated in the Distribution and Connection Networks.

As mentioned earlier, the Connection Network was built by twisted pair copper access lines (telephony and data), coax (cable-TV) systems and wireless access systems (mobile telephony). The coverage with copper access and mobile was 100% and with cable-TV app. 30%

Data rates was typically ISDN 64Kbit/sec and dial-up modems with data rates beyond 64Kbit/sec. Fibre optical cables were provided for the high end business segment.

The potential for introducing higher speed internet access via the cable-TV systems was under investigation.

The general growth in capacity consumption of data access led to the introduction of the xDSL (Digital Subscriber Line) technology, installed on top of the copper access network. The expectation was that this technology, opening initially for capacities in the range 128-512 Kbit/sec, would only be of interest for the high and middle size business segments and not of interest for private end users or small enterprises.

Over the next 5 years, the number of connections exceeded 1 million, completely dominated by the private end-users and with a capacity over 2 Mbit/sec for more than 35% of the connections.

With respect to coverage with xDSL/cable-TV type of broadband access, Denmark is amongst the leading countries in the world.

DDN and ICT infrastructure

Aalborg University took the initiative of putting focus on the ICT infrastructure in the North Denmark project (DDN). ICT infrastructure was selected as one of the four main topics in DDN.

The North Denmark ICT infrastructure year 2000

Knowledge about the ICT infrastructure is in general not publically available, which makes it difficult to give a more precise picture of the situation in year 2000.

The general situation in North Denmark was not much different from similar rural regions in Denmark at that time.

Tele Denmark (TDC) was the overall dominating Danish operator in fixed networks. Sonofon had a strong position on the wireless infrastructure in a region with wireless technology as a strong base for R&D on an internationally high level. Telia-Stofa had a strong position on cable-TV, an area which also counts several major, user-owned systems, facing the upcoming digitalisation process of the TV signals and the accompanying rather costly investments in upgrading the systems.

Some international operators crossed the region with fibre optical cables as part of their international activities on establishing global transmission connectivity. This could open for new possibilities for the region seen in an international perspective and in particular as support for some of the initiatives for closer cooperation with the neighboring Nordic regions.

In Aalborg city and a in a few more of the larger cities in the region, some fiber optical systems were already established by a variety of operators and local initiatives, but almost completely without any kind of mutual coordination. Even the municipalities providing the digging permissions did not posses a complete picture of where the cables and ducts were placed or an overview over the available used and spare capacity.

Some years before, the regional municipality had taken an initiative together with a regional bank to make a plan for a dedicated fiber structure, but the plan was never implemented.

DDN visions for the ICT infrastructure

In 1999, Aalborg University contributed to the DDN preparation phase with the description of a number of ICT infrastructure problems to be handled if the overall idea of the DDN project as a base for a future ICT based society in the region at large would be realistic.

It is interesting to note that the potential convergence between the wired and wireless networks was formulated as a goal for the first time.

The preparatory work of Aalborg University was adopted as framework for the tendering material formulated by the DDN working group with representatives from public and private interest groups in the area.

The DDN tender

The following specific goals were formulated in the call for tender:
- Geographical coverage with capacity and functionality
- Inter working between the various transport forms

The Evolution of the Danish ICT Infrastructure since 2000

- Convergence in the user access
- Increased mobility and global access to the ICT society independent of geographical position
- Reduction of ICT infrastructure cost
- Enhanced accessibility and quality
- New infrastructure technologies
- Improved competition
- The knowledge base for operation and development of infrastructure should be kept in the region
- Promotion of unification and totality without getting closed solutions and monopolization.

In the tender material, two groups of important objectives had to be met.

The first was the complete geographical coverage, sufficient capacity, mobility and cheap access to the global ICT world and cheap transport of information.

The other was the requirement for regional protection against larger errors in the infrastructural components. This point became particular actual, as the whole region in the preparation phase experienced an almost 100% breakdown of all communication in the region for a whole day in connection with a loss of a power supply.

In order to concretise and illustrate the framework for the tender, four sub-areas were selected and possible scenarios given.

DDN projects on ICT infrastructure

From the tender, four winner projects were selected:

Bitvognen
A project aiming at establishing a platform for improved communication in the rural area communities with the global society. Components in the project was broadband access, IP based high quality video distribution, testing of new technologies, etc.

Nordjysk Netforum (NJNF) and KMD Netbroker
A double-project aiming at establishing a neutral, long-term strategic operator and vendor development plan for the ICT Infrastructure in the North Denmark region and establishing a new type of enterprise acting

as an ICT Infrastructure broker between the end-users and the ICT Infrastructure service providers inside the framework of the long term strategic development plan.

The long term strategic development plan for the ICT Infrastructure in the North Denmark region produced by NJNF obtained one of the highest scores in the following overall evaluation of the DDN initiative. In particular, credit was given for the already registered influence on the evolution in other regions adopting the principles in the strategic plan provided for North Denmark.

Personal Mobile Broadband Services (PMBS)

A project aiming at providing a new type of flexible, mobile internet terminals in cooperation with one of the local information service providers.

TV2/North-Digital

A project aiming at establishing a terrestrial based, interactive IP based digital TV-channel distribution network.

NJNF after the DDN period

The steering committee for the NJNF project made a proposal to the North Denmark Region for the follow up on the ICT infrastructure work after the end of the DDN initiative.

The committee proposed the establishment of a knowledge center for ICT infrastructure placed at Aalborg University financed through an expected portfolio of strategic planning projects in the region but also from a number of other regions that had closely followed the DDN project and expressed a strong interest in getting access to the know-how gained in the NJNF project.

The goal was to ensure that the know-how of NJNF would be kept together in order to support the initiatives to establish a next generation ICT infrastructure. With a close linkage to the planned Center for TeleInFrastruktur (CTIF) at Aalborg University, fast dissemination of new research results could be ensured and contribute to the potential for bringing the North Denmark region in front in this field.

Aalborg University was prepared to host the center but the North Denmark region was not prepared to take the risk in the initial financing.

The final result was that the employees in NJNF established a private, independent company of their own, keeping the NJNF name. Initially, the company was based on contracts with a number of regional and local municipalities, but these contracts have been followed by contracts with a number of electricity distribution companies entering the fiber to the domestic market as foreseen and pointed out in the NJNF project.

CNP, Center for Network Planning

CNP, Center for Network Planning, was founded in January 2004 based on an agreement between the Institutes of Business Studies, Electronic Systems, Mathematics and Planning at Aalborg University and hosted by the department of Control Engineering at the Institute of Electronic Systems.

CNP was established in order to strengthen the base for research, special studies, education, training and dissemination of results within the field of Network Planning and with special focus on the development of the next generation ICT Infrastructure.

The Network Planning research area ideally deals with all aspects of analysing and planning ICT networks. Taking the limited resources at CNP into account, some specific areas have been chosen for the research work in this first period.

In CNP, the focus has been on planning ICT Infrastructure with the aim of providing useful results in the planning process for next generation fibre optical based broadband ICT infrastructure and the convergence towards an integrated wired and wireless, unified infrastructure for 4G.

The following initiatives have been identified and initiated:
- Description, development and analysis of network structures
- Structural Quality of Services, SQoS, based network planning for wired and wireless infrastructures
- Analysis of Growth Limits
- Model for Automatic Planning of ICT Networks (MAPIN)
- Intelligent ICT Infrastructure, I3
- Establishing international contacts and cooperation

Part of the research activities has been to identify and describe a general framework and uncover missing research fields of importance for the planning process. The close relations with the educational system, the feedback from the external dissemination of result activities through the CNP knowledge center and the cooperation within CTIF form a valuable base for keeping the research strategy up-to-date.

CNP is working for closer cooperation between researchers across institutions and disciplines, as well as for closer cooperation with similar research institutions and commercial companies nationally and internationally. CNP is in the process of establishing a new research team based on relatively young researchers as only a very limited number of established researchers exists in this new field. In order to ensure an internationally recognised level of research, participation with papers in conferences and journals has been prioritised in order to gain qualified feedback and at the same time to establish a base for exchanging knowledge with existing as well as new cooperative partners.

The research dealing with formulation of theories, proofs and simulations, investigating the SQoS concept invented and formulated in CNP, has brought some new structuring principles into play that have proven to be superior to the present state of the art in structuring principles.

The results are major contributions in:

- Methods to ensure global and documented properties across the Wide Area Networks, WANs.
- Considerable improvement in the utilisation factor of the network resources with respect to network capacity.
- Establishment of a base for the introduction of new routing principles simplifying the routing process and reducing the network management overhead for keeping the routing information up to date including the time taken to stabilise the network in break-down situations.
- Improved and new algorithms in the field of automatic generation of network plans, based on available Geographical Information Systems, GIS, based documentation, including expansions from 2D to 3D algorithms.
- Investigations in the problem of identifying growth limits in large scale networks.

During the period, NJNF and the knowledge center of CNP have until now been involved with strategic planning for an area covering close to half of the Danish population and has obtained a position as leading in this field – recognized in Denmark as well as internationally.

Conclusions and reflections

The communication world will change dramatically over the next decades. If we want to influence the evolution in order to move in a direction where the result satisfies our wishes and expectations, more efforts are needed to understand the strategic steps to be taken including the obstacles to be removed.

The DDN initiative was a unique opportunity to highlight the needs in an expected future ICT based society, and in this context to highlight the requirements for an ICT infrastructure.

Some key elements and problem areas in the strategic process were investigated in the NJNF project under the DDN initiative. One of the major achievements might have been the efforts to establish general awareness of the needs for a new infrastructure in the population and in particular in the more rural regions in Denmark.

Today, the political awareness in the local communities is high, but the clear message did unfortunately not reach the national level in due time to take the needed steps to establish the necessary framework for research, development and education as well as some needed regulatory steps to ensure an evolution that could have brought Denmark into a unique position in the ICT based society. This is particularly strange seen from the outside and in the light of the results from the governmental initiated and sponsored DDN initiative.

New elements relevant for the ICT infrastructure, such as more emphasis on development of network management and security schemes must be taken into account and brought into a common framework programme if we want to design architectures able to encompass our needs in the future network.

Some specific requirements and consequences for the infrastructure of an explosive growth in bandwidth demands and new applications were highlighted. Reducing the burden of the upper layers, efforts to compensate for an incomplete underlying network and dynamical support for the fast changing complex logical connectivity patterns are requested.

The Structural based Quality of Service (SQoS) approach taken at Aalborg University, allowing for topological routing in large scale networks, could be an important step in meeting these requirements. This approach in combination with enhanced automatic planning tools for integrated wired and wireless broadband planning could be a cornerstone in a converging process leading from the present unsatisfactory state of the art towards the picture of a well organized future intelligent ICT Infrastructure.

Part Three
Politics & Organisation

Local Political Deliberations on the Internet

Lars Torpe

> Based on experiences from experiments with e-democracy in the municipality of Hals and a number of other Danish municipalities, the article tries to assess the potentials of the Internet for political deliberation. Political deliberation is seen here as a broader concept than political dialogue and, in an assessment of the potentials of e-deliberation, three main questions are addressed: 1) Which new tools are constructed to open for citizen involvement in local politics? 2) Does the use of these tools lead to more public debate and have new actors become involved in the debate? 3) Is anyone listening and does anybody respond to what is discussed on-line?

Introduction

In later years, several scholars have voiced doubts as to whether the Internet is an adequate medium for political deliberation. In this article, I shall try to assess this position in the light of some experiments with e-participation that took place in Hals, a little municipality outside Aalborg, Denmark from 2002 to 2004. For obvious reasons, several of the critical assessments have been influenced by the work of Jürgen Habermas and his view on public deliberation (Habermas, 1962, 1996). The article will develop a different approach to the public sphere and to public deliberation. On that base, the following questions are addressed: 1) Which new tools are constructed to open for citizen involvement in local politics? Such tools can be seen to form new political opportunity structures for citizens. 2) Does the use of these tools lead to more public debate and have new actors been involved in the debate? In other words, to what extent is something new added to the political public? 3) Is anyone listening and does anybody respond to what is discussed on-line? This is essential for being able to talk about political deliberation at all.

The Internet as a political public

In relation to democracy, the Internet can be seen as a particular structure of communication that, like other media, supports individuals communicating with their environment. In this context, focus is on the local political public as a sphere between the local institutions of authoritative decision-making and implementation and the local citizens. In normative democratic theory, this sphere is constituted on a principle of free will and opinion formation that apply equally to all citizens. To protect and to give meaning to this principle, theories of deliberative democracy have emphasized *public deliberation* in particular.

In the famous Habermasian interpretation, public deliberation is equated with dialogue as a special form of rational communication. In a perfect functioning public sphere, particular interests are excluded; only rational, impartial arguments count (Eriksen & Weigaard, 2003: 277). The normative ideal for political decision-making is thus a peaceful conversation with the aim of reaching consensus on the common good. Such an understanding has met some critics. Not only has it been deemed unrealistic. It has also been rejected on a normative basis because it misconceives the nature of political decision-making in modern, pluralistic societies. In- stead it has been stressed that deliberations on the public good are not peaceful, but conflict-ridden. They are not spontaneous but essentially rule-governed, and they are not an end in it self, but oriented towards problem-solving and thus towards good governance (Schudson, 1997). Furthermore, political deliberations take place among individuals and groups with conflicting interests, motivations and resources and not only among people who are equal and hold the same values. Finally, in modern societies, political deliberation must have a broader meaning than just "face to face" conversation. Spectators who receive arguments and information are also part of the game (Slevin, 2000; Thompson, 2001). Therefore, public deliberation is not to be equated with dialogue, but should be seen as an integrated part of modern systems of mass-communication.

In this context, public deliberation will be understood as *non-coercive forms of arguments circulated between transmitters and receivers in open spaces based on mutual expectations of being listened to and of having some sort of response.* On the one hand, public deliberation is a broader term than "face to face" dialogue. On the other hand, it excludes propaganda, advertising, etc. where a response is not expected. Furthermore, open spaces mean spaces, where activities are visible and to which access is not restricted. Finally, deliberations do not aim for consensus. Rather, the ideal can be stated as an open-ended contestation of discourses, where consensus is a possibility, not a necessity (Dryzek, 1996) and not a normative ideal either.

Focus is thus on the role of the Internet as a vehicle for political transparency and public, political deliberation. In media-theory, the concept of *communicative affordance* is used to describe the opportunities of a certain media to support the communication of individuals and authorities with their environment (Finnemann, 2005; Jensen & Helles, 2005). In theories of democracy, a parallel concept is used, namely *political opportunity structures* or opportunity structures for political participation. The focus is here on the specific properties that characterize various channels connecting citizens with political authorities. Both media-theory and democratic theory indicate that the media or the channels in question enable certain forms of action and interaction.

In this context, the main focus is upon how the Internet has been shaped to constitute a new channel between citizens and local authorities, which opens for new opportunities for local political participation. The main concern is the relationship between representatives and represented. It is, therefore, also possible to see the Net as an opportunity structure for the communication of representatives with the represented.

Institutional opportunities may vary from locality to locality depending on how the new channels are shaped and thus on how new opportunities are created for local political deliberation. Speaking in market-terms, the creation of opportunity structures represents the "supply-side" of the local political public (Norris, 2003). Supply should, however, not only be conceived as a matter of web-design. It is also a matter of investment of time and money in collecting and presenting information and organizing political debates via the net.

To give an idea of the democratic potentials of ICT at the local level, the supply of ICT-mediated forms of communication should be seen in relation to the demand of citizens for such ICT-mediated solutions. By holding the two sides of supply and demand together, one may get a more realistic account of the democratic potentials of the Net contrary to the exaggerated positive and negative statements of its role that have flourished in the last ten years.

In the following, I shall take a closer look at the shaping of ICT-mediated opportunity structures at the local level and at the use of these structures by those who have access to the Internet. The overall question is what the Internet adds to the political public with regard to political deliberation. The main concern here is not the character of the processes of interaction (see chapter 9 for a contribution on that subject), but the potentials of the Internet for including more and new citizens into processes of local deliberations; both as actors and spectators. Two main questions are addressed: 1) Does the Internet add something new to the local public in terms of citizens involved and issues raised? 2) Is anyone listening among citizens and in particular among the elected representatives? In the long run, the success or failure of a medium depends not only on its ability to mobilize citizens but also on its ability to serve as a channel for influence on policies. First, this requires that some of those who are empowered to take decisions, i.e. the elected political representatives, listen and respond. To what extent is that requirement fulfilled?

The data-material

From 2002 to 2004, some experiments with digital democracy took place in the municipality of Hals outside Aalborg in Denmark. These included various institutions from community level to the whole municipality. In this article, I shall concentrate on the municipality level. During the period, four major on-line consultations were held: Two concerning the budget in 2002 and 2003, one concerning a new development plan for the municipality and one concerning a proposal from a national commission to amalgamate smaller municipalities. Besides these four consultations, a free debate took place at the web-portal called *hals.dk*, where everybody was invited to express opinions and to make proposals.

Hals is compared with two other municipalities, namely Soelleroed, located close to Copenhagen and Odder, located south of Aarhus in Jutland. These three municipalities cover the main feature of the variations of Danish municipalities. Hals is placed at the countryside: Approximately 11.000 inhabitants in an area of 190 km2. The municipality of Odder has approximately 20.000 inhabitants and covers and area of 220 km2. But contrary to Hals, most inhabitants live in the provincial town of Odder. As a suburb to Copenhagen, Soelleroed has approximately 32.000 citizens in an area of 40 km2. The density of the population is therefore more than 13 times as high in Soelleroed as in Hals - with Odder ranging in the middle.

While the supply of e-instruments for information and deliberation are determined by the local council, we must assume that the demand for these instruments are affected by some of the same factors that influence off-line forms of participation, namely on the one hand individual resources for participation, mainly indicated by the level of education, and on the other hand motivation for participation, mainly indicated by the degree of interest in local politics and the orientation toward local politics, for instance through local newspaper reading. However, also traditions or habits of local involvement, which can be called participation-readiness, are assumed to play a role. Table 2 gives an overview of the differences in the allocation of educational resources, of the motivation and of the off-line participation in the three municipalities.

	Hals	Odder	Soelleroed
High school or similar	39	40	71
No vocational training	13	10	4
Very and somewhat interested in local politics	65	72	70
Read local newspaper daily	37	20	7
Participated in a local meeting	15	25	6
Contacted a local politician	13	15	8
Signed a petition	15	40	6
N	1012	545	1102

Table 2: Hals, Odder and Soelleroed – differences in the level of education, in local political motivation and in local political participation. Percentage of Internet-users

As appears, Solleroed has a concentration of persons with high resources, while Hals and Odder is rather similar among internet-users. There are no big differences between the three municipalities concerning interest in politics, whereas the citizens in Odder and notably in Hals are more frequent readers of local newspapers than the citizens in Soelleroed. These differences are repeated if we look at the measures for local participation, although it appears that citizens in Odder are somewhat more active than citizens in Hals.

In every municipality population, surveys have been carried out: In Odder and Soelleroed in 2003, in Hals in 2001 and again in 2004 (Olsen et.al. 2004; Hoff

& Marckmann, 2004; Torpe, 2005). Additional data-material consists of interviews with politicians, civil servants and citizens in the three municipalities, but also data from a nationwide survey about the use of media is included (Hoff & Jauert, 2005; Olsen & Rieper, 2005; Torpe et.al. 2005).

The supply of tools for e-participation in three municipalities

Tools for e-participation can be related to *information, consultation* and *active participation* (OECD, 2001). [1] The third category includes activities where citizens decide the matter themselves. This is however rarely the case. It is therefore more adequate to let the last category include activities, where initiatives to influence the political agenda or to participate in processes of decision-making and implementation are taken "from below" – by citizens themselves, contrary to the second category where citizens respond to initiatives taken "from above". Both forms of participation can lead to deliberations between citizens and between citizens and authorities.

In later years, new ICT mediated opportunity structures for participation have been created at local level (Torpe & Nielsen, 2004; Torpe et.al., 2005). These include both tools for consulting citizens on specific matters, for instance through electronic citizen panels and permanent e-forums, where citizens within some broad ethical guidelines are able to debate freely. A survey from 2005 shows that 25 percent of all Danish municipalities have established on-line discussion forums in various forms (Torpe et.al, 2005). Such forums are also present in the three case-municipalities, Hals, Odder and Soelleroed. In all three cases they have been used for both free debates, to consult citizens on specific matters and to collect feedback.

According to several evaluations, the websites of Hals, Odder and Soelleroed belong to the best half of municipality websites in Denmark (www.bedstpaanettet.dk ; Torpe & Nielsen, 2004). In 2004 and 2005, Odder has even been ranked as number one among all municipalities. Odder has paid special attention to the information side by hiring a journalist to edit and present the local stuff. But Odder has also made a specific effort to include citizens by

---

[1] For an overview see: Coleman, Macintosh & Lailjee, 2005.

inviting them to build their own website linked to the municipal website and to offer support for that purpose. Hals differs from most other municipalities in Denmark by having organized several e-consultations on different matters from 2002 to 2004. These consultations were part of some experiments with e-democracy in Hals supported by a regional ICT-programme called "The Digital North Denmark".[2]

The use of e-instruments for political deliberation

As mentioned above, 25 percent of Danish municipalities have an electronic debate board and thus offer opportunities for deliberation. However, a spot check in January 2005 revealed that in more than 60 percent of the municipalities there were no postings. Only in two municipalities, more than 10 postings were found during a whole month, namely in Odder with 43 postings and in Hals with 221 postings. Even with only one posting, Soelleroed is above the average. On this basis, one could easily get the impression that citizens are not interested in discussing local politics on-line. This is, however, a too hasty conclusion, because, unlike Odder and Hals, most municipalities have only done little to stimulate the debate. In fact, many of the municipalities have done nothing else than provide the software. Here, not only citizens but also council members and civil servants are total absent from the debate.

	Hals N=1012	Odder N=546/950	Soelleroed N=1102
Send postings to online local debate forums	4	3	1
Spectators to online local debate	38	31	11
Regular spectators to online local debate *	18	5	1
Written a letter to the local newspaper on local affairs	5	4	2

* defined as having visited the discussion forum at least once a month

Table 3: The use of on-line discussion forums in Hals, Odder and Soelleroed.
Percentages

---

[2] For further information see: www.detdigitalenordjylland.dk

In Hals, more than 1800 letters were posted on the debate forum over a three year period: From approximately 200 the first year over almost 600 the next year to more than 1000 the third year (Torpe et.al., 2005). However, as appears in table 3, these postings are produced by only four percent of the internet-users corresponding to 3 percent of the whole population in Hals. Moreover, 10 persons account for 60 percent of all postings (Torpe et.al., 2005). It is, thus, the same few people who are active in the discussions.

The majority are spectators. In Hals, 38 percent of the internet-users are spectators in terms of having visited the debate forum once. 18 percent have visited hals.dk at least once a month and can therefore be called "regular spectators". This is a somewhat higher proportion than in Odder and Soelleroed and a difference that cannot be explained by referring to individual resources or to participation-readiness. It must be explained by the fact that more was done in Hals to motivate citizens to participate in "on-line" deliberations. Examples of that are some of the e-consultations that were held during the period, where information about plans and proposals were made accessible at the municipal website, where announcements were made about the consultations in the local newspapers, and where citizens were asked to contribute to the debate (for an elaboration of what was done in Hals to stimulate on-line deliberation, see chapter 9 and 10).

Seen in relation to what was done to facilitate e-participation, the rather small proportion of net-participants may seem disappointing. However, rather than looking at the figures in isolation they should be compared with similar forms of off-line participation. Hals offers an opportunity for such a comparison. In autumn 2003, a consultation took place over some new development plans for the municipality. Citizens were invited to comment on and to discuss the plans at several meetings and on the on-line discussion forum "hals.dk". It appears that approximately the same proportion of citizens can be labelled active in terms of being actively involved in writing letters to the local newspapers and sending postings to the on-line discussion forum. But compared to participation in meetings, more citizens followed the debate on hals.dk. While four percent have attended one of the meetings, eight percent have read the contributions to the debate on hals.dk. Thus twice as many followed the debate on-line as off-line. One may perhaps think that those who attend a physical town meeting are more actively involved in the debate than those who follow the on-line debate. This is, however, not true. Normally, only a few takes the floor. Most of the participants in town meetings are passive listeners.

As expected, there is an overlap between on-line and off-line spectators. Almost one third of those who followed the debate online have also attended one of the meetings. But, the two thirds, who did not, represent an expansion of the public. As such, something *more* is added to the public. Generally, this is also the case since the proportion that attends town meetings has not decreased subsequent to the opportunity to deliberate on local matters on-line was created (Torpe et.al. 2005). The same proportion of citizens who have participated in at least one town meeting in 2001 has also participated in a town meeting in 2004, namely 12 percent. There are thus no indications that on-line participation replaces off-line forms of participation.

So even if the expansion may be less than some would have expected, the Internet did add something more to the public of Hals with regard to political deliberation. The question is now, whether something *new* is added as well – whether the new on-line channel has a potential not only for mobilizing more participants but also for mobilizing new participants.

Is something new added to the local political public?

Newer research has shown that on-line activists largely resemble traditional political activists (Ward et.al. 2005). If this is correct, it may even be the same persons who are active "on-line" and "off-line" and the same topics that are discussed. If that is so, the Internet only facilitates communication between those who would communicate anyway. Let us first take a look at the social and political divisions of the participants on the Internet compared with similar off-line activities and from that proceed to the question of who is represented and what is presented in the on-line channel compared to the off-line channels.

As shown in table 4, the same picture appears for on-line and off-line forms of participation in local politics: Men are more active than women, the middle-aged and the elderly are more active than the young, and persons with higher education are more active than persons with lower education (table 4). For those who had hoped that local political participation via ICT could help overcome existing divisions, the result is disappointing. The findings for Hals are in accordance with the general picture of on-line and off-line political participation at the national level except for the younger generations, who are politically more active on-line than off-line (Tobiasen, 2005). The same is, however, not the case at the local level. At this level, the younger generations are just as passive on-line as off-line.[3]

	Participated in a town meeting*	Written a letter to the editor*	Read postings on hals.dk**	Send postings to hals.dk***	N
Men	19	6	14	6	478
Women	12	3	11	3	531
16-29	7	1	5	2	174
30-39	10	4	8	1	234
40-49	14	6	16	5	233
50-59	21	7	16	8	233
60 +	26	5	16	5	130
School low	14	3	11	4	226
School middle	15	4	12	4	353
School high	15	6	15	6	392

* within the last year
** weekly, monthly or less frequent
*** from 2002 to 2004

Table 4: Off-line and on-line participation distributed on gender, age and education. Percentage of internet-users

Apparently, social divisions are transferred from off-line forms of participation to on-line forms of participation. But, does this also mean that by and large it is the same persons who are active in both channels? The answer is both a "yes" and a "no" (Torpe et.al., 2005). Firstly, a "yes", because there is an overlap of issues discussed in the local newspapers and in the digital forum. But, also a "no": Some of the issues raised in the digital debate-forum do not appear

---

[3] The differences for age and education would increase if the basis of comparison is the whole population and not only the net-users. There is also a social divide in the access to the Internet. In Denmark where about 80 percent of the population have access there is an under-representation of low educated people and of the elderly. However, these divides have decreased in later years and are likely to decrease further in the years to come (Goul Andersen, 2003). To have a similar basis of comparison, we have chosen to base the analysis on the Internet-users.

in the newspapers and visa-versa. There is namely a tendency that issues close to the citizens take up more space in the on-line discussion forum than in the newspapers. In the on-line discussion forum, we meet clients who complain about the way their cases have been treated by the local administration, and we meet people who are worried about the local traffic and who are unsatisfied with the way the municipality manage the snow clearing. Why do we find more of such stuff in the online discussion forum than in the newspapers? First of all, it reflects what people are concerned with and secondly, it reflects that that there is no filter or editing at the on-line discussion forum. Citizens are free to put any subject on the agenda and some of the issue raised may seem too "small" and too "specific" for the local newspapers.

Secondly, a "yes", because there is a massive overlap of persons engaged in local political activities "off-line" and "on-line". Almost half of those participating in town meetings also follow the discussion on hals.dk. Even more pronounced is the overlap for the active citizens on-line. 61 percent of the on-line activists have attended a town meeting during the last year, 32 percent are members of a political party and 36 percent have written a letter to the editor. Moreover, the frequent users of hals.dk constitute a rather small group for whom it has become part of their identity to comment on local political issues. As one of them states: *On hals.dk you almost feel as a family* [interview with an active user]

But at the same time "a no" because further investigations show a more subtle result (Torpe et.al., 2005): Very few of the participants, less than 10 percent, have never been active in politics before. Furthermore, a comparison between those who write in the newspapers and those who post letters to hals.dk shows that there are more representatives of the local elite, i.e. from interest- and political organizations, in the local newspapers, whereas what can be called "ordinary citizens" take up more space in the on-line discussion forum.

All in all, the "social divide" seems to be the same in both channels. Thus, we find no indications that the internet-forum is less representative than off-line forums. Furthermore, it seems that at least some new participants are mobilized. In that sense: what is added to the local political public is not only something more, but also something *new*. There are, however, also indications that for some of the very frequent contributors it has become part of a lifestyle to go "public" on hals.dk. Now and then, the discussion forum is turned into something that resembles a chat-room, in which participant small talk to each other in the same way they would talk to each other as neighbours across the hedge. Not all talk is equally important in relation to public opinion-formation and policy-making.

Is anybody listening, is anybody responding?
To make oneself heard, it is important that someone is listening, not least among those who are in a position to take action, i.e. local politicians and civil servants. However, in an on-line discussion forum, this cannot be taken for granted. In Hals, as we have seen, 18 percent of the internet-users corresponding to 12 percent of the entire population visit hals.dk on a regular basis. This constitutes a somewhat smaller audience than that of conventional media, where 40 percent follow local politics on a daily basis. It is therefore important that most council members visit hals.dk. Out of the 13 members, who have answered the question, five follow the discussions on a daily basis, four follow the discussions several times a week, two follow them less frequently and only two never follow the discussions. All the leading members of the Council are among those who visit hals.dk frequently. Some of the members of the Council are also among the most frequent contributors to hals.dk Among the 10 persons that account for 60 percent of the postings on hals.dk (see above) are four members of the Council including the social democratic mayor and the liberal leader of the opposition.

We also asked the members of the council to assess the importance of hals.dk compared to other media and channels. From this appears that hals.dk has become a more important medium in the eyes of the politicians. In 2002, only four council members stated that hals.dk is an important medium for a politician. In 2004, the number elevated to nine. Among them are all the leading politicians. Hals.dk is, however, still regarded as a less important medium than local newspapers and also regarded as less important than for instance "face to face" contact to citizens.

No doubt, there is a threshold for new media to make a breakthrough in public. An important factor is how many citizens use the medium, because this determines, at least to some degree, how much attention the political elite will pay to the forum. It is impossible to say how many citizens should follow the discussions before that threshold is passed, but with no more than 12 percent of the entire population as regular participants, there is a risk that hals.dk could be politically marginalized. It is therefore important that relatively many politicians in Hals pay attention to the new medium, but also the interplay between hals.dk and the local newspapers is important. On several occasions, the local daily newspaper has referred to the discussions on hals.dk. One of the reasons for that attentiveness and that so many members of the Council have followed the debate could however be that hals.dk was part of an experiment on e-democracy supported by The Digital North Denmark. We still need to analyze the situation under more "normal" circumstances.

Conclusion

As shown, the employment of the net in local politics leads to an extension of the public. Not only is something more added to the public with regard to information and deliberation. In a limited sense, something new is also added in terms of issues debated and persons involved. It is not the introduction of a new medium that makes a difference in itself. Success or failure seems to be closely related to what is done in the municipalities. In Odder and Hals, more participation was generated contrary to most of the municipalities, where nothing was done to stimulate participation. However, even in Odder and Hals it is not possible to speak of a breakthrough of e-democracy. Rather, ICT-mediated forms of information and deliberation supplement older forms of political communication. In the future, this can turn out to be of great importance in parallel with the need of local politicians to find alternative ways of communicating with the citizens, not least to compensate for the decreasing importance of party-communication and the continuing decrease in local newspaper readings.

Did we confirm the sceptical views of the democratic potentials of the Internet that were outlined in the introduction of this article? Some of them were: It is true that in most Danish municipalities the interactive potentials of the Internet for constructing two-way-communication with the citizens are not utilized. This is part of a general picture including public authorities, companies and NGO's as well (Jensen & Helles, 2005). It is also true that the municipalities in which the interactive potentials are used, relatively few citizens are actively involved in political deliberation activities on the Internet and even in Hals, where citizens were invited to participate, less than 20 percent followed the discussions on a regular basis. Furthermore, it is true that on-line-participants resemble those active off-line, and it is also true that much of what is discussed in the on-line discussion forum is the same as what is discussed in the local newspapers.

However, in an assessment of the democratic potentials of a new medium, the differences we observe, even as small as they are, could be of more importance, namely because the on-line discussion forum did not only add something more but also something new to the local political public. Furthermore, it was important for the relative success in Hals that the local politicians followed the debate and some of them furthermore took active part in the deliberations on-line.

References

Coleman, S., A. Macintosh & M. Lailjee (2005). *E-Methods for Public Engagement: Helping Local Authorities communicate with citizens*, Published by Bristol City Council for The Local eDemocracy National Project.

Davis, Richard (2005). *Politics online. Blogs, chatrooms and discussion groups in American democracy.* New York/London: Routledge.

Dryzek, John S. (2002). *Deliberative democracy and beyond. Liberals, critics and contestations*, Oxford: Oxford University Press.

Eriksen, Erik Oddvar & Jarle Weigård (2003). *Kommunikativt demokrati. Jürgen Habermas' teori om politik og samfund*, København: Hans Reitzels Forlag.

Finnemann, Niels Ole (2005). The cultural grammar of the internet. pp. 65-92. In: Klaus Bruun Jensen (ed), *Interface://Culture – the world wide web as political resource and aesthetic form.* Copenhagen: Samfundslitteratur

Hoff, Jens & Bella Marckmann (2004). *Internet og det lokale demokrati i Odder kommune – dokumentation af en spørgeskemaundersøgelse*, MODINET Working Paper no. 10.

Hoff, Jens & Per Jauert (2005). Internet, politisk kommunikation og offentlighed i en dansk kommune. In: Hoff, Jens & Kresten Storgaard (red),

Informationsteknologi og demokratisk innovation. Borgerdetagelse, politisk kommunikation og offentlig styring. København: Samfundslitteratur

Jensen, Klaus Bruun & Rasmus Helle (2005). 'Who do you think we are?' A content analysis of websites as participatory resourdes for politics, business and civil society, pp. 93-122. In: Klaus Bruun Jensen (ed), *Interface://Culture – the world wide web as political resource and aesthetic form.* Copenhagen: Samfundslitteratur

Loftager, Jørgen (2004). *Politisk offentlighed og demokrati i Danmark*, Århus: Aarhus Universitetsforlag.

Norris, Pippa (2004). *Building knowledge societies: The renewal of democratic practices in knowledge societies*, UNESCO World Report.

OECD (2001). *Promise and problems of e-democracy. Challenges of online citizen engagement.*

Olsen, Leif et.al. (2004). *Borgernes brug af Søllerød Kommunes hjemmeside – dokumentation af en spørgeskemaundersøgelse*, AKF Forlaget.

Schudson, Michael (1997. Why conversation is not the soul of democracy. In: *Critical Studies in Mass Communication* 14, p. 297-309.

Slevin, James (2000). *The internet and society*, Cambridge: Polity Press.

Thompson, John B. (2001). *Medierne og moderniteten. En samfundsteori om medierne*, København: Hans Reitzels Forlag.

Torpe, Lars & Jeppe Nielsen (2004). Digital communication between local authorities and citizens in Denmark. *Local Government Studies.* Vol 30, no. 2 pp. 230-244.

Torpe, Lars (2005). *Borgerdeltagelse på Nettet. Digitale demokratiforsøg i Hals Kommune.* Modinet working paper no. 14. Center for Media and Democracy. University of Copenhagen.

Torpe, Lars, Jeppe Agger Nielsen & Jens Ulrich (2005). *Demokrati på nettet. Offentlighed, deltagelse og digital kommunikation.* Aalborg: Aalborg Universitetsforlag.

Ward, Stephen, Rachel Gibson & Wainer Lusoli (2003). Online participation and mobilization in Britain: Hype, hope and reality. *Parliamentary Affairs*, vol. 56, no. 3.

Digital Municipality Planning – Experiments with the Use of ICT-Tools in Democratic Processes.

Jeppe Agger Nielsen

> In the last part of the 1990ies, E-government gained a more significant role and the use of ICT in the planning process was put on the agenda in Denmark. In this paper, the objects of closer examination will be the dialogue and communication possibilities in digital planning. The paper investigates whether it is possible to involve more citizens in the decision-making process by using ICT and thereby strengthening the democratic aspect. The theoretical starting point is Robert A. Dahl's criteria (enlightened understanding and effective participation) to what ought to apply for the democratic process. A case study in the municipality of Hals represents the first systematic, empirical research results of the dialogue and communication possibilities in digital planning in Denmark. The results point in the direction of the Internet being a suitable media when it comes to the involvement of the citizens, but it ought not to be alone in this. The use of ICT in the planning process is only in its infancy and should be seen as a supplement to the traditional channels. The results from the municipality of Hals indicate that other municipalities too can benefit from using ICT in the physical planning, not least as a tool to create more visibility.

Introduction

In later years, the information and communication technology (ICT) has gained a much more significant role than earlier when it comes to physical planning in the municipalities in Denmark. An indication of this is that a large number of municipalities publish their plan material on the Internet. A screening of all 271 municipalities in the spring of 2004 shows that 173 municipalities published their municipality plan on the Internet (whereof 48 are plan strategies) (Arleth, 2005).

The use of ICT in the planning process or digital planning gradually came on the agenda in the last part of the 1990ies. The development must be seen in relation to the fact that, during this period, E-government and digital administration started to play a bigger role. On one side, the increased demands on efficiency improvement and modernization of the public sector, and on the other the citizens' wishes for more and better service, provided a fertile basis for digital solutions in the hope to rectify this pressure. By and large, digital administration has been considered a Columbus-egg in the modernization of the public sector. Moreover, the new technologic possibilities provide new potentials for planning. Interactive visualizations, Geographic Information Systems (GIS), analyses of vast quantities of data, dialogue and exchanges of information independent of time and place are examples of tools that have been brought along with the technological development and have made some dimensions available which was not possible through analogue planning (Larsen & Lassen 2003). Hereby not said that digital planning by definition is better than analogue planning, but merely that the digital tools open up to some extended possibilities in relation to both the visualization aspect as well as the dialogue and communication aspect.

In this paper, it is especially the dialogue and communication possibilities in digital planning that will be the objects of closer examination. In other words, the question is whether it is possible to involve more citizens in the decision process by using ICT and in doing so create a democratic improvement. More concretely, the focus will be on the parts of the planning stage concerning the involvement of the public such as communication between authority and citizen. In other words, the bead will be pointed explicitly towards the processes in "digital planning" where the citizens have an opportunity to express their opinion and less attention will be on "the digital plan" itself. However this does not mean that the digital product is of less importance for such an approach. Among other things, it is going to be interesting whether the strength of digital media as an always accessible "information base" and visualization tool will have a spill-over effect on the citizens' interests and involvement. Here, the logical basis is that increased access to better and less complicated information will result in a growing interest among the citizens, and make them capable of following and partake in the debate about physical planning. When it comes to changing municipality plans, it is statutory that the citizens have the opportunity to object to the proposal presented by the municipal council whether the plan is digital or not. Thus, during the hearing phase, the citizens have the opportunity to raise objections to the proposal made by the political decision makers. Such objections or statements do not usually become subjects of public discussion, but instead they end on the tables of the administration and municipal council. The question is whether the Internet promotes public interest and increases the political expression of opinion on this area.

To make some suggestions to whether ICT-tools can help to promote democratic influence in the planning process, we are going to involve the municipality of Hals' composition of a digital municipal plan as a case. Especially two circumstances seem to make the municipality of Hals interesting. First, the municipality is among the only ones who have developed a fully Internet-based digital plan with interactive opportunities and GIS-functionalities so far. Second, the municipality has had focus on the "external dimension of organization", i.e. the communication with the citizens, etc. and not so much on the "internal dimension" such as efficiency improvements by linkage to the underlying specific systems and implementation of Electronical Case- and Document Handling (ECDH). In other words, the dominating parts of the project have been of democratic character and not so much about the administrative aspect (Larsen, 2004). The pivotal point in this paper will be the external dimension and the democracy aspect, rather than the administrative dimension.

Since the beginning of 2002, the municipality of Hals has, as a part of the project "The Digital Democracy" (see Torpe this book for more information) put energy into developing a new digital municipality plan. Several linear metres of paper plans have now been replaced and grouped in a new digitalized plan tool. The plan is publicly available on the web page of the municipality of Hals (www.halskom.dk) and, it is now possible – day and night - for politicians, citizens and skilled personnel to collect information from the traditional municipality plans' main structure and frame section on e.g. district plans and the county bonds on environmental protection. We are here talking about the first fully digital municipality plan in the country, complete with a digital pre-process followed by a digital hearing stage (Det Digitale Demokrati, 2004).

Besides creating the product itself, the process in connection with the development of the digital municipality plan has been an important part of the project. In other words, the municipality of Hals has tested the use of ICT-tools in democratic processes throughout the process. In the following, we will examine whether a democratic strengthening is traceable when using this procedure of citizen involvement.

To examine a domain like this, it is essential to make clear upon which benchmarks the evaluation should be based. The theoretical starting point is Robert A. Dahl's criteria to what ought to apply for the democratic process (Dahl, 1989, 1998). The two criteria used in this connection are: Enlightened understanding and effective participation. *Enlightened understanding* means that the citizens in any decision process must have opportunity to form an opinion on the matters in question. This has to be done on basis of free and sufficient information. *Effective participation* means that all citizens must have the opportunity to express their opinion on matters that have to be democratically decided. Effective participation does not require that the politicians always succumb to the citizens, but that all citizens have the opportunity to practice influence on the decision-making of the politicians. In the literature on democracy there is distinction between a collective and an individual dimension of effective participation (Petterson et. al. 1989). The collective dimension refers to participation in the common formation of opinion and will. When it comes to physical municipality planning it could for instance be participation in a debate at a citizen meeting or on an Internet portal. The individual dimension however, is about the opportunity each individual citizen has to practice influence on one's own situation, for example through the opportunity to make objections to the proposal for a new municipality plan.

The set off, the present study is thus based on two of Dahl's known prescriptive criteria for the political process. The agenda is not to make a manual, but rather to set some reference points, which the municipality planning process can honour to greater or lesser extent. Despite the fact that the criteria were developed prior to the common spread of the Internet, they seem to be useful also when it comes to studying digital democracy. Encouraged by Dahl's criteria, it will be examined whether ICT can contribute in the municipality planning process through:

- An expansion of the citizens' *opportunity structures*. Here, the bead is pointed towards the tools provided by the municipality to involve the citizens in the planning process. Including the possibility to gain access to information, the possibility to the expression of opinion and debate.
- The extent to which the citizens *make use* of the ICT-tools they are given. Thus it is examined if ICT can contribute in the course of planning to involve/engage the citizens and strengthen the communication between authority and citizens.

It is to be kept in mind that it is very hard to isolate the influence of ICT when for example it comes to involvement of citizens in the planning process. The fact that ICT, in the present case, has been used as supplement and not as replacement for the traditional channels (the local press, meetings with citizens, etc.) does not make the exercise less complicated. Therefore, the purpose is not to evaluate the attempt, but rather to make a suggestion to where ICT seems to have its opportunities and limits in the digital planning process.

The layout of this paper is structured in three parts. First, we are going to take a closer look at what characterizes a digital plan and digital planning. Second, we will document the process of the preparation of the digital municipality plan in the municipality of Hals such as the citizens' *possibilities* of gathering information, of expressing their opinion and of debating through ICT. And finally, it is examined *to what extent* the citizens of the municipality of Hals have made use of the new information, communication and dialogue opportunities. The data used in this study is a postal questionnaire survey sent to a representative segment of the citizens of the municipality of Hals in 2004. On top of this there is a series of interviews with people who have been directly involved in the digitalization process as well as documents from working groups, etc.

Analogue and digital municipality planning

In Denmark, the municipal councils are responsible for the overall municipality planning, including e.g. the establishment of a municipality plan. The plan has to contain and specify the politically defined goals for the development of the municipality and can be seen as the linkage between the regional plan on one side, and the regulations of the district plan on the other. In the so called planning act, a number of regulations for shape and contents are elaborated, among other things it is said in section 4: *"the main structure states the superior goals for development and area usage in the municipality such as development of homes and workplaces, traffic service, service supply, allotments and other recreational areas"*. Beside the main structure, the municipality plan consists of a frame section, where the scopes for the district planning are fixed. In other words, a municipality plan is the governing guidelines of a municipality for the development over a number of years. The concern is about how homes, service functions and industries are to be arranged in relation to each other, about traffic service, tourism, etc.

As initially mentioned, it is now the majority of the municipalities who publish their municipality plan on the web page. But what is a digital municipality plan and digital planning? To begin with, it is essential to distinguish between the two forms. Where a digital plan refers to the product that is available, typically via the Internet, digital planning refers to the process in which digital tools are implicated in the preparation of the plan. Digital planning stands in contrast to the analogue planning where no electronic means are applied. Basically, the digital plans and digital planning are mutually independent. For example it is possible to work out an entirely digital plan and then publish and print it on paper. On the other hand, it is also possible to make a hand written paper plan, scan the documents and publish the plan on the net. In practice, the two procedures often interact and the publication of a plan on the net can for example constitute an element of the total digital planning process. (Larsen & Lassen 2003).

There is a big difference in how far the municipalities have come towards digital planning and establishment of digital plans. A large part of the municipalities have published their plans on their homepages, but only few operate with actual digital planning. As pointed out earlier, a screening of all municipalities' homepages shows that 64 percent of the municipalities have published their municipality plan on the net. It is typical that the plans are published in PDF-format as done by 141 municipalities (52 percent), while very few operate with more developed digital plans (Arleth, 2005). The municipality of Hals is, as stated previously, among those municipalities who have adopted the entire digital process both in relation to digital planning and publishing of the product. Other municipalities, such as Aalborg, Esbjerg and Hadsund have also worked out "real" digital plans where the potentials of the web-mediasuch as hyper links and "live" maps are used. There is no doubt that digital plans give the citizens some obvious service advantages. On the other hand, there are also some aspects you should be aware of. On the positive side, a digital plan is among others available to interested citizens 24 hours and the digital media open to some new visualization opportunities. To make use of the offer though, it is required that the citizen has access to the net as well as some ICT-capabilities seem necessary to navigate in a digital municipality plan. Although the majority of all Danes have access to the net today, there is still a group of nearly 15 percent that does not have an Internet connection (Danmarks Statistik, 2004). On top of this, a gap exists in both age difference and geography. The questionnaire survey of the municipality of Hals shows that 34 percent of the citizens in 2004 did not have access to the Internet. It is probably only a question of time before almost all Danes has access to the net, but for now there is a considerable group of people that cannot make use of the offer in practice.

The municipality of Hals is among the few municipalities that have a fully digital plan tool published on the Internet at present. The model, which is implemented on the homepage of the municipality of Hals, is not just a copy of a paper plan but an interactive, net-based solution with GIS-functionalities. What characterizes the digital municipality plan of the municipality of Hals is that it is "a real digital municipality plan. Before, it (edt: the digital municipality plan) was made with a starting point in a paper plan, and then it is transferred into the digital media. Now, we are simply doing it the other way around... Now we have tailored it for the digital media, and then we believe that it is no longer necessary to consider the traditional method, but rather to think the book through in a whole new way. The things are connected in a whole new way for the first time ever" [interview, representative from Sven Allan Jensen A/S, 2002]. The fact that "the things are connected in a whole new way" means a.o. that the digital solution, beside the traditional contents of a paper plan, also includes other types of the municipality plans. Here, we are thinking of for instance district plans, theme plans and other spatial details of the administration. Furthermore, when it comes to the construction of the municipality plan, the digital version is disparate from the paper edition. The plan is built according to a "citizen logic" so interested citizens in a foreseeable manner are able to find the information that is required. Therefore, the traditional subdivision of the municipality plan – the main structure, a frame section, a review section and an appendix of maps - has been changed. Now the plan is approached through a theme, through a city area or through the individual estate. For example features such as "Your map" and "What applies for me" exist to help make the plan more present to the individual citizen

Finally, it has to be mentioned that the language in the municipality plan has been adapted to the digital media. Traditionally, in common plan material, a lot of words are written which poorly fit the digital plan [interview, representative from Sven Allan Jensen A/S, 2002]. The language in the municipality plan is more "journalistic" in its character, and focus has been on easy-to-understand expressions instead of long texts.

In spite of the advantages of the digital media as a tool for visualization, the contents of the plan are still diverse and (probably) complicated to many citizens. Nevertheless, according to the planners of the municipality of Hals, the digital municipality plan makes it easier to navigate through the many details. In addition to this it is seen as an advantage that all plan details are collected in one place and that the citizens can be sure that the material available are updated. (Det Digitale Demokrati 2004).

Electronic forms of dialogue and communication

One of the central aspects in connection with the revision of the municipality plan was to involve the citizens in the planning process through ICT. In the project application to TDD is says that the ICT-tools are to be *"put to full use in all phases of the process"* (Det Digitale Demokrati, 2001). In the following, we are going to review the planning process in chronological order and take a look at the supply of ICT-tools and to what extent the citizens exploit the offers, respectively. However, we are going to start by providing insight into the procedure used by the municipality of Hals during the construction of the municipality plan. Indeed, the construction is vital to the way in which the ICT-tools have been applied. The municipality of Hals chose to maintain the revision principles and methods applied earlier, which a.o. include appointment of work groups and citizen meetings. The appearance of ICT did not mean that the municipality changed the process of citizen involvement, but that the ICT-tools were implicated as an extra element. Table 5 provides an overview of the time lapse.

Through a number of years, there has been a tradition of establishing the municipality plan in a certain way in the municipality of Hals. Rather than one complete revision of the municipality plan for example every fourth year, "mini municipality plans" for smaller limited areas and theme plans are continuously worked out when needed. In connection with the transition to a digital plan tool, the scene was set for a total revision of the existing municipality plan with special focus on the subjects. The subjects were a) a new Town Model for Gandrup, b) a new Town Model for Ulsted and c) a new Rural District Policy for the municipality of Hals. Thereafter the district plans were –together with the additional elements- incorporated into a complete digital municipality plan for the entire municipality.

Time	Activity
Spring 2002	The municipality of Hals holds three citizen meetings. Three work groups are established for Town Model Ulsted, Town Model Gandrup and the Rural District Policy, respectively. At the same time, the work on developing the digital platform is initiated. Sven Allan Jensen A/S is in charge of the work.
Summer 2003	The platform for the digital municipality plan is finished. The proposal for the digital municipality plan is published on the homepage of the municipality of Hals. Now, the citizens have an opportunity to investigate the municipality plan.
Autumn 2003	The proposal of the work groups for the digital municipality plan is presented to the politicians in the technical committee and in the town council.
Autumn 2003	The politicians make changes in the proposal.
Winter 2003/2004	The digital municipality plan is sent to public hearing. The municipality holds citizen meetings, initiates debates on the municipality plan on hals.dk and offers the possibility of sending in objections electronically.
Spring 2004	The town council considers the received objections and formally approves the digital municipality plan.

Table 5: Overview of the time lapse

The process of the revision of the municipality plan can be analytically divided into four phases. The first is a preliminary phase where the municipality is collecting input for the plan. The second is a development – or process phase, where the municipality plan is in the work out. The third is a hearing phase, where the citizens are heard and offered the opportunity to make objections. And finally, the fourth is an approval phase, where the politicians approve the final plan.

The preliminary phase

Project "digital municipality plan" in the municipality of Hals first aired in the spring 2002. Three citizen meetings set off the citizen-involvement-part. The meetings were, by tradition, well visited, with for instance just about 100 participants in Ulsted.[1] In continuation of the citizen meetings, work groups on the three chosen areas were made each with 16-20 members. In the preliminary phase, the Internet was *not* actively used in the communication with the citizens. The municipality of Hals used the traditional methods in the form of citizen meetings and the establishment of work groups, but they did not initiate electronic debates as a supplement to the citizen meetings in this phase. If you are to follow the words of the project application it must be said to be in conflict with the intention of fully using ICT-tools in all of the planning phases. One of the reasons was that the planners of the municipality of Hals estimated that the citizens were not ready at that point to use the digital tools.

Other municipalities in Demark have tried to involve the citizens through ICT in the preliminary physical planning phase. The municipality of Aarhus is an example of this. In 2002, the politicians of the municipality decided to prepare a traffic plan for the central section of Aarhus. It was emphasized that the citizens

---

[1] In the municipality of Hals it has been custom that quite a lot of citizens have participated in the citizen meetings when a municipality plan is made. This is, according to a planner from the municipality, due to the procedure used: "... *when the citizens are used to being close it is because we make municipality planning in a certain fashion out here. In the places where you talk every fourth year about municipality planning and say what we want with the municipality, it is hard to get the citizens involved. It is too airy, it is too far away, it does not mean anything to the individual and then you cannot obtain involvement. We talk municipality planning with one community at a time. People are more able to comprehend their own local community than the entire municipality as a whole*" [interview, planner at the municipality of Hals, 2002].

were to have a real opportunity to participate, and in the spring 2003, an idea debate was going on for eight weeks. During the idea debate period, the municipality used a multi media strategy in the contact with the citizens. The traditional citizen meetings were among other things supplemented with the opportunity to debate on the net, as a net-based citizen study was conducted. The latter was a direct mail study, which was made possible with the help of cooperation with the town portal www.aarhus.dk. Each week aarhus.dk circulated a newsletter[2] by e-mail and in February 2003, the subscribers were encouraged to participate in an electronic survey about the traffic plan for the central section of Aarhus. The municipality received roughly 1000 answers from readers and the town portal seemed to function as a door opener to the involvement of the citizens. In addition, 72 letters were written on the municipality debate forum. The debate was advertised on aarhus.dk, which probably had a positive effect on the number of letters. It is assessed that the digital initiatives have made a payoff in the form of increased activity among the citizens. Traditionally, the citizen meetings in Aarhus attracted very few citizens, and especially in the idea phase they succeeded in involving a much larger number of citizens through ICT than normal in the physical planning (Ryolf & Høj, 2004).

The development phase

Where the municipality of Hals did not choose to use ICT-tools in the preliminary phase, the intention in turn was to use ICT in the development phase. It was the intention partly that the internal communication in the work groups, and partly that the contact from the work groups to the "base", including interest groups, associations, etc., should be through the digital media (Det Digitale Demokrati, 2004). The hopes, however, were never fulfilled.

> *"The work itself in the work groups has not been digitalized, it goes on as usual with paper back and forth. In the beginning, we tried to send information through e-mail and have a common closed homepage only available to the members of the work group. But it just did not*

---

[2] In 2003, aarhus.dk had about 11.000 subscribers. By the beginning of 2005, this number amounted to 25.000.

> *work – we experienced that people only had half of the material ready for the meetings. It just became too difficult."* (interview, planner of the municipality of Hals, 2004)

The digitalization of the work flows stranded a.o. on the fact that not everybody had access to the Internet just as some of the participants only used the media from time to time. Moreover, it is generally quite difficult to send and represent heavy plan material containing maps and illustrations through e-mail. The fact that the platform for the digital municipality plan was not ready until the summer of 2003 only complicated the digital communication in the work groups even more (Det Digitale Demokrati, 2004). In short, the ICT-tools did not change the workflow, and the planning process in the work groups proceeded "in the same way as always".

As noted, it was also the intention that ICT was to strengthen the communication between the work groups and their "base" (associations, institutions and local communities). However ICT did not play a part in this area either. It seems that there are at least four explanations for this. First, as mentioned, they did not manage to power up the workflow internally in the work groups, why it was not natural to digitalize the communication externally either. Second, the groups were big (16-29 participants), which meant that relatively many local groups and associations were already directly involved in the process. Third, the "Town-Model-concept" means that the audience is limited and that the communication between citizens takes place over the hedge, in the local store, in the sports club, in the bank, etc. instead of and not through e-mail. And finally, the platform for the digital municipality plan was not ready until the summer of 2003, for the citizens to try out the digital solution on the homepage of the municipality of Hals.

In the fall of 2003, the work groups presented their respective suggestions to the political level and the suggestions were processed in both the Technical Committee and in the town council. After the political treatment, the suggestions were incorporated in the proposal to a digital municipality plan for the municipality of Hals. The additional plan material was moreover updated and digitalized. In connection with the political treatment, the digital plan was used as the primary media, and the municipality plan was not circulated in paper format. The political treatment meant that some parts of the work group suggestions were adjusted. Among the most spoken of cases, as well as politically as in the public, was probably a case on area division for homes in Ulsted, where a unanimous town council altered the proposal of the work group. As we are to see later, this also resulted in a debate on the net as objections were made to the alterations of the town council.[3]

The hearing phase

After the adjustments made by the town council of the suggestions set forth by the work groups, the proposal of a digital municipality plan for the municipality of Hals was presented for public hearing and debate for 10 weeks from the end of October 2003 to the beginning of January 2004. In the hearing phase, some new dialogue tools were put into use. As a supplement to traditional citizen meetings, articles and press releases in the local papers, the Internet was introduced in two areas. First, it became possible to publicly debate selected topics from the proposal on the portal of www.hals.dk. Secondly, it became possible to electronically send in objections/hearing answers to the municipality. Before we clarify in more detail the citizen's use of these possibilities, we are going to take a closer look at the citizens of Hals's knowledge of the hearing and through which channels they kept themselves informed of the hearing.

A survey showed that 35 percent of the users of the Internet knew that the municipality had presented the proposal of a new municipality plan for public hearing.[4] Even though the basis of comparison is not very extensive, earlier studies indicate that the knowledge in the municipality of Hals is basically at the same level as in other municipalities. A questionnaire survey in the municipalities

---

[3] In short, the case was about where a new area for single family buildings was to be built. The work group had suggested placement in the central neighbourhood of Ulsted. The background for this was to make a slow road to school possible and to create a more united town. The town council had decided to put a suggestion to a public hearing. The suggestion was to move the neighbourhood to the southwestern part of the town. The arguments were, that the area was well placed for the commuters who were driving to Aalborg, and that the area would provide opportunity to make some more exciting buildings.

[4] It appears that gender and education does not play a significant role when it comes to the proportion of individuals knowing about the hearing. On the contrary, the group of individuals under the age of 30 is underrepresented. In the meantime, this is not a big surprise as young people are less interested in local politics.

of Ribe, Sorø and Glostrup in 1994 shows that 27, 27 and 30 percent of the citizens, respectively, were aware of the latest public hearing of the municipality/district plan (KMD Dialog, 1994). However, it comes with the story that the knowledge of the municipality hearing was higher in both Gandrup and Ulsted who were the two directly involved local areas. 46 percent in Ulsted and 39 percent in Gandrup answered that they had knowledge of the hearing.

	Yes	N
Knowledge gained on the proposal on the municipality homepage	24	539
Press coverage on the proposal about the municipality plan in local newspapers	88	551
Participation in meetings about the proposal	11	539
Heard the proposal mentioned among neighbours, friends and family	52	539
Discussed the proposal with neighbours, friends and family	46	545
Sent in comments to the municipality on the proposal	3	544
Read discussions on the proposal on hals.dk	22	544
Wrote input to discussions on the proposal on hals.dk	2	545

Note: the percentages are distributed between those who said they had knowledge of the hearing.

Table 6: Distribution of answers from citizens of the municipality of Hals, with knowledge of the hearing on a new municipality plan: (percentages)

When the citizens are asked where they have discussed and learned about the digital municipality plan, it is not surprising that the traditional ways of communication dwarfs the role of the net (table 6). 24 percent of the citizens with knowledge of the hearing – which equivalates about 8 percent of all citizens – learned about the proposition on the municipality homepage. In comparison, 88 percent read about the proposition in the local papers and 46 percent discussed the proposal with neighbours, friends and family. However, it is interesting that 22 percent read debate contributions about the proposal on www.hals.dk, which is twice the number of people who attended citizen meetings on the topic. The intention of the electronic debate on hals.dk was exactly to reach more citizens than by the physical citizen meetings, which must be said to have been successful. We are now going to take a closer look at the extent of the debate on hals.dk and what topics have been discussed.

The electronic debate on hals.dk was initiated immediately after the physical citizen meetings on the two Town Models and the Rural District policy. A paper written by the mayor initiated the debate and the starting point was taken in the major discussions at the citizen meetings.

	Town Model Gandrup	Town Model Ulsted	The Rural District Policy	Total
Number of papers	69	13	6	88

Table 7: Contributions to debate/discussion on hals.dk regarding the municipality plan of Hals

As table 7 indicates, a debate was created on the net on some of the central elements of the digital municipality plan. In total, 88 contributions were received whereof approx. 75 percent concerned The Town Model of Gandrup. The 88 contributions were established by 21 debaters whereof two were from the town council and one was from the administration. The contributions mainly carried on the discussions started at citizen meetings and new topics were not introduced. On the contrary, only few of the hearing answers/ objections were published on the portal. Of the 13 objections (see table 8), four of them found their way to the public through hals.dk.[5] The citizen study also supports the impression of public objections through hals.dk. It shows that about half of the citizens sending objections to the municipality were also active in the debate on hals.dk. This is actually a noticeable result because the public seldom gains knowledge of objections as these normally end up at the tables of the administration and the political decision makers. In other words, it must be seen as an advantage to the public debate that the hearing answers are presented in the public space and not only communicated within the administrative and political system. Along with the above, it is a limited number of objections and a small number of people we are dealing with here.

---

[5] A single objection was reproduced in complete form while other debaters presented their views more informally. The earlier mentioned case on home development in Ulsted is an example of this. Three members of the work group each wrote a paper on hals.dk and later they authored a final objection against the proposal of the town council on the location of home areas.

The planners of the municipality of Hals were convinced that the digitalization of the plan material increased the level of knowledge among the citizens in the municipality and improved the communication in the hearing phase *"...by having the plan on the net it gives a better contact with the citizens, because they are informed beforehand. That is maybe the primary gain, that the citizens are better informed'* (interview, planner of the municipality of Hals, 2004). It also seems that the citizens of the municipality of Hals used the Internet for search of information on plan material. Close to 30 percent of all citizens of the municipality of Hals thus said that they, at some point, obtained information on area plans or district plans on the municipality homepage. The result seems essential; especially because such a great share of the citizens probably would not collect information on the municipality's plan material at the municipal office. According to the planners of the municipality, , the citizens were better informed especially on the citizen meetings, but also in the debates taking place online.

General objections	Objections to Town Model Gandrup	Objections to Town Model Ulsted	Objections to the Rural District Policy	Total
3	5	2	3	13

Table 8: Objections regarding the municipality plan of the municipality of Hals

If it proves correct, the digital planning tools have played a significant role in relation to "dressing the citizens better" and to qualifying the municipality plan debate. This must be seen as an important result and in the optics of Dahl, contribute to better-informed and enlightened citizens to benefit the democracy.

As mentioned, it was not only possible to debate online, but also possible to send in objections electronically. From the platform of the digital municipality plan on the home page of the municipality, it was possible via a prefabricated dialogue box to directly send in objections to the administration. As table 8 illustrates, 13 objections were submitted in the public phase. Whether the number is large or small can be difficult to determine. However, a planner of the municipality of Hals explained:

> "When you have had the citizens involved in this way, many things are already clarified. So with the traditional processes there are not so many objections. Most of the associations and interest groups are already involved in the process." (Interview, planner of the municipality of Hals, 2004)

There were both general objections from the county of Northern Jutland, The Danish Nature Conservation Association's Local Committee of the municipality of Hals and the Directory of Food Industry and 10 objections from local citizens. About half of the objections were sent electronically, while the rest were sent by ordinary mail [interview, planner of the municipality of Hals, 2004]. Even though an amount of 13 objections is not a whole lot to base an argumentation on, the electronic delivery of approximately 50 percent seems to point toward the fact that the digital media is useful in this area. In time, when more and more citizens become confident with the media it is very likely that the electronic delivery of objections is going to be the norm. The possibility to send objections electronically has to be seen primarily as a service improvement to the citizens. Many will find it easier and faster to send an e-mail in preference to posting a letter. The potential seems particularly large when the citizen, as in the municipality of Hals, is able to send the electronic objection directly from the platform of the digital municipality plan. Whether the possibility to send in electronic objections contributes with new inputs to the political process is another question, about which our data does not allow us to say anything consistent.

The approval phase

In continuation of the public phase, the town council considered the received remarks and objections to the proposal of a new digital municipality plan for the municipality of Hals. On basis of the objections, a number of adjustments of the municipality plan were made, and on a town council meeting in the spring 2004, the adjustments of the plan were formally approved. It would be interesting to know which part the electronic debate and the possibility to send in objections electronically played in the municipal, political process. However, from the existing data material, it seems hard to say anything certain about whether the

ICT-tools have improved the politicians' basis of decision and affected their decision making process. Though we asked a number of town council politicians in the municipality of Hals at the end of 2003, to what extend the debates on hals.dk affected the political decisions, none of them could give any examples that the debate on hals.dk had directly affected the political decisions in committees and town council. It was added though that the debate on hals.dk had set political tracks "in detail" (Torpe & Ulrich, 2004). When it comes to the meaning of the digital communication regarding the political process in connection with the physical municipality planning, ICT has probably only played a marginal role.

Recapitulation

Today, in more than 60 percent of the Danish municipalities, it is possible to find plan documents on the homepages. During the last years, the municipalities' homepages have gone through notable changes and there is reason to believe that the ongoing development, where more and more municipalities publish plan information on the Internet will continue in the future years. Most plans are published in PDF-format, while only a few of the municipalities offer the citizens fully digital plan tools. The municipality of Hals is among the leading in this area and has by help of e.g. GIS-functionalities made an entirely digital municipality plan. Along with the development of an Internet-based plan tool, the municipality has experimented with ICT during the planning phase in the dialogue and communication with the citizens. It is mainly the last mentioned aspects we have clarified in this paper.

It turns out that the possibilities of the Hals-citizens both in relation to gathering information, in the expression of opinion and in debates have been expanded in connection with the digitalization of the planning process. When it comes to consultation of the citizens in the planning process, the municipality of Hals used a multi media strategy. Besides the traditional channels such as citizen meetings and paper ads, the citizens have gained additional possibilities for expression of opinion and debate in the form of a variety of ICT-tools. The ICT-opportunities have not turned the citizens involvement processes "upside-down", but rather operated as supplementary elements. As supplement to the village-hall-method, it has been possible in the hearing phase to debate on www.hals.dk. In this connection, the citizens were urged to publish any objections on the portal. As supplement to send in objections by mail, the citizens had the similar possibility via e-mail. It goes with the story though, that the ICT-tools were not introduced until a good while into the process and the initial idea phase proceeded without involving ICT.

To the question on whether the citizens used the possibilities at their disposal, it shows that the citizens apparently wanted to collect information on plan material on the net. Just barely every third citizen in the municipality of Hals has been seeking information on plan material on the municipality homepage. Something therefore indicates that the digitalization of the plan material has increased the openness and the visibility concerning the physical planning in the municipality. It does not seem likely that every third citizen has been to the municipal office to get information about the municipality's plan material. In a Dahl-context ICT seems to lay out the ground for informed citizens. It must also be determined that is has been possible to create a debate online. In the hearing phase, 88 papers were authored on the portal hals.dk. In relation to this, it must be seen as a strengthening of the democracy, that a lot of objections, which does not usually get published, were presented and discussed. Hals.dk has probably not had an initiating function in relation to new debate topics, but to a higher degree continued and developed the discussions started at the previous citizen meetings. One of the purposes of the electronic debate on hals.dk was also reach out to more citizens than possible in the physical citizen meetings. From this consideration it seems interesting that there are radically more citizens, who have read papers on the proposal on hals.dk, than citizens attending the citizens meeting concerning the proposal.

The possibility of sending in objections electronically was also used. About half of the 13 objections were sent in by e-mail. The possibility to do this is primarily to be seen as a service improvement to the citizens, while it is more uncertain whether it produces new inputs.

The study of the experiments in the municipality of Hals represents the first systematic, empirical research results of the dialogue and communication possibilities in the digital planning. The results point in the direction of the Internet being a suitable media when it comes to the involvement of the citizens, but it ought not to be alone in this. The use of ICT in the planning process is only in its infancy and should be seen as a supplement to the traditional channels. The results from the municipality of Hals indicate that other municipalities too can benefit from using ICT in physical planning, not least as a tool to create more visibility. A number of precautions ought to be taken though, when the results are generalized to other municipalities. On one hand, the total digital project on democracy in the municipality of Hals has contributed to increase the attention on the digital municipality plan, and has in this way given the process a lift. On the other hand, there are also aspects of the Hals-case that indicate that other municipalities will be able to obtain even more radical results. Hals did not succeed in testing the possibility to involve the citizens by means of ICT in the idea phase. The experiences from the municipality of Aarhus show that there is an existing potential in exactly that phase of the decision process. Additionally, the "Town-Model-concept" in the municipality of Hals means that the public is limited, which means that a lot of the "necessary" communication will take place in the physical space. That is why bigger units immediately seem to magnify the need to use ICT in the planning processes.

If you try to look into the future, there seems to be a need for further experiments with digital tools in the physical planning. The reform of municipal structures in Denmark containing larger municipalities should create further ground to plait the digital possibilities into the communication between authority and citizen.

References

Arleth, Mette (2004). *Future tools for area administration and public participation.* Paper, for the conference CORP 2005, University of Vienna, February 22-25 2005

Dahl, Robert A. (1989). *Democracy and its Critics.* Princeton University Press

Dahl, Robert A. (1998). *On Democracy.* New Haven, London. Yale University Press.

Danmarks Statistik (2004). *Informationssamfundet Danmark – It-status 2004.* Danmarks statistisks trykkeri, København.

Det Digitale Demokrati (2001). *IT-kompetenceudvikling – digitale demokratiforsøg i Hals Kommune*. Et konkurrenceforslag i projektkonkurrencen Det Digitale Nordjylland.

Det Digitale Demokrati (2004). *Statusrapport, marts 2004*.

KMD Dialog (1994). *Own statistical data from citizen investigations in Glostrup, Ribe og Sorø kommuner*.

Larsen, Torben Kjeldgaard (2004). *Informations og kommunikationsteknologi i den fysiske planlægning*. PhD thesis (forthcoming).

Larsen, Torben Kjeldgaard & Lassen, Claus (2003). *Digital planlægning – nye dialogformer med borgere og omgivelser*. Landinspektøren, juni 2003.

Petterson, Oluf et. al. (1989). *Medborgarnas makt*. Stockholm: Carlssons.

Ryolf, Per & Høj, Brian (2004). Slides from a seminar "E-demokrati i praksis", at the central library in Aarhus d. 24. November 2004.

Torpe, Lars & Ulrich, Jens (2004). Åbenhed og borgerdeltagelse via ikt – forsøg og erfaringer fra Nordjylland. *Det Digitale Nordjylland – ikt og omstilling til netværkssamfundet?* Aalborg Universitetsforlag 2004.

Part Four
Interaction & Communication

Inclusiveness as a Parameter in Design of Online Interaction with Public Authorities

Ellen Christiansen

> Design of web communication between citizens and public authorities is in need of a sustainable strategic perspective involving citizens directly in design, completing and transcending current accessibility and cost effectiveness goals. Inclusiveness is suggested as the loadstar for design, in product as well as in process of development. Citizens should have the option to tailor their online access to public authorities, and a discourse of inclusiveness should dominate labels, navigation and organization. The paper begins with a review of state-of-the-art of interaction design strategies for Danish public online services, where focus is on accessibility and cost-effectiveness. Then, the inclusiveness-discourse is introduced and explained in terms of a prototypical list of design parameters comprising common language, first person agency, personalization, disclosure of mutual dependencies and responsibilities, and community-awareness. Finally, the paper discusses how to organize a development process under the auspices of inclusiveness, and suggests user driven innovation as a part of an integrated design and evaluation approach.

Introduction

Why don't they just send out the digital signature? Why do we have to apply for it – I keep forgetting, and every once in while, when all of a sudden I could use it, I am stuck.' Since 2004, where I started to focus on the digital signature aspect of e-governance, I have heard many complaints about digital signatures. Underlying the complaints is always the same discourse: 'them' is an external authority trying to do something to 'us'. Users or 'wannabe-users' or 'ought-to-be-users', experience management rather than leadership, alienation rather than participation, helplessness rather than respect, when it comes to contact with public authorities via the web, and this experience jeopardizes the citizen-attitude, which is the mother of self-motivated, responsible and caring behavior in a society. Inhabitants, who feel trusted, participate more vigorously in fulfilling the duties of being a member of society. Communication with public authorities should invoke a sense of inclusiveness in those, who use them.

The idea of citizenship is by some anthropologists claimed to be as old as the idea of a human community, while sociologists like to link it to western civilization, particularly the ancient Greek and Roman worlds. Due to globalization, world citizenship, as expressed in the UN declarations, is acknowledged at the political arena to be important to peace in the world, while, by the same token of globalization and migration, people all over the world feel pressures to place their loyalty closer to home, avoiding to take responsibility beyond their own and their families' best interest - hence the importance of supporting the sense of citizenship wherever possible.

The notion that sense of citizenship build on sense of being included was shared by the authors of the American declaration of the rights and duties of man. In the preamble it says: *'All men are born free and equal, in dignity and in rights, and, being endowed by nature with reason and conscience, they should conduct themselves as brothers one to another. The fulfillment of duty by each individual is a prerequisite to the rights of all. Rights and duties are interrelated in every social and political activity of man. While rights exalt individual liberty, duties express the dignity of that liberty. Duties of a juridical nature presuppose others of a moral nature, which support them in principle and constitute their basis. Inasmuch as spiritual development is the supreme end of human existence and the highest expression thereof, it is the duty of man to serve that end with all his strength and resources. Since culture is the highest social and historical expression of that spiritual development, it is the duty of man to preserve, practice and foster culture by every means within his power. And, since moral conduct constitutes the noblest flowering of culture, it is the duty of every man always to hold it in high respect.'* (Quoted from the webpage http://www.cidh.org/Basicos/basic2.htm). Although constantly abused, these words are still the common ground on which communication about organization of society rests and builds, worldwide. Hence, the idea that inclusiveness leads to sense of citizenship when it comes to design of interaction with public authorities online should build on this very same ground. Reality seems however, somewhat different.

The digital signature issue came up while I was teaching a course 'ICT in organizations' for undergraduates at Aalborg University, Humanistic Informatics. The case of introduction of digital signature to Danish public e-services was part of the course syllabus. The students applied for a digital signature and kept diary of their experiences, and in the end we handed in our material to the people in TDC, the company in charge of this service[1], and a TDC representative visited us in return and gave a talk about the digital signature as a public online service. We learnt about the heavy demands on security, cost-benefit calculations, and about experiences from TDC's digital signature hotline. TDC really appreciated the students' diary notes, especially their questions about what to use it for, and, as a direct outcome, TDC decided to put information about possible uses for the signature on the application webpage. The students and I realized the complexity of the routes of decision making between the ministries, vendors involved, municipality- and county-offices, all represented in dedicated boards interacting with consultants. We surfed the web-portal oio[2], http://www.oio.dk/, 'public information online', which gives an overview of initiatives regarding public information and services online. Reading through the pages on this site provides insight into the complexity of decision-making in these matters. As mentioned, the course was about interaction design and organizations, and in the beginning, the students wanted to talk to the designers of the interfaces we looked at, but coming to understand the complexity of the organization around the design of these interfaces was discouraging. Our energy was drained, before we got started on the actual planning of contacting designers.

At the same time, also in 2004, Nyvang and I analyzed the discourse of the national strategies for public online services, and found little focus on user experience. We found that self-motivation is not an issue, neither at the strategic level nor at the level of evaluation of public online services in Denmark. We

---

[1] TDC is a Danish-based European provider of communication solutions
[2] OIO – Offentlig Information Online (public information online) is a website and an electronic newsletter offering information, knowledge and access to tools in relation to IT in the public sector as well as public sector communication.

suggested, then, that design guidelines addressing self-motivation should be implemented at the political strategic level, in the system architecture, in the information architecture, and in the design of interaction (Christiansen & Nyvang 2005). Here, I try to go deeper into the user experience and describe the experience of inclusiveness, and design implications thereof. The prime implications are that design of communication between public authorities and citizens needs guidance from an idea, an overall perspective, other than, - but not contrary to – the operational concerns now in focus, and that this guiding idea should foster citizenship among citizens. To be practical and concrete, I suggest a solution, by which the users can experience inclusiveness without having to wait for a re-design of all Danish public online services, and I suggest user driven innovation as a way of realizing this solution through design. Such initiative should of course be evaluated before recommended as a policy, and inquiry into whether a user driven approach to designing for inclusiveness will in fact lead to users experiencing inclusiveness should be done at first.

Inclusiveness and the interfaces to online communication with public authorities in Denmark

Governance is about regulation of power, and power is regulation of rules, processes, and behavior of a system. The way power is distributed between inhabitants is constitutive to a society, and digitization impacts distribution of power globally as well as locally: participation or policing are two very different approaches to communication, and the direction of communication reveals who is supposed to do what to whom. Citizenship is the outcome of enculturation, a state of mind, stemming from the experience of 'legitimate peripheral participation' (Lave and Wenger 1990), and a sense of being at home. The way inhabitants of a nation build loyalty and commitment, come to obey rules and positively contribute to the reproduction of society's institutions, is shaped by their experience of participation: experiences from kinder garden onwards build a general attitude towards the institutions of society: am I included or am I marginalized? Recent research in Denmark shows that a great deal of the choices in a family's grocery shopping is influenced by the kids, which of course build self-confidence, but expectations as well. These same kids are likely to expect active signs of welcome from public institutions, they will assume they have choices, just like their parents, who are said to be 'shopping schools' and 'shopping churches'. It is in this context, the interfaces of public online services communicate. A moral statement like the famous Kennedy-dictum 'Don't ask what America can do for you, ask what you can do for America' or the classic social democratic slogan 'Know your rights and do your duty', both embodying the idea of citizenship, are met with the counter question 'What's in it for me?'

Design of interaction with public authorities is, however, a challenge. Contrary to the need of buyers, those seeking contact with public authorities are in some state of difficulty – many would in fact prefer not to need the contact. Hence, if on top of the anxiety caused by their errand they are to experience anxiety using the mean of communication, a negative user experience is spoken for – since, as pointed out by Calvin Mooers '*An information retrieval system will tend not to be used whenever it is more painful and troublesome for a customer to have information than for him not to have it*' (Peter Morville, 2005, p. 44).

In this case, everything that would help create the reverse experience: one of self confidence in managing the task, of feeling at home, and of satisfactory completion of the errand should be top priority amongst designers of interaction with public websites. The more so since research on the interaction of online communities has pointed out membership patterns as important to an online community's stability and vitality (Maloney-Krichmar & Preece 2005). This seems however, not to be the case. The criteria for evaluating interaction, we can find via the oio-web portal, and in research on social aspects of online interaction, seem solely to focus on operability issues, which is of course crucial, but not sufficient to establish a mutually respectful dialogue.

As for now, the quality assessment of the Danish public authorities' way of communicating online is in the hands of the Danish Ministry of Science, Technology and Innovation, IT & Telestyrelsen (the National IT and Telecom Agency), which has established an institution 'Top of the web' (http://www.bedstpaanettet.dk, English version) to assess and stimulate high quality on the public web services. Criteria comprise usability (navigation, language and point of departure in user needs), online self-service, openness & usefulness, and technical accessibility. In 2006, users of some of the public service sites were involved in assessing quality through questionnaires, which in the first half of 2006 was such a success that the providers put up a limit of

5000 completed questionnaires, in order not to disrupt traffic[3]. The 'Top of the web'-evaluation covers four categories: form, content, practical value, technical accessibility, and in the presentation of the criteria, the authors emphasize that *'a user should be able to find his or her way around the website - effortlessly. Regardless of their level of expertise, users should have no problem finding the information they need - quickly and easily - and the language used should be simple.'* Regarding content, the authors focus on usefulness: *'the degree of quality depends on the users' potential benefit from the information given. Thus, obviously, it is imperative that the site not only be kept up to date, but that it also offers relevant self service options.'* The closest the 'top of the web'-criteria formulations come to the issue of inclusiveness is when they emphasize openness as a criteria regarding content: *'Users should be able to get some idea as to who is making the decisions and how it is possible to influence a decision-making process. But openness is also about complying with the needs of the user; e.g. by enabling him or her to ask a question and receive an answer electronically.'*

The user questionnaire covers navigation, overview, text, waiting time, and graphic design, experience and likeability. Apart from user evaluation, the other main criteria in the 'top of the web' are technical accessibility (browser, colors and more). At the practical level of design, a resource center KIA[4] (in Danish http://www.oio.dk/tilgaengelighed/kia) has been established to help designers make sure that the governmental 'handicap no hindrance'-plan is implemented. In fact, accessibility is a main focus of the national strategy for public services online as confirmed on the official national Danish website on public information online www.oio.dk: *'It is an essential task to support and promote the quality of public communications, ensuring that the focus remains on the citizens. An important element is the public sector's digital communication to citizens. The focus is not only on technical IT solutions, but also to a great extent on the*

---

[3] This information is only available in Danish at http://www.bedstpaanettet.dk/Content?content=90 beginning of October 2006

[4] The National IT and Telecom Agency established the Competence Centre IT for All (KIA). KIA was established according to the action plan 'Disability no Obstacle', published by the Minister for Science, Technology and Innovation in January 2003. As part of the eEurope 2005 action plan – with the aim to ensure a true and universal information society involving all social groups – KIA participates in the eAccessibility expert group, which is providing advice to the eEurope Advisory Group in the area of eInclusion.

communications provided by the public sector through the Internet, which must be easy to understand, easy to use and remain coordinated across the sector'. A big issue in accessibility is the digital signature, which allows the user to not only get and send information, but also to complete interactions. In 2005, 22% of public authorities received at least ¼ of all documents from citizens in a digital version. Another big issue is a portal that will give the inhabitant only one entrance to all public online services. When the state budget for 2007 was negotiated between minister of finance, municipalities and counties, in the summer 2006, the parties agreed on financing and maintaining a personal website for each and every inhabitant in Denmark, a 'citizen portal' (Borger.dk) with a 'my page'-facility. In 2008, 40 mio. DKK. is on the budget for this, and a pilot version involving some public services is to be released, and at least in 2012 this portal is supposed to be up running. The idea is to 'personalize information with respect to the needs of the citizens' sparked by an OECD report from 2005, which pointed out the risk of Denmark not using the web efficiently for public service. The OECD report also suggested a stronger focus on the users. The portal is to be developed on top of 'borger.dk' (citizen.dk), which is a conglomerate of danmark.dk and netborger.dk (netcitizen.dk). In 2006, the realization of these plans has shifted hands from KMD[5] to a consortium consisting of KL (the union of municipalities in Denmark), 'Den digitale Taskforce' and IT & Telestyrelsen (the National IT and Telecom Agency).

For the citizens, however, it still is a matter of pull, and of making an extra effort, to access public authorities online: While Erhvervs- og selskabsstyrelsen (the Danish Commerce and Companies Agency) sent out a digital signature in September 2005 to 8.000 new enterprises giving them access to self service on virk.dk[6] – the government-citizen part is still on demand – individual citizens are themselves to sign up to get a signature. This is a disturbing priority, from the point of view of creating a sense inclusiveness among citizens.

---

[5] KMD is a software house and the main provider of software solutions to Danish municipalities.

[6] Virk.dk is a web portal to a web of public and private information and digital service regarding commerce. It is developed in a partnership between Erhvervs- og selskabsstyrelsen (the Danish Commerce and Companies Agency) and the private enterprise Krak.

As can be seen from the above overview, the public authorities themselves focus on accessibility, while research in political strategy such as the research center for public sector process rebuilding, http://www.pprgovernment.com/, is applying a cost-effectiveness perspective, which comprises accessibility *as well as* task performance: If a citizen is going to leave the country, build a house, or start up an enterprise, there are lots of permissions to be obtained, lots of authorities to approach, and lots of forms to fill in. An evaluation of public websites from the public sector process rebuilding research center, published July 2006, accuses the administration of not utilizing the potential for rationalizing labor, cutting budget *and* offering the citizens better online services, by cutting through existing divisions of labor and generating entirely new case-handling routines. The report does, however, not offer suggestions with respect to how users could be better met by having the opportunity to express their need. Here, a seeming mystery surfaces: Why is it so difficult to apply an accessibility *plus* task performance approach in the public sector, when it has been done successfully in commerce for years.

If we look over the fence from public to commercial service, customer experience is being researched, and many people nowadays have personal experience buying online. The Amazon.com shopping experience has evolved over some years, and because of its' success in attracting customers, the architecture of this interface has become the mother of interface architecture for online commerce. It seems not so far fetched for public online communication to learn from the insights gained in online shopping, where customer loyalty has always been a big issue. When it comes to the art of bonding with customers, Amazon.com has managed to transfer customer loyalty from trading in the physical world. As a customer at Amazon.com, you are welcomed by name, and they have special offers for you based on their tracking of your previous interaction, without restraining themselves from showing all the other options for buying. In case of complaints, you use the 'trace your order'-facility, and less than 24 hours later you receive apologies, a good explanation, prognosis for delivery, and a discount because of the inconvenience the delay or whatever has caused you. Navigation options and invitation to check status on our interaction surrounds the core service of buying and selling. As a customer, you leave the interaction with the feeling of being treated with respect and having one's needs taken seriously. Why should public websites not be able to give inhabitants the same? Figure 9 depicting the author's intro-menu line at Amazon.com illustrates the point: a 'welcome', recognition of the customer, and the categories of products Amazon.com meets the customer at a glance.

Welcome	Ellen's store	Books	Electro-nics & Photo	Music	DVD	Video	Soft-ware	PC & video-games	Home & garden	Toys & games

Figure 9: The author's intro-menu line at Amazon.com

User experience is a context issue; something outside of the technological materials and the repertoire of forms related to the application area, in this case web-site forms. When accessibility is measured, as we see in 'Top of the web' (http://www.bedstpaanettet.dk), or when cost effectiveness is measured, as we see in the survey coming from the research center for public sector process rebuilding, (http://www.pprgovernment.com/), the subject of analysis is what is available via the computer screen. The users' situation when dealing with the screen content is not considered: what is the life-situation, how does the actual physical setting look, what is considered normal behavior there, how does the user prefer to be met, etc. Apparently, people in Denmark order tickets via the Internet for soccer and for music, they order cheep flight tickets, and they vote in pop-quizzes, etc. But we do not know exactly *how* they do it, how much people help each other, and in what ways, and we do not know the diversity of ways in which ordering and paying via the Internet are carried out. When we hear that, in 2005, 22% of public authorities received at least ¼ of all documents from citizens in a digital version, we do not know whether these citizens accomplished the interaction themselves or had children/grandchildren/neighbors do it for them. Hence, we cannot conclude that ¼ of all grown up inhabitants are in command of the Danish public online services, let alone happy using them. But simple reasoning can help us see that a healthy, coherent and socially sustainable democratic society need more than ¼ of the population to feel included and acting as responsible citizens.

The quality of inclusiveness

When it comes to interface design, experience qualities such as 'inclusiveness' must be translated into tangible characteristics in order to guide design. The following list of parameters to consider is prototypical, a first start, to be underpinned by research. The inclusiveness parameters are generated partly by looking to the Amazon-example above, partly by considering what constitutes a home-experience: you feel contained as you are, you have a point of orientation, to leave from and return to, and you can make the given resonate with your needs and preferences through changes you are able to make yourself.

Common language is mandatory should communication be successful. Hence there should be ways in which to make all citizens speak freely in their own language, when communicating with public authorities, also on the web.

First person agency (Laurel 1991) makes the action on the website something I do. Labels saying 'Watch this!' or 'looking for at short cut? Indicates that I have the power to choose; that someone, who wants to help me, is now trying to guess what my plans are. This is different from formulations such as 'We offer you the opportunity' or 'To make a short cut you click on ...', where I have to feel grateful, because someone is doing something to or for me.

Personalization is an option that is common on many commercial websites: the site remembers prior activity and allows you to continue where you left last time – everything looks as when you left – very much like at home - the site may greet you by name, etc. In case of communication with public authorities, this feature may easily tip over and signal surveillance, hence personalization should only be optional, and designed in line with e-banking, where respect for privacy is part of the product brand.

Disclosure of mutual dependencies and responsibilities is an important point should the quality of experiencing inclusiveness foster citizenship in the 'declaration of human rights'- sense. The Amazon-experience indicates ways to support this, for instance by offering information on consequences for environment and additional cost, or by offering other options, like when your are a blood donor and you are asked, if you are willing to sign up for organ donation, too.

Community – awareness is, as already mentioned, well researched as a feature, which is important for an online community's stability and vitality (Maloney-

Krichmar & Preece 2005). In communication with public authorities, where sense of membership is both the precondition and the goal, a potential double communication of mutual rejection may jeopardize trust; hence the interaction should be as unambiguous as possible. But small things can be done: people who sign up for a place in kindergarten may want to know what options are close to their residence, and if these pop up effortlessly together with names and addresses of sports clubs and other activities in walking or biking distance, the family gets the sense of being part of a community.

This provisionary list of parameters of inclusiveness does not contradict the lists of criteria already in use in evaluation of accessibility and cost effectiveness. On the contrary: If practical circumstances block communication, no sense of inclusiveness is fostered. If the workarounds created by online routines leaves no time to process requests or slows processing down, no sense of inclusiveness is fostered. On the other hand design for inclusiveness is not just a few more bullets on the designer's checklist. It is a different approach to design, suggesting agile development, and developers who listen to the grass growing, and know how to fertilize this growth.

Transparency, reflection and innovation are aspects of action, also when action turns into unconscious operations, as when you interact with a website you know. The more you can do on your own, the more you innovate. This has to do with the double sided nature of action: by doing something, we learn *a way of doing*, as described by Gregory Bateson in his systemic learning theory (Bateson 1979/2000). A user experience of inclusiveness lies in the deutero-learning of being respected and met. For example: with the offer to put in tax-information online comes an important second order reflective message about the way the tax-system/tax-authorities see the relationship between inhabitants and the tax-institution: partnership or policing. The message comes with the wording of the prompts, it comes with names and functionality of the navigation bars, it comes with the ease of use, and it comes with the constellation of the setting of use. The citizen will either experience his or her capacity as extended, feeling more competent in managing one's own life, or inhabitants will slide into lacunas of learned helplessness (Christiansen & Nyvang, 2005). This goes for decision support systems and knowledge management systems in general: they have to be experienced as tools by their users, implying that users have to feel competent when using them (Christiansen 2001). The institutions of a nation materialize in expected and unexpected ways in everyday life, and no design can guarantee a positive outcome, but designers can strive to provide experience of inclusiveness by taking the information ecology of the inhabitants into account and shape the feedback accordingly. From feeling included follows a feeling of responsibility, from which self-regulation grows. To experience that trust is placed in you invokes gratitude, it makes you feel indebted and ready to give. The architect and philosopher Christopher Alexander describes a constellation of fit between form and context which invokes in the actor a feeling of pleasant recognition and support, of being contained in a way open to interpretation and transformation as 'the quality without a name' (Alexander 1979). Feeling included has this quality.

Building a user experience when designing for inclusiveness

The government and administration in Denmark make quite an effort to support more extensive use of web communication between citizens and public authorities. To spark engagement at all levels in society and make the design process transparent, a web portal gives an overview of the initiatives regarding public online services http://www.oio.dk/. Visiting this portal leaves a clear impression of the complexity of the web of organizations, institutions, boards, committees and vendors involved in creating public online communication. The developmental road to a menu bar comprising boxes with all public core services initiated with a Welcome box, followed by the personal Ellen's box, as the one depicted in figure 9 seems long, despite the previously mentioned 'my web'-plan within the borger.dk (citizen.dk) strategy to be fully launched in 2012.

From within the communities of systems developers and interactions designers there is, however, a lot going on at the moment, regarding ways to include end users in the development of computer applications. Three areas are of specific interest, when considering how to involve citizens directly in the design of online communication with public authorities. One is the drift towards agile development including on site customers in case of large projects (Larman 2005). The other is Web 2.0 development, where all of a sudden a mix of personal and corporate blogging, and peer-to-peer sharing of knowledge and resources have caught on so forcefully that it no doubt will dramatically change the level of self-regulation of interaction on the Internet. And finally, the ideas of user driven innovation, dating back to the 1950ies and earlier, have gained a renaissance due to new possibilities of lean production opened by computer technology.

This indicates that it is on the practical, political and bureaucratic level we find the real challenge, when it comes to involving citizens in developing citizen-interaction with authorities. Changing today's 'Look what we have got for you, provided you sign in and do so and so'- discourse to a 'My interactions'-discourse saying 'From where I am now, I want to look at my interactions with so and so' represents a front-end problem, as have been dealt with above, but indeed also a backend problem of compiling a cross-bureaucratic sum of the interactions of one person with all aspects of public service. In principle, this has been possible since 1969 thanks to the introduction of a unique identifier, the civil registration number. In 2006 it is, however, still not possible for a person by way of this number in one click to get an overview all instances of information linked to a number. For those who are persistent, have a digital signature, and are computer literate, yes, a lot of personal information can be found, but it is certainly not a walk-up-and-use facility.

To generate Ellen's box, a set up menu could be designed, which could be included in the welcome box, where I could click through the available categories of data about my interactions with public authorities, so that I have in front of me all my contacts – whilst, at the same time, through the labels of the other boxes, I am aware that there are other contacts available to me in case I need them.

Before taking action on such a design idea, however, we need to know if this is what will simultaneously

a. make public administration more efficient
b. make citizens sense their community and feel included
c. be an effective technical solution

The only we way to get to know is by involving citizens, administrators, politicians and technicians and designers in practical design. For some reason, the division of labor in society prevents us from even think through this idea. An example, right now in the making, is encouraging, though.

In a research project 'The FEEDBACK-project', on feedback motivated electricity saving in private households funded by ELFOR, Kanstrup and I employed user driven innovation as part of both the conceptualization and the construction of design concepts (Kanstrup & Christiansen 2006). We worked with eight families, who told us about their ideas about energy saving, who used our mock ups, and who themselves designed and re-designed prototypes, all of which gave us insights into where, when and how they were motivated to receive information about their consumption of electricity. A similar project, probably in a somewhat larger scale could be launched concerning a personalized interface to all public online services. A resent report on the ways that user driven innovation is employed in marketing (Grunert 2006) gives both an overview and a convincing argument for the key insights to get user experiences, preferences, habits and values from this way of researching. The message is that users need to be situated in real use situations in order to be able to bring out innovations. The key is therefore to begin with the citizen-life world instead of in the formal top down structure of public administration. The governmental strategy to be presented summer 2007 involves all relevant ministries, and according to the work plan receivers of public service are going to be involved. There is no indication, however, that involvement will exceed meetings and questionnaires.

Summing up: Reviving the collective resource approach to systems development

This paper began with the voice of a citizen asking *'Why don't they just send out the digital signature? Why do we have to apply for it – I keep forgetting, and every once in while, when all of a sudden I could use it, I am stuck.'* I have analyzed why such a question can be posed, and what could be done to eliminate it: At present, designers of online communication with authorities know very little about the difficulties faced by citizens who want to communicate with public authorities online, let alone their preferences. Moreover, the designer have no loadstar for their design other than concerns for operability spelled out in accessibility and cost effectiveness, By turning this development situation up side down, by including user innovations from the very start it would be possible to include focus on the very mission of the communication between citizens and authorities: the mutual effort to sustain society.

In the preceding sections, I have argued for 'inclusiveness' as a key quality of the communication between citizens and public authorities, also in online communication, should this communication foster a sense of citizenship different from a policing (emphasis on duty) or a service (emphasis on right) rhetoric - a mutual right and duty relationship.

This quality was broken down into a provisionary list of five parameters to design for and to evaluate: common language, first person agency, personalization, disclosure of mutual dependencies and responsibilities, and community-awareness. The last section of the paper discusses why and how including user driven innovation would be a feasible solution: To design with inclusiveness as a loadstar requires that also the development process becomes inclusive, for which we are fortunate to have a long and world wide recognized tradition in Scandinavia.

Acknowledgements

This paper has benefited from collaboration with Anne Marie Kanstrup, in specific in the FEEDBACK project, and with Tom Nyvang on issues on self-regulation and democracy in relation to design. I am grateful for comments and inspiration in the review process, too.

References

Alexander, C. (1979). *The timeless way of building*. New York: Oxford University Press.

Bateson, G. (1979/2000). *Steps to an ecology of mind*. Chicago: University of Chicago Press.

Christiansen, E. (2001). *Knowledge Management in a Thinking System*. Paper presented at *IRIS 2001*, Ulvik, Norway, Aug.11-14, 2001

Christiansen, E. & T. Nyvang (2005). *On the importance of supporting self-motivation among end users of eGovernmental services*. Paper presented at the 2nd Workshop eGov Workshop, 14-15 February 2005, Copenhagen Business School, Copenhagen

Ehn,, P. & M.Kyng (1987). The collective resource approach to systems design. In: G. Bjerknes, P. Ehn & M. Kyng (eds.), *Computers and democracy: a Scandinavian challenge,* pp. 17-58, alderhot, England: Aveburty

Grunert, Klaus G. (2006). Innovation i fødevaresektoren: En tværfaglig opgave. (Innovation in food sector: A crossdisciplinary challenge). *Momentum,* No 1, vol 4. årgang, pp 28-30, 2006.

Kanstrup, A.M. & E. Christiansen (2006). *Selecting and engaging innovators: Combining democracy and creativity.* Paper submitted for NordiCHI2006, Oslo, Oct. 14-16, 2006

Kanstrup, A.M. & E. Christiansen (2005). *Model power – Still an issue.* Paper presented at a workshop at the fourth decennial Aarhus Conference 'Between sense and sensibility' Aug. 20-24, 2005

Laurel, B. (1991). *Computers as theater.* Addison-Wesley

Larman, C. (2005). *Agile and iterative development.* Prentice-Hall

Lave, J. & E. Wenger (1990). *Situated learning.* Cambridge University Press.

Maloney-Krichmar, D. & J. Preece (2005). A multilevel analysis of sociability, usability and community dynamics in an online health community. *ACM Transactions of Human-Computer Interaction,* vol. 12, 2.

Morville, P. (2005). *Ambient Findability.* O'Reilly.

Communicating Across Sectors in Health Care – A Case of Establishing New Infrastructure

Ann Bygholm

As part of a project, the Municipality of Aalborg, the Department of Care for the Elderly and Disabled decided to implement electronic exchange of information between on the one hand the municipality and the hospital, and on the other hand between the municipality and the general practicing doctors. The idea behind the project was that switching from communicating through telephone and letters to electronic information exchange would mean a more correct exchange of information and also a faster and more holistic treatment of the citizen involved. A well-known standard, EDIFACT, was chosen for exchange of information involving an extension of the standard, but from a technical point of view it should not be difficult to make the systems of the involved partners communicate. Still, numerous problems were encountered between the partners in the implementation and use of electronic exchange for communication and coordination of work with senior citizens. The problems were due to a mixture of factors among which the technical were not the least, despite the fact that this factor ought to have been fairly easy "in principle".

In this paper, I will argue that the main problems anticipated were not due to neither the technology nor the work practice but to the relation between them. Thus, it is not solely a question of more/better technology or more adequate work practice but rather a question of establishing a proper balance among them. I address the problems involved in application of ICT for communication and coordination in terms of the concept of infrastructure thus focussing on the relation between systems, work practices, organizations, and knowledge involved. Understanding ICT systems as infrastructure, as opposed to understanding ICT as a system or a tool, contributes to a more differentiated acknowledgment of the problems involved and thus also to building a better foundation for anticipating them in the applications of ICT in complex work settings.

Introduction

Work in the health care sector is highly dependent on cooperation between persons and institutions both because of increasing specialization and because coherence in performance and course of events is important for the quality of the service. This put an increasing demand on communication and coordination between partners in the health care services and the use of ICT is seen as an important issue to make sure that relevant information is available at the right time for the right persons to utilize in the right situation. Effective and secure communication and cooperation between partners in the health care sector by the way of ICT could seem as a fairly straight forward task to accomplish, but it has proven not to be. It is a complex endeavour involving both technological innovation and organizational change.

In Denmark, ICT has been on the political agenda since 1995 when the first national strategy for information technology in the health care system was launched (Ministry of research 1995). In continuation of the national strategy, two initiatives were started, one focussing on establishing a health data network and the other on developing electronic health patient record systems (EPR). These initiatives have had a profound effect on the further development of ICT in the health care sector until today.

The health data net was based on a small experiment back in 1990 using EDI communication between pharmacies and medical practices ("Amager trial") and further experiments in different regions led to the formation of a nation wide project, MedCom in 1994 by important stakeholders in the area. The purpose of MedCom was to develop standards for the most common communication flows between medical practices, hospital and pharmacies. When the national strategy was launched, the task of developing the health data net was given to MedCom who expanded and disseminated the technology and standards all ready developed to cover a wider range of actors such as general practitioners, specialists, dentists, hospital wards and departments, radiology departments, laboratories, pharmacies, home nursing sector, regional and local authorities. Recent activities involves transferring the communication among the various partners to an Internet based data network and the development of a health portal shared by health professionals and citizens. (MedCom hompage).

The development of EPR was less well defined from the outset. In the national strategy from 1996, it was stated that the use of IT for recording patient information and clinical data holds a large potential for rationalizing and gives the possibility for increased openness and quality in the treatment of patients. The ministry of health and the counties cooperated in order to initiate and stimulate development of EPR on hospitals, with the aim of creating a national standard, by funding 13 regional and local projects, and in addition to this one project, the EPR-observatory was funded to monitor, collect and disseminate experiences from the regional project. In the next strategy, IT in hospitals (2000-2002), the EPR-observatory's working area was expanded to include an identification and description of all relevant EPR projects in Denmark and also to include descriptions on information modelling in relation to the work done in this area by the national board on health. The EPR-observatory continued this work under the latest strategy for IT in the health care sector (2003-2007). Thus the EPR-observatory has mapped the national development and diffusion of EPR by a series of investigations based on questionnaires and interviews. In addition, a number of central themes has been examined, e.g. information modelling, data communication and integration. Since 2000, these investigations have been published in annual reports and presented at national conferences every year. The mapping includes descriptions of the development and use of four different information models, among these the generic model (G-EPJ) developed by the national board of health, various proposals for integration platforms and problems concerning re-use of data for research and development of quality (EPR observatory homepage). Although much has been achieved, the aim of the original strategy, to develop a national standard for EPR, has not been reached. At the moment, the work with EPR is under reorganization and a government organ has been appointed to lay down guidelines for the further work with EPR in Denmark. A new strategy for ICT in the health care sector is on the way, focusing on centralization and integration in order to promote the needed flow of communication, coordination and cooperation in health care services.

The project that is in focus in the following is only a small piece of the whole picture, but it illustrates some of the problems and challenges in using ICT in communication, coordination and cooperation in a concrete context from the perspective of the clinical users. I argue that the main problems are due to a misfit between technology, work practice and organization, thus focusing on understanding ICT as a working relation more than as an object or tool in complex work settings. Levels of problems are identified in the use of the new communicational infrastructure. First, I start by discussing the relational role of ICT in terms of the infrastructural aspects of technology and here I draw on the work of Star and Ruhledger (1996) and Hanseth (2002), secondly, I describe the case and the methods used for collecting data, thirdly, I analyse data from the case, and finally, I conclude on the challenges involved in establishing a new infrastructure.

ICT system as infrastructure

Machines and tools are the widespread metaphors for information technology that have been shaping the thinking and understanding of design and implementations. Different metaphors reveal different aspects of technology and also different perspectives on what it is we want to achieve with technology.

Machine metaphor

Inherit in the metaphor of a machine is a kind of automation; a machine is performing a piece of work that to some extent replaces the work of a human. The steam engine was a breakthrough for the industrial revolution in converting power from steam into movement and originally the machine metaphor conveyed the focus on automation of muscle power. The use of the machine metaphor within the area of ICT transfers the focus on automation from muscle power to brain power, such as office automation which is the designation of the use of computer systems to execute a variety of office operation. The perhaps most complete display of the machine metaphor within the area of ICT reveals itself in the field of artificial intelligence. Research on artificial intelligence is concerned with producing machines to automate task requiring intelligent behaviour, such as problem solving, speech and pattern recognition. Although the ambitions of artificial intelligence, which was initially formulated in the late 1950, never totally fulfilled the ideas, techniques and results from the discipline is with us in a variety of applications e.g. expert systems, intelligent search agents and the use of robots in various forms of production. The point here however is that the metaphor of a machine conveys the idea of systems that perform automatically without the interventions of humans.

Tool metaphor

The tool metaphor has had a great impact on the whole area of ICT development and implementation. The Scandinavian tradition on system development founded in the late 1970, which later became known as Participatory Design outside Scandinavia, is in a way founded on this metaphor. The idea of a tool as the basic perspectives on ICT development borrows meaning from traditional crafts in understanding ICT as an extension of traditional tools and materials used within a given craft or profession. In order to design good ICT tools then, the designer must understand the specific work process, which the tool is intended to support. Focus on work processes is thus a key point; "Work Oriented Design" was the title of Pelle Ehns dissertation from 1988 where the tool perspective on ICT development was introduced (Ehn, 1988). "Design at Work" (Greenbaum & Kyng, 1991) and "Contextual Design" (Beyer & Holtzblatt, 1998) are other examples of influential publications based on the tool perspective. Cooperation between designers and users is of paramount importance for this design philosophy since the users are in possession of the fundamental knowledge of work processes that forms the foundation for design of ICT tools. Thus, the development of methods and techniques to support the cooperation between designers and users is in focus. For example the use of muck-ups, prototypes, scenarios, and video observation, i.e. techniques that promote a concrete understanding of the domain of work and which facilitate a shared understanding of the existing work practice and the role of the coming ICT tool. The metaphor of a tool makes us think of the task that people are supposed to accomplish with the ICT tool and it conveys the idea of the ICT systems as something that support work and is in the control of humans.

The use of one metaphor does not necessarily exclude another and even if there is a kind of history in the use of these metaphors, meaning that the machine metaphor came "before" the tool metaphor, the perspectives conveyed by different metaphors provide supplementary perspectives on ICT systems. Also other metaphors, e.g. text and ecology (Nardi & O'Day, 1999), have been proposed in order to focus on different elements and problems in the development and use of ICT systems. Here, however, I will proceed discussing the implications of the use of infrastructure as a metaphor.

Infrastructure metaphor

The traditional conception of an infrastructure is something that is just there, ready-to-use, completely transparent and not to question e.g. the water system, the electricity supply, the railway, the road system, telecommunication, the mail services and the Internet. In this conception, there is a tendency to understand infrastructure as "hardware", something that is built and maintained and then sinks into the invisible background. Something to be noticed only when it breaks down. But as Edwards (Edwards 2003) points out, infrastructure is socio-technical in nature, meaning that not only hardware but organizations, socially communicated background knowledge, general acceptance and reliance, and near ubiquitous accessibility are required for a system to be an infrastructure.

According to wiktionary (http://en.wiktionary.org), infrastructure means "an underlying base or foundation especially for an organization or system" and "the basic facilities, services and installations needed for the functioning of a community or society". The definition provided here also point to the fact that the development or evolvements of ways to deal with this underlying base are equally important for the understanding of infrastructure. Telephony is possible because transmission of signals over a distance involving electromagnetic waves by electronic transmitters is possible, but also because of the invention of an appropriate appliance, the telephone, which can be used for the purpose, because enough people want to use, own and pay for a phone so there is someone to communicate with and because the whole service is highly organized making sure that is possible to make calls to the ones you want to talk to. The road system is built in order to afford transportation, nowadays primarily transportation by car. This implies that there are cars (automobile industries), which people can afford to buy, that they have access to roads, are able to drive (driver license), and can drive safely (traffic regulations) and so on. Furthermore, it is difficult to separate the development of the "base" from the development of services and regulations. It is difficult to separate the development of roads (base) from the development of cars and the other services and installation needed to make the road system function as an infrastructure. Infrastructures are formed by use and are always under development; they grow by use and it is the use context and use practice that define whether or not something becomes an infrastructure.

The designation of the term infrastructure to ICT systems came in to focus by the Clinton Administration's Policy initiative on National Information Infrastructure (NII) from 1993; this was later followed by EU by launching eEurope, which, similarly to the US plan, aims at making the European Union the most competitive and dynamic knowledge based economy in the world developing modern public services trough widespread availability to an information infrastructure (Fomin, 2003, eEurope Resolution, 2003). These plans describe visions for the use of ICT for different areas of society like business, health care, education, etc. By these initiatives, information infrastructures became a key issue in international politics and economy. Star & Ruhledger (1996) and Hanseth (2000) a.o. discuss how the metaphor of infrastructure forms the thinking and understanding of development and implementation of ICT systems.

In contrast with the metaphors of machine and tool, the metaphor of infrastructure put forward the relational side of ICT systems. Both Hanseth and Star and Ruhledger suggest different dimensions to characterize an infrastructure, which I will present here in order to frame my discussion and analysis of the task from the Municipality of Aalborg. While focusing on use and use practice, Star and Ruhledger mention eight different characteristics, that is *embeddedness* (integrated in social structures and practices), *transparency* (can be used without removing focus from the task), *reach or scope* (goes beyond individual tasks or processes), *learned as part of membership* (an inherent part of an organization), *links with conventions of practice* (shapes and is shaped by practice), *embodiment of standards* (builds on standards and conventions), *building on an installed base* (must relate to existing technologies), and *visible upon breakdown* (looses transparency and is drawn in focus when it breaks down). Very much in line with this, but with slightly more emphasis on the necessary technical prerequisite for an infrastructure to function as such, Hanseth (2000) suggests that an infrastructure is an *evolving* (evolves continuously), *shared* (must function as a shared resource or foundation for a community), *open* (lack of borders in how many elements it may include, how many users may be using it and also in the sense that there are no limits to who might contribute to its design and deployment and that the development time has no beginning and no ending), *heterogeneous* (including sub-infrastructures based on different versions of the same standard or different standards covering the same functionality), *installed base* (backward compatibility which also means that the existing heavily influences how the new can be designed and that infrastructures are considered as existing already, never developed from scratch).

These dimensions suggest "an infrastructure, which is without absolute boundary on a priory definition" (Star and Ruhledger, 1996) and also points to the fact that infrastructures cannot be understood independently of their use. An ICT system is becoming an infrastructure in relation to the involved technical, social and organizational element and in relation to the organized practices within which it functions. It is evolving over (long) time, it does not have a fixed group of users or use practices, and it is a dynamic, ongoing process with no fixed centre of control. It both forms and is formed by use. The metaphor of infrastructure put to foreground the fact that ICT systems are never designed from scratch, they always build upon exiting tools and practices. Hanseth proposes the term "cultivation" instead of design to put emphasis on this dynamic and bring up the resemblance to a living organism. In this he draws on Dahlbom and Janlerts' (1996) distinction between construction and cultivation as two very different ways of thinking of design, construction denoting the process of selecting, putting together and arranging a number of objects to form a system, whereas in cultivating we interfere with, support and control a natural process.

To get a deeper understanding of the sort of problems arising in this "natural process", Star and Ruhledger turn to Bateson and his understanding of communicative systems. Communication in Bateson's terms is an extensive and far reaching concept referring to the kinds of phenomena that cannot be understood in terms of physical laws. His study of communicative behaviour included problems from very different domains e.g. schizophrenia, alcoholism and the communicative system of whales and dolphins. Regardless of the particularities in the concrete problem involved, Bateson's focus was on understanding the general laws and patterns of communication. Inspired by Bertram Russell's theory on logical types, Bateson pointed out that human communication operates at several levels of abstraction. The levels are organized in a hierarchical structure such that the above level is about the sub level. The level that is about communication is called meta-communication, and the level that is about meta-communication is called meta-meta-communication and so forth. In the distinction between the content and relationship level of a message, the relationship level is about the content. The relationship or meta-communicative level is used to classify the content level of the communication, to inform on how to understand the message. Bateson points out that there is a gulf between the meta-message and the message. A gulf that is of the same nature as the gulf between a thing and the word that stands for it, or between the members of the class and the name of the class (Bateson 1972, 247). Bateson's understanding of learning corresponds to his theory of communication in the sense that learning is communication and like all communicational phenomena should be understood as a hierarchy with different levels.

The number of identifiable levels in human communication is not fixed but similar to Star and Ruhleder I use three levels as relevant for understanding the problems involved in the process of creating/ re-creating an infrastructure for communicating across sectors in health care. Level one problems appear as matter of fact problems, like not knowing how to send or receive a message or not succeeding in having two systems communicating with each other. Level two problems can be seen as a result of not knowing how to use the system properly in the use context, like not knowing when the sent messages will be received and acted upon or not knowing what is wrong when a message can not be communicated properly. Level two moves the problems into a wider context and is about classification of, discussion and reflection on the problems involved in using and running the system. Level three is one step more abstract, and put questions to the values and basis of the work done like what kind of information do we want to share, who is entitled to use the system and legal issues in connection with exchange of information. An issue raised on level three is concerned with the fundamental issues and values in the concrete practice, in this case the care practice.

Electronic exchange of information

The Municipality of Aalborg, the Department of Care for the Elderly and Disabled undertook together with Aalborg hospital and four general practitioners a project "Exchange of information in the health care sector". The project was part of "The Digital North Denmark" (DDN), a large-scale experiment with ICT technology (2000-2003) with the aim of investigating the condition for 'network society' and a 'learning region' by building on exiting competences in the region. DDN was partly funded by the government and based on project offers within four themes. The projects within DDN were conducted by consortia of private companies and public institutions and could get a maximum of one third of the total project sum from the government. One of the themes was digital governance and within this theme there was a special call for projects within the health care sector. The project from the Municipality of Aalborg was one in a total of nine projects within the health care sector in DDN (further description of the DDN project can be found in Dirckinck-Holmfeld et al. 2004 and for projects within the health care sector in Bygholm and Boisen 2004). The project from the Municipality of Aalborg ran from 31.1.2001 to 31.12.2003.

The case description is based on interviews with main actors from the involved organizations and the project leader. Besides, various documents including diary notes and minutes produced during the project is used, as well as an evaluation report done by the responsible organization after the end of the project.

Point of departure for the project was the fact that the exchange between the municipal home care section, the hospital and the general practitioners was growing and, at the beginning of the project, the message exchanges were of the order of more than 400.000 thousand per year. Thus, the aim of the project was to use electronic communication to "…improve quality in cooperation and information exchange between municipality, hospital and general practitioners to the benefit of the citizens" (project application p. 4.). More specifically, the purpose was to gain "higher security for correct information, more coherent treatment, more quick and effective way of communication, more rational use of resources, and a simplification of work" (project application. p. 4).

The project was initiated by the Municipality of Aalborg and included, apart from the medical wards at the hospital and the general practitioners, The Danish Healthcare network (MedCom), the IT supplier partners – that is Rambøl Informatic (Municipality of Aalborg), B-Data (Aalborg Hospital) and the four suppliers to the general practitioners (EG Data Inform, Acure, Ascott Software and Profdoc).

The project was divided in two parts, one focusing on exchange of information between the Municipality of Aalborg and Aalborg Hospital and one focusing on exchange of information between the Municipality of Aalborg and the involved general practitioners. The project was organized with a steering committee with representatives from the involved partners, one working group for each part of the project and some working groups focusing on specific problems e.g. rules of consent and security.

The project was based on structured EDI messages, in which an electronic form, an exchange standard, can be exchanged between systems through a closed net, VANS-net. The exchange standards are developed in cooperation with The Danish Health Care Net, MedCom.

Work with electronic exchange of information was started before the DDN project began. Thus from 1999, there has been an exchange of admission and discharge advice between the Municipality and the hospital. The advice communication is a single automated orientation on whether a citizen is admitted or discharged. Building on these experiences, the idea was to extend and supplement this communication allowing for a more detailed communication between the partners on for example data care, training and medication. During the project, admissions reports from municipality to hospital were developed together with warning reports sent by the hospital to the municipality to warn of completion of treatment, discharge reports from hospital to municipality and correspondence messages which is a message based on free text to communicate between the partners. The part of the project that was concerned with the communication between municipality and general practitioners had no former experience on electronic exchange to build on. During the project messages were developed for prescription renewal, correspondence messages, and home care status. When the project was initiated there were very few standards available for exchanging information between local authorities and other partners in the health care sector. Thus, through cooperation between the project and MedCom, the project came to function as an incentive and pilot project for developing these standards and, based on the experiences gained during the project, the standards were more easily implemented by the way of MedCom in other parts of the country.

The first phase of the project was used to specify content in the six new EDI messages, to ensure that technical communication between the municipality's care system, the hospitals patient administrative system and the four involved systems used by the general practitioners were technically possible and also to test the developed solutions. Specification of content was organized by MedCom and carried out in two different working groups; one group for communication between municipality and hospital and in this group there were representatives from the municipality and the hospital in Aalborg as well as from other municipalities and hospitals in Denmark; one group for communication between municipality and general practitioners which only involved doctors from Aalborg. The messages developed were later distributed to most of the country and for the main part also converted to XML format. This phase also included teaching of hospital personnel. Second phase was used to further development of messages, tests, teaching and transition to operation for part of the solutions.

In sum, you could say that the project took its point of departure in well known technology and standards for electronic communication, that is EDI messages through the VANS network, a number of new standards for exchange of information was developed within the EDI framework and tested in cooperation with MedCom, which seemed to be a manageable task. Thus, the major challenge foreseen by the project was to make electronic exchange of information a natural part of the daily work of the involved partners.

Analysis and discussion

Below I will present and discuss two stories from the case - one, which focuses on the development, techniques and standard, and another which focuses on work practice, communication and collaboration. The stories illustrate the tangled nature of the problems experienced in the development and use of electronic exchange of information. It is stories that illuminate the fact that finding explanations and solutions on what seems to be relatively straight forwards tasks can be an extremely complex process involving all sorts of issues, technical and non-technical.

Techniques and standards

Exchange of information between the partners depended on the ability of the involved systems to send and receive messages technically correct, that is both senders and receivers of information used MedCom standards and EDI syntax in exactly the same way. The very idea of testing systems, after the new messages were developed, was to ensure that these matters were respected. During most of the project period, errors kept coming up which meant that messages were not transferred at all or they were wrongly transmitted. It should be a manageable, although perhaps a time demanding process, to correct these errors so that the messages could be transferred properly. But it was not, and the complications were due to several reasons.

First of all it was difficult to localize the errors because of the many involved systems. Was the failure due to one or another system, to errors in message syntax, to problems with the Vans-net or something quite different? Some of the problems had to do with a shift to new version of the care system, problems in the capacity of the server, periods of peak load, and even power failure. These experiences also lead to the recognized need for rules for non-electronic exchange of information as these situations can not always be avoided.

Another thing was the commitment from the involved partners - especially the vendors of the system used by the general practitioners. They had agreed in being part of the project but not necessarily specified to what extent they were able and willing to prioritize the work, e.g. how quickly they could correct identified failures. These systems were quite different, three of them were windows-based and one was based on DOS, and the extent of necessary corrections in the system varied a lot. After more than two years, most failures were corrected though, and, from a technical point of view, exchange of information between municipality and doctors was possible. Before the project ended a new version of the system former based on DOS was launched. The new windows-based version of this system did not include the possibility to exchange EDI based messages through the Vans-net. In a broader context, this makes sense because there where a lot of commotion and changes in standards and principles for organizing data in the health data net at that time, but for the involved doctors and for the project as such is was a draw back, meaning that the doctors could either keep the old version, which for other reasons were a problem or loose the possibility of electronic exchange of messages, the messages that they used quite some time to take part in the specification of.

There were continuous problems and failures with messages for re-ordering medicine in one of the systems used by the general practitioners and, in the last part of the project, the assumption was formed that the problem might be due to inconsistencies in the medicine data used by that system. In Denmark, the registration of medicine is organized by two providers, Danish Medicines Agency (lægemiddelstyrelsen) and the medicine catalogue from the Danish Medical Association (den lille grønne). The system with the failures used the catalogue from the Danish Medical Association whereas the other three systems used by doctors and the municipality's care system used the catalogue from the Danish Medicines Agency. These two catalogues should be identical in principle, but it turned out they were not. They had terminated the cooperation and were (unintentionally) moving apart. At the time, this came as a surprise for other important stakeholders, e.g. the Pharmaceutical Association, of course they would have noticed it later on, but as a consequence of the problems in the project, the owners of the two catalogues were advised to renew the cooperation, which they did. This did not solve the problem though and a reprogramming of part of the system was necessary to make exchange of re-ordering of medicine work from this system, which was done after the end of the project.

The whole issue of technical communication and exchange of EDI standards seemed at the outset as a well defined task with known solutions, i.e. a level one problem, but it turned out to be more complicated. Some of the problems had to do with the combination of testing new EDI messages with several systems, which had not performed EDI communication before. Thus, there was a collision of several level one problems and, in order to address these, the project had to broaden the frame for examining the problems; it became level two problems. One example of this kind of broadening was the supposition of the inconsistency in data between the two medicine catalogues. This turned out to be right; there were inconsistencies in the two catalogues which of course were unacceptable and could have turned into a discussion of the sanity in having two instead of one medicine catalogue and thus be an example of a level three problem. In fact, this discussion took place around a year after the project had ended. On initiative of the Ministry of the Interior and Health, a new organization was formed to establish one single medicine catalogue in Denmark. The fact that one of the vendors chose to launch a new version without the possibility of sending and receiving EDI messages is also a level three problem. There was a contradiction in interest between this vendor and the rest of the project, which meant that this vendor gave no priority to backward compatibility at this point, probably for good reasons, which however lay outside the scope of the project.

The story about techniques and standards shows that problems connected with developing and exchanging new EDI messages were not solely a question of agreeing on the content and making the technique work. All sorts of other problems interfered which had very little to do with exchange of EDI messages, such as inadequate organization of medicine catalogues and contradicting interests.

Work practice

Use of the system was especially difficult at the hospital that used an old fashioned patient administrative system (PAS) and, besides, the involved staff (at seven medical wards) had no experience in using ICT in their work. Thus, before being able to exchange information electronically with the municipality, the hospital needed new hardware (which there were not really room for), training of the staff, and establishment of support structures. Training of staff was a challenge because of the inexperience in using ICT systems among the staff, because of the old fashioned and time consuming interaction style in the hospital's PAS, and also because of the number of the involved staff members (approximately 300 persons). Use of PAS especially caused problems because of the unfamiliarity of the command based interaction style, which was unknown to most users regardless of level of computer knowledge. For each of the seven wards involved, about four persons were trained for one day in use of PAS to exchange information with the municipality. The training contained both theoretical and practical issues. In connection with the training, three different kinds of manuals were prepared, one very extensive describing everything in detail, one less extensive presupposing a basic knowledge of procedures, and one single laminated sheet describing the most important procedures and commands. Especially the last one was highly used.

The staff participating in the training was supposed to teach the remainders in their wards, and thus function as super users. The problem was not that the trained staff could not use the system, but more that it was an extremely time consuming task to send messages, the system operating with many different types of screens that should be accessed in at certain order and was difficult to navigate in. For an inexperienced user, it could take around an hour to send a message and demonstrating the process for another nurse could easily take one and half to two hours. To use such an amount of time without being interrupted was almost impossible. The trained users had no change in other working obligations and it was difficult to fit in this extra task. Of course the work load connected to exchange of messages with the municipality was reduced as the experience with the use of the system grew and two of the wards actually succeeded in making electronic exchange a part of daily work, whereas others were overwhelmed by the initial troubles. The problems connected with communicating through the PAS were not a surprise for project management but from the start it was considered more important to experiment with electronic communication than to wait for at new EPR system. One of the incentives for the medical wards was the possibility of reduced telephone communication, which is also very time consuming.

Apart from being difficult and time consuming to interact with the system, there was a need for new routines to ensure that sent messages were actually received at the municipality within an acceptable time limit. These routines were especially needed at the municipality and at the hospital where many people were involved in the exchange of information. Thus, agreements on cooperation were set up before the implementation and these were revised several times during project. For example it was first agreed that the hospital should send two warning reports on all patients. One within the first 48 hours after admission and the second after the time of discharge was agreed upon. This was revised during the last period of the project so that two messages should only be sent in case of long admissions or in case of a major change in the need for homecare after discharge, whereas only one where needed for shorter stays at the hospital. Another change had to do with the time for sending the discharge report; in the beginning the deadline was the day of discharge, which later on was changed to the day before discharge. The discharge reports were especially difficult to fill in and print and as a consequence they were very often not sent electronically. A basic guideline in the set of agreements was the division of messages in two categories: emergent and un-emergent messages. Emergent messages were messages that had to be acted upon within 24 hours and those had to be phoned to make sure they were received and understood by the right persons. An un-emergent message, which is a message not needing action within 24 hours, could be sent electronically. This was unexpected compared to the expectations expressed in the project application concerning "…a more quick and effective way of communication…" by using ICT for communication. As for the whole set of agreements it turned out that, due to many different interpretations of the agreements, they got increasingly detailed which in turn made them less accessible for the staff. At the end of the project, a large part of the staff in the municipality and at the hospital were still not sufficiently familiar with the agreements to use the system accordingly. It was also realized that there was a continuous need for coordination of agreement for both electronic and non-electronical communication between the partners. Thus instead of one infrastructure for exchange of information between the institutions they now had two and double communication became a result of this, i.e. they used both the phone and the system to communicate the same information just to be sure that messages were actually received.

According to law, sending more detailed information on the patients need for e.g. care, training and medication between the partners needed a personal consent for each message. In practice this was not always possible and one of the solutions that was examined and discussed with the legal authorities was the possibility of a general consent from each citizen receiving care. This was however considered a breach of the law, thus information could only be exchanged if consent was given for each message. Personal consent was indispensable no matter other conditions. There was nothing new in the law, the same conditions count when information is exchanged between two persons on a telephone. Use of electronic communication however changes and broadens the context for information exchange, what can be said in an oral phone conversation between two people is not necessarily suited for wider distribution in a writing based media. Moreover, electronic communication gave a possibility of exchange of valuable information that was not accessible before. In fact, that was the whole idea of the project, but in many cases this information exchange could not be carried through because it was illegal. This problem is not only a problem for this project but appears in almost all attempts to use information on patients to coordinate the treatment and care. It has been on the political agenda several times in the last ten years. And this year, the Minister of Health has proposed a change in the law in order to facilitate the exchange of information across different institutions in the health care sector.

The story of work practice shows the complexity of the many issues involved in the attempt to change from one infrastructure to another. Some of the problems were due to the complicated interaction style demanded by the old system and to computer inexperience among the staff. These are examples of level one problems and were handled by training and by producing manuals. The fact that it was such a time demanding task so send and receive messages and the doubtfulness concerning the rules for exchange of information to some extent questioned the rationale of using the system seen from the point of view of the hospital staff. The agreements that should solve the problems got rather complicated in order to cover all situations. The necessity of operating with two different lines of communication did not afford the work practice at all and results of these level two problems were in many cases double communication, i.e. more work instead of less work for the staff. Adding to this, and coming from a societal context, there were whole issues of patient consent which questioned the legality of the basic intensions and goals behind the project.

Concluding remarks

The case shows the comprehensive and complicated process of introducing infrastructural changes. In this case, the change meant that the staff, instead of one way of communicating, had two separate ways and this meant that communication among the partners, a least for a number of instances, resulted in double communication (extra work). Moreover, the problems involved are of all kinds and tangled in all sorts of ways, only some of them within the controls of the partners involved. Even if the hospital got a new system that could afford the exchange of information in a proper manner and the agreement made it obvious when to do what, this would not provide an answer to the legal an ethical questions involved in exchanging information. Here, there is a contradiction between the aims of ensuring a coherent treatment on the one side and the protection of integrity of the citizen at the other side.

Also, attention should be paid to the evolving character of infrastructural technology, meaning that the time involved in creating these changes is often seriously underestimated. An example from the county of West-Sealand illustrates this (MedComs homepage and personal communication). It is about exchange of prescriptions between pharmacists and general practitioners. Electronic exchange of prescriptions by the way of EDI standards has been possible since 1997. Although 56% of the general practitioners at that time had the technical possibility of doing this, i.e. they had computers allowing them to communicate Edi standards; only 9% of them used the possibility. When the medical association decided to pay for the electronic exchange (fee to Vans vendor), the use went up to around 14%. The breaking point came in 1999 when the hospitals started to send laboratory reports and other information electronically to the general practitioners. Then the use of the service increased to more than 40%. This example shows that a well functioning electronic communication is not enough in itself to motivate use. Only when more facilities were offered, returns of investment of time were considered appropriate by the general practitioners to use the electronic exchange. Only the balance between the time invested and the benefits gained were in balance. Ciborra and Hanseth (2000) state that "infrastructures tend to "drift", i.e. they deviate from their planned purposes for at variety of reasons often outside anyone's influence" (p.4) and as a concluding remark of this paper, I will say that realizing the dimensions of the task is a part of the solution.

References

Bateson, G. (1972). *Steps to an ecology of mind.* Ballantine.

Beyer, H. & Holtzblatt, K. (1998). *Contextual Design, Defining Customer-Centered System*, Morgan Kaufmann Publishers, San Francisco

Bygholm, A. & Boisen, E. (2004). Implementering og informatisering (Implementation and Informating). In: Dirckinck-Holmfeld, L.,Dalum, B.,Ulrich, J.& Boisen, B. (eds.), *Det Digitale Nordjylland – IKT og omstilling til netværkssamfundet.* Aalborg Universitetsforlag. (Digital North Denmark – ICT and change to network society)

Ciborra, C. U. & Hanseth, O. (2000). Introduction. In: Ciborra, C.U., Braa, K., Cordella, A., Dahlbom, B., Failla, A., Hanseth, O., Hepso, V.,Ljungberg, J., Monteiro, E., and Simon, K.A. (eds.), *From Control to Drift. The Dynamics of Corporate Information Infrastructures.* Oxford University Press, NewYork, 2000.

Dahlbom, B. & Janlert, J.E. (1996). *Computer Future, mimeo.* Department of Informatics, Gøteborg University.

Dirckinck-Holmfeld, L.,Dalum, B.,Ulrich, J.& Boisen, B. (eds.) (2004). *Det Digitale Nordjylland – IKT og omstilling til netværkssamfundet.* Aalborg Universitetsforlag (Digital North Denmark – ICT and change to network society)

Edwards, P.N. (2003). Infrastructure and Modernity: Force, Time, and Social Organization in the History of Sociotechnical Systems. In: Misa, T.J, Brey, P. and Feenberg, A. (eds.), *Modernity and Technology,* MIT Press, Cambridge, MA.

eEurope Resolution, Brussels, 28 January 2003, http://europa.eu.int/information_society/eeurope/2005/

Ehn, P. (1988). *Work-Oriented Design of Computer Artefacts.* Stockholm, Arbetslivscentrum

EPR-observatory, homepage http://www.epj-observatoriet.dk/

Fomin, V.V. (2003). *The Role of Standards in the Information Infrastructure Development, Revisited.* MIS Quarterly, special issue workshop on standard making, Seattle, http://www.si.umich.edu/misq-stds/proceedings/

Forskningsministeriet (1995). *Fra Vision til handling – Informationssamfundet år 2000.* (Ministry of research: From vision to action – information society year 2000). http://videnskabsministeriet.dk/site/forside/publikationer/1996/it-politisk-handlingsplan-1995---fra-vision-til-handling/html/index.htm

Greenbaum, J. & Kyng, M (Eds.) (1991). *Design at Work: Approaches to Collaborative Design.* Lawrence Erlbaum, Hillsdale, New Jersey.

Hanseth, O. (2000). The economics of Standards. In: Ciborra, C.U., Braa, K., Cordella, A., Dahlbom, B., Failla, A., Hanseth, O., Hepso, V.,Ljungberg, J., Monteiro, E., and Simon, K.A. (eds.), *From Control to Drift. The Dynamics of Corporate Information Infrastructures.* Oxford University Press, NewYork.

MedCom Homepage, http://www.medcom.dk/wm109991

Ministry of the Interior and Health (2004). *National IT strategy 2003-2007 for the Danish Health Care Service*, Copenhagen.

Nardi, B.A. & O'Day, V.L. (1999). *Information Ecologies, Using Technology with Heart*, MIT Press, Cambridge, Massachusetts.

Star, S. L., Ruhleder, K. (1996). Steps toward an Ecology of Infrastructure: Design and Access for Large Information Spaces. *Information Systems Research* 7(1): 111-134.

Sundhedsministeriet (1999). *National IT strategi for sygehusvæsnet 2000-2002* (National strategi for hospitals 2000-2002). Copenhagen.

Implementation of ICT in Government Organizations - User Driven or Management Driven?

Tom Nyvang & Camilla Roseeuw Poulsen

> Organizational implementation of ICT is crucial to the success of most modern organizations. To push development of the knowledge that will help organizations to successful implementation projects, the paper develops a theoretical framework of implementation that integrates the influence of hard- and software, mandate, culture and knowledge, conditions for learning in the organization as well as the goals of the implementer. The theoretical framework is used to analyze two cases of organizational implementation. The main difference between the two cases is found in the mandate issued by management and the subsequent distribution of implementation initiative in the organization. One implementation is primarily user driven and the other primarily management driven. The paper concludes that both of the two cases gained from both management and user drive. Management drive leads to coordination and integration of overall strategy and the implementation of ICT. User drive leads to integration of the new ICT in a sustainable practice at the micro level in the organization. Neither of the two cases did however reach the full potential of interaction between macro and micro level in the organization.

Introduction

The potential gain from ICT (information and communication technology) in organizations is substantial, but implementing ICT for whatever reason in an organization offers challenges to all members on all levels of the organization. Several papers in this book deal with similar or closely related issues. Kanstrup & Bertelsen focus on local IT support as a way to integrate IT (or ICT) in an organization. Rose shows the double dance of humans and technology which is also crucial to the understanding of organizational implementation. Simply making a technology available does not mean that it will be used.

This paper aims to deal with the implementation challenge by investigating the complexity of organizational implementation of ICT. In doing so, it defines implementation as *the process leading from one practice to a new practice where the new practice is characterized by use of ICT.* In addition, implementation is understood as a mix of management processes, social processes, and processes in which competent individuals decide to start using ICT.

We will deal with the implementation challenge by developing a theoretical framework that presents new insights into the complexity of implementation processes. We will, in addition, apply the framework on two cases to show the dynamic relationship of management drive, user drive and learning processes in the organization when ICT is implemented. The underlying assumption is that to meet the implementation challenge the first step is to shed light on the often invisible or little valued implementation effort carried out in organizations around us every day. In that respect, we have a lot in common with other authors in this book; Madsen who argues that the infrastructure is not just there even though we often may think so and Kanstrup & Bertelsen who shed light on local support.

The rest of this paper is divided into three main sections: Theoretical perspectives on implementation of ICT in complex contexts; two cases of implementation of ICT – two cultures and strategies; and discussion and conclusion.

The paper is based partly on research done in the project Virtual Learning Environments and Learning Methods (ViLL) by Tom Nyvang and partly on research done in the project implementation of EPJ (Implementation of electronic health records) by Camilla Roseeuw Poulsen. The ViLL project was part of the Digital North Denmark program, but this was not the case for the "Implementation of electronic health records" project.

Theoretical perspectives on implementation of ICT in complex contexts

In the literature, inspiration on how to interpret and understand organizational implementation of ICT can be found in at least three disciplines: Systems development, organizational learning and theory on diffusion of innovations. We do thus devote the following paragraphs to further elaboration on the possible contributions from the different research traditions.

Theories and methodologies on systems development do, not surprisingly, focus on development of ICT, but stress different issues as core challenges to the development. The focus has traditionally been on management of development projects by means of linear processes organizing system engineering from idea and system requirements to system design, programming and technical test (the socalled waterfall model). Research and practice are however to an increasing extent moving in another direction by stressing that development of ICT in most cases is development of more than a technical system and should thus involve future users in an iterative learning cycle that allows the system to develop in and with context (Beyer & Holzblatt, 1997; Dahlbom & Mathiassen, 1993; Larman, 2003; Vliet, 1993). Current trends in systems development thus inform us that ICT, or in other words information systems, are ideally developed not only in the use context, but also in short iterations that allow both developers and users to continuously learn about the potential of a specific piece of software and the development of use (Larman, 2003). In other words, iterative user involved development promises to be the fastest and cheapest way to develop the right kind of ICT for a specific purpose. User driven innovation is another perspective on systems development that advocates a high degree of user involvement in development of ICT – perhaps the highest possible degree (Hippel, 2001; Jeppesen, 2003; Land, 2000; Thomke & Hippel, 2002).

Based on the system development theory and methodology, it is reasonable to assume that implementation of ICT in complex organizations is ideally an iterative user involving process since the system and use practice ideally develop hand in hand. Bearing the iterative aspect and the concept of user driven innovation in mind, we may even have to understand organizational implementation as an ever ongoing process, not as a one time event. This conception of implementation as an ongoing design, interpretation and reinterpretation process is among others supported by Spinuzzi (2003).

Theory on organization and organizational learning contains relevant aspects since implementation of ICT is closely linked to organisational changes according to theory on systems development. However, the focus on ICT is traditionally relatively blurred as a review of a number of prominent sources shows (Argyris, 1999; Bakka & Fivelsdal, 2004; Von Krogh *et al.*, 2000; Wenger, 1998; Wenger *et al.*, 2002). These sources only show that technology in general is one of more components of the organization. The same sources do however inform us about the dynamics of organizations and do in that way help us to highlight prominent constrainers and drivers of change (including implementation of ICT) in organizations. According to Wenger, learning in communities of practice[1] equals negotiation of meaning that is a process of participation and reification. Although a community of practice does not fully equal an organization, the duality of participation and reification is relevant here since it once again stresses the importance of a collaborative practice in organizational development (with ICT). Von krogh, Ichijo and Nonaka stress a similar complex understanding of knowledge in organizations since it is *justified true belief, individual and social, tacit and explicit (Von Krogh, Ichijo et al. 2000, p. 30)*. As a consequence, knowledge creation cannot be managed, only enabled: Instill a knowledge vision, manage conversations, mobilize knowledge activists, create the right context and globalize local knowledge. This may of course seem to contradict the formal structure of many organizations with a fine grained division of labour and management hierarchy. In reality, it depends on the kind of management philosophy and subsequent granularity of division of labour in the organization.

The last body of theory relevant to understanding organizational development we want to mention here is activity theory (Engeström, 1987, 1999; Engeström *et al.*, 1999). Activity theory stresses that individual and social development is influenced by tools in use, culture and division of labour between different individuals or collectives. According to activity theory, human practice is driven by overarching motives, subordinate to the motives are the conscious day to day goals or even more specific goals, and subordinate to the goals are the conditions under which goals are pursued. Some research has already been done in relation to implementation of ICT from the perspective of activity theory (Nyvang, 2005, 2006; Nyvang & Johnson, 2004).

---

[1] Wenger (1998) defines practice as *doing in a historical and social context that gives structure and meaning to what we do* (p. 47).

Based on the organizational development theory and methodology, it is reasonable to assume that implementation of ICT in organizations can be interpreted as a collaborative learning process that is influenced by the organizational and to some extent societal context. That context is comprised by culture, tools, division of labour, motives, goals and conditions for engaging individually and collectively in the learning process which implementation of ICT is understood as here.

Theory on diffusion of innovations focuses on the process of adopting new technologies (Rogers, 1995). Rogers defines diffusion as:

> *"... the process by which an innovation is communicated through certain channels over time among the members of a social system. It is a special type of communication, in that the messages are concerned with new ideas." (Rogers 1995, p. 5)*

Rogers does not only look at ICT or for that matter communication of innovations in formal organizations. His definition does however also catch elements of implementation of ICT in organizations when he defines a social systems as *"... a set of interrelated units that are engaged in a joint problem-solving to accomplish a common goal"* (Rogers 1995, p. 23). It is *joint problem-solving* in particular that resembles organizational implementation as our case studies will show. With reference to joint problem solving, Rogers also points towards issues that are more thoroughly discussed in the above mentioned research literature on organizational development and learning. Rogers puts the innovation decision process at the core of the diffusion process. The process has five steps: Knowledge, persuasion, decision, implementation and confirmation (Rogers, 1995, p. 163).

Compared to the call for iterative methods from systems development literature, innovation adoption seems surprisingly linear here, but the last step, conformation, indicates a potentially iterative process that analyses, implements and evaluates. Another of Rogers' important points is that the speed with which an innovation is diffused through a social system depends on the relative advantage, compatibility, complexity, trailability and observability of the innovation (Rogers, 2003, pp. 229-265). An innovation may, in other words, be easier or harder to implement depending on these attributes. Rogers has however also received some critique because he tends to overlook the complexity of an adoption. It seems as if adoption is either full adoption or none at all (Bøving & Bødker, 2003; Gallivan, 2001).

Based on the diffusion of innovations theory, it is reasonable to assume that communication about the relevance and relative advantage of the new ICT is crucial to implementation of ICT in an organization. It is also important to note that the individual members of an organization tend to adopt on the basis of which adopter category they belong to. No matter if the implementation is user driven or mandated the inclusion of all adopter categories is a challenge.

There is no unified framework for neither analysis nor design of implementation processes that includes all the considerations and challenges we have discussed in this section. The three disciplines represent three different foci and approaches to the implementation field. First, systems development focuses on the development of the ICT to be implemented but to a lesser extent on the organizational aspects. Second, organizational learning focuses on organizational learning and development, but to a lesser extent on the role of ICT. Third, diffusion of innovations focuses on the decision processes associated with implementation of ICT, but to a lesser extent on the organizational change and development of work practices associated with implementation of ICT in an organization. It is however also important to stress that each of the three research traditions offer a variety of positions, perspectives and conclusions that sometimes contradict each other.

All three foci offer important aspects to the understanding of implementation of ICT in organizations. We cannot really choose one above the other as the best and most suitable one. Instead, we chose to introduce and develop a new a framework for thinking about implementation of ICT in organizations that integrates the influence of hard- and software, mandate, culture and knowledge, conditions for learning in the organization and the goals of the implementer.

Towards a framework for evaluation of implementation processes

The framework we want to present here is heavily inspired by activity theory and the work done on genres and activity theory by Clay Spinuzzi (Spinuzzi, 2003).

He characterizes genre as *tradition* and as his unit of analysis (Spinuzzi, 2003, p. 41) and draws on activity theory to analyze genres with special emphasis on contradictions, discoordinations and breakdowns in the activity system that indicate the failure of a genre to handle a specific situation in a specific context. This is relevant to our analysis of implementation of ICT in organizations because it provides an opportunity to integrate the different relevant issues discussed earlier into one theoretical and analytical framework.

We adopt the distinction between the macroscopic (cultural-historical, unconscious), mesescopic (goal directed, conscious) and microscopic (habitual, unconscious) levels of an activity (levels well known in activity theory). We likewise adopt the identification of the activity system, contradictions, discoordinations and breakdowns as means of analysis.

We do, however, suggest a development of Spinuzzi's activity system that focuses the generalized model of the activity system towards implementation of ICT in organizations drawing on our review of relevant theoretical and methodological positions. The main differences between Spinuzzi's original model and the one we suggest is that the mediating artifact *instruments* has been split into *hard- & software* and *mandate*[2]. We have also added *conditions for learning* as a new mediating artifact. Finally, we have changed the wording of other parts of the model to better grasp implementation of ICT in organizations.

---

[2] We define mandate as an official or authoritative command.

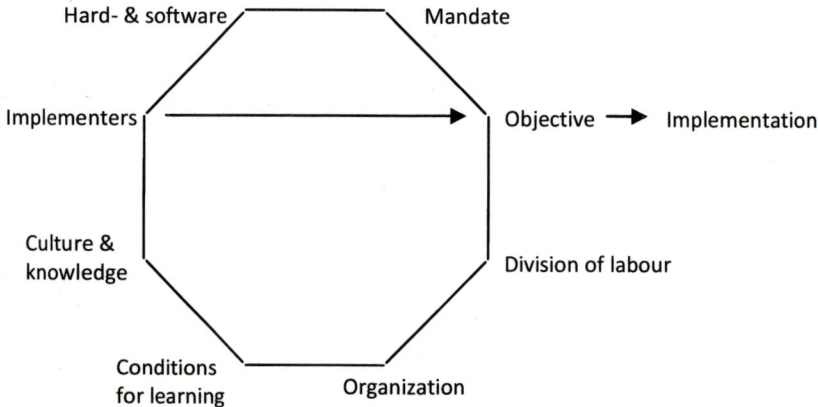

Figure 10: The revised version of Spinuzzi's activity system. It has been revised to accommodate the issues that influence the implementation process

The *implementer* or *implementers* are part of an *organization*. Cultural-historical theory generally talks about subject or subjects. Spinuzzi has chosen to talk about collaborators in his case. We have chosen the term implementers to specify the focus of the model. Spinuzzi and cultural-historical theory in general refer to community where we choose organization and we are aware of at least some of the potential risks of using that term. In the cultural historical tradition, community normally refers to the fact that we are always part of some sort of community – and that division of labour mediates between that community and the task. First and foremost, there is no evidence supporting that all subjects are members of a (formal) organization in general. We do, however, introduce organization instead of community in the model to underline that we are targeting organizations. We have thus chosen to use organization in a manner that is close to the original term community.

We have split *instrument* into *hard- & software* and *mandate* to underline that implementation processes are mediated not only by the instrument and its characteristics as they are perceived by the implementer, but also by the mandate attached to the new technology. According to the diffusion research tradition there is normally going to be some sort of mandate or perceived mandate in an organization – it may be strong, weak, precise or diffuse. It is in either case relevant to the implementer if use of a specific piece of hard- and software is mandatory and what the specific content of a mandate is. It is, however, important to notice that the model does not imply that a mandate is always followed by the implementers – just that the mandate influences the implementation process.

Conditions for learning have been added because an organization always provides certain conditions for learning – conditions that must be expected to influence the outcome of an implementation process as discussed earlier in relation to systems development and organizational development and learning. Once again, it must be stressed that an organization always offers certain conditions for learning even if learning is not on the official agenda of the organization.

Culture and knowledge is also a modification compared to Spinuzzi's original model since he focuses on *domain knowledge*. The re-introduction of culture as a mediating artifact (closely related to knowledge in a broad sense) is rooted in the cultural-historical tradition on which Spinuzzi also draws heavily.

Division of labour is a mediating artifact also used by Spinuzzi and well-known in the cultural-historical tradition. Division of labour is always present in organizations and often challenged during implementation of ICT. The analysis will show that this is also the case in the two cases we have studied.

After this short introduction of our theoretical framework, we move on to operationalizing the framework and introducing our cases studies.

Two cases of implementation of ICT in public organizations – two cultures and strategies

The aim of this section is to analyse two cases of implementation of ICT in organizations. Both cases are from Danish public institutions, one case from a university and another case from a hospital. The cases are chosen because they represent different approaches to implementation and different cultures and, as such, contrast each other. For more details on the cases, we refer to the following sections. However, before moving on to the cases, we need to say a few words about how we use the theoretical framework as a means of analysis.

We aim to uncover the problems and challenges that arose in the implementation processes. In the terms of our theoretical framework we search for contradictions between different mediating artefacts in the activity system.

Contradictions are important because they arise when existing knowledge and ways of doing fail. They are important because activity systems always strive towards resolution of contradictions which means that contradictions are also drivers of change (Spinuzzi 2003).

Implementation of ICT in higher education – user driven

The first case study focuses on implementation of ICT in the program Human Centered Informatics, Aalborg University. Human Centered Informatics is an educational program within the humanities offering both bachelor (3 years) and master level (bachelor + 2 years) education and has approximately 500 students. It combines communication, organization and ICT studies to provide students with the tools necessary to be critical, but constructive, participants in the evaluation and construction of ICT and new media.

Methodology

The project moved through four iterations involving gradually more students until the full educational program including all teachers, students and administrative staff were involved. The project also used different change and research strategies as shown in table 9.

Itera-tion	ICT implementation	Involved	Goal	Research method	Data
1.	5th semester of Human Centered Informatics. Teachers free to choose technology.	6 teachers, 21 students	Document existing implementation procedures.	Pilot study of existing practice.	Interviews, ICT.
2.	3rd semester of Human Centered Informatics. Teachers have to use the same technology for communication.	20 teachers, 80 students.	Develop, use and document new implementation procedures.	Action research.	Interviews, ICT.
3.	4th semester of Human Centered Informatics. Teachers have to use the same technology for communication.	30 teachers, 160 students.	Develop, use and document new implementation procedures.	Action research.	Interviews, ICT.
4.	All semesters and specializations of of Human Centered Informatics.	60 teachers, 500-600 students.	Use implementation procedures.	Case study of practice.	Interviews, ICT.

Table 9: Research design

Analysis of the implementation process

The case study builds of data from four iterations of the research and development project. This leaves us with a large amount of data and a corresponding number of challenges and contradictions between different mediating artefacts. In the following report from the case study, we focus on four prominent contradictions that arose during the implementation process. These contradictions were identified as prominent because they persisted through several iterations or because they were identified in a significant number of interviews.

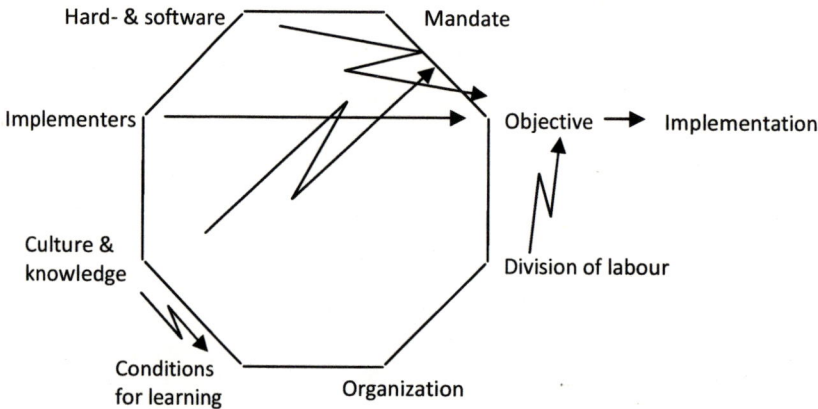

Figure 11: Prominent contradictions in the case of implementation of ICT in an organization, Human Centered Informatics

Hard- & software – objective contradiction

The teachers, students and administrative staff all faced the new hard- and software offered to them with a set of expectations and objectives. Objectives were grounded in the practice they knew and the challenges they had experienced. It is on the one hand not surprising that objectives arise from something else than knowledge about specific hard- and software, but it is on the other hand obvious that this can lead to contradictions between objective on the one side and hard- and software on the other side. This contradiction did for example show when some of the students acknowledged that the new software, Quickplace, had something to offer that was in line with some of their objectives. It could help them organize files produced and shared in their project group. They did however also express concerns grounded in the design of Quickplace:

Student 5: [...] You feel that the system does something while you look the other way. I have never ever programmed anything which may also make me feel uncertain about my own competencies. Then I think, perhaps it is me that don't understand what it is that I have done. And 'shit', what have I gotten myself into? Because if I have messed up my hard drive it is not just fixing it again. I have to find someone else that volunteer to do it for me... (After iteration 2)

The design of the specific software scared some users off even though the functionality in principle seemed to match the objectives of those users. As stated in the quote, some of the users felt insecure about the consequences of using the software. Others sections of data indicate insecurity about the stability of the new software and backup procedures. The iterative design of the implementation project fortunately allowed for the specific contradiction to be resolved by a combination of redesign and improved communication about the software, backup and other procedures.

The iterations of the implementation project followed the well-known semester rhythm in the organization. Shorter iterations could have speeded up the process, but would have been difficult and time consuming to implement without loss of productivity and quality due to contradictions with the traditional rhythm of change in the organization.

Culture & knowledge – conditions for learning contradiction
The university is a research and educational institution and, to a large extent, accordingly provides sound conditions for learning. Nevertheless, a contradiction arose between culture & knowledge and the conditions for learning in the implementation process. It was a contradiction between the conditions for the teachers to learn to facilitate learning with ICT by providing a common tool (Quickplace) on the one side and on the other side a culture in which the individual teacher chooses method and tools for his or her teaching. This is illustrated by the words of one of teachers. First, he describes his use of Quickplace:

Teacher 1: I don't think that I have used Quickplace very much. I pretty much use it to stay updated about what's going on. And it is a lot easier than if you have to search in news groups, web pages or similar places. (After iteration 2)

He then goes on to talk about his own active use of Quickplace:

Teacher 1: And if I think it over I may have a bad consciousness, because I have felt that I probably should have published something in Quickplace to keep it collected in one place, nice and homogeneously. I just didn't take the time to do so [...] because I have the other course, the course in [theme of course] which is web-based and has a rather large web-site. (After iteration 2)

The teacher clearly has good reasons for using Quickplace – he lists some of them himself: It is easier to stay informed and publish information where it is easily found. He does, however, also stick to his usual way of teaching for a good reason: He has invested a lot of effort in building and improving a large web-site in the past – a web-site that cannot easily be imported into Quickplace. He has thus been engaged in an iterative development process of his own, there is nothing bad to say about the material he developed, and what he did was rooted in the culture. What happened was that the introduction of Quickplace actually threatened the learning trajectory that he was on himself.

Culture & knowledge – mandate contradiction
The initiators of the project and the management of Human Centered informatics saw the implementation project as an opportunity to develop ICT supported communication and learning in the organization. The aims were to develop quality, efficiency and flexibility in communication, teaching and learning. These aims were of course too broad for anyone to disagree with.

In the first three iterations of the project, the aims of management and project initiators contradicted the mandate. On the one hand, the management had decided to join the project, but, on the other hand, participation of members of the organization was not mandatory. This was, however, in congruence with the culture of the organization where teachers (and for that matter students too) traditionally had a high degree of freedom in choosing method and means for communication and facilitation of learning. When the project moved into the fourth iteration, use of a common piece of software and certain communicative practices (Lotus Quickplace) were made mandatory thus contradicting the tradition and culture in more ways. Firstly, mandatory use of a specific tool contradicted the culture (this was indicated in the culture & knowledge – conditions for learning contradiction). Secondly, the remediation of communication led to a contradiction between mandatory use of ICT and what some of the users regarded the best and richest communication:

Teacher 2: I have a principle with project supervisors. I use e-mail unless it has to do with the exam. They receive that on paper. And I have discussed it with [one of the supervisors] because they wonder why. And my answer was that in respect of the students you need to have a piece of paper in front of you. And he wrote back that it actually did make sense to him. He thought it sort of gave something more... (After iteration 4)

Some of the students discussed the same issue in an earlier interview:

Sudent2: It is more tangible then, isn't it? But I do, however, think that it may have to do with adaptation because I think that my attitude towards digital stuff in contrast to paper stuff has changed this semester. [...] I think that digital is just as acceptable as paper

Student3: I would still prefer an old-fashioned letter. (After iteration 2)

The contradiction between the mandate and the above quotes may however not be a long lasting one. The perception about what the best communication is seems to be changing as indicated by student2.

Division of labour – objective contradiction

The contradiction between division of labour and objective is a contradiction between different perspectives on what the division of labour should be – different perspectives that are rooted in different objectives. We observe that when teachers on the one hand acknowledge the need for a tool like Quickplace to develop a more efficient communication while they on the other hand are concerned that the tool will increase the number of individual inquiries:

Teacher2: [...] I think we have to thoroughly consider whether Quicplace and similar things in fact increases the number of individual inquiries we receive. (After iteration 4)

This view is shared by other teachers. They foresee that the implementation of new tools like Quickplace may develop a *service culture*:

Teacher3: It does create the expectation that everyting is available there. That is my concern, that you create a service culture – or the expectation of a service culture. (Before iteration 2)

The teachers define service culture as a culture in which the students act lesser and lesser independently while they expect the university to take on more and more of the workload and responsibility that used to be on the students. One of the students gives the following example:

Student2: Some things have been better than before. The fact that you find all files and so on from the teachers in one place. In the past there has been many many many problems finding your way around the different web-sites to locate it, right? And it is my impression that people [students] are very pleased with this. And that they more frequently during lectures ask the teacher to upload something to Quickplace where they used to ask the teacher to put it on his or her web-site. (After iteration 2)

The prominent contradiction here seems to be the contradiction between the objectives of teachers and students as expressed in the desired division of labour. Both parties implement Quickplace to change the division of labour in favor of themselves and their own conception of what the best learning environment is. Teachers want students to be more involved in the learning process and the students want more information and support from the teachers to ease their way towards a degree. There is no obvious way to dissolve this contradiction – both teachers and students have good reasons for arguing the way they do. These contradicting views represent a prominent contradiction in the present case, but they may also in a broader sense be rooted in the development of a (modern) mass university. We are however not going to look deeper into that here – just mention it as an example of structures in society reaching into the present organization and even being visible in a concrete implementation project.

Implementation of electronic health records in a hospital – management driven

The focus of the second research project is the implementation of an electronic health record system (EHR- system) in an orthopaedic surgical unit in a Danish hospital. The background for the implementation is the nationwide effort to develop and implement electronic health records as a means to improve and facilitate exchange of health related data, thereby benefiting the health sciences and improving communication between health professionals resulting in a higher level of information and improved treatments for the patients.

In the present case, the decision to develop and implement an EHR system was made on the county level in cooperation with representatives from the county hospitals. This meant that the use of the EHR system was mandated for all local units. Likewise, consideration for the quality and uniformity of data left little room for personal adjustments of ways of working with the EHR. The implementation strategy was developed centrally and consisted of designating responsibles at various organizational levels, informing through several official channels, supplying super user support at the local level and a training programme to ensure that all health professionals knew what was going to happen and what their role and responsibilities with regards to the system would be. In other words, a very different approach from the one employed at Aalborg University. The roll-out took place during the fall of 2004 and the spring of 2005.

Methodology

The implementation process was followed by 21 semistructured research interviews with key informants at different organizational levels from hospital management to clinical staff to ensure that different perspectives on the implications of the process were represented. Likewise, since the differences of opinion were often related to professional roles and responsibilities towards the system, respondents were chosen to ensure that all involved professional groups were represented. Finally, since opinions have a tendency to vary over time, interviews were conducted at different fazes of the implementation process.

Analysis of the implementation process

Seen from an adoption perspective, the implementation process was highly successful, since, after one year of implementation, the EHR was an integrated part of the daily work in most parts of the unit. That the overall result of the process was pervasive utilization of the system does not however mean that there were no contradictions, discoordinations and temporary breakdowns during the process nor that the objectives behind the implementation were necessarily realized. In the following report from the case study, we focus on three prominent contradictions.

210 Interaction & Communication

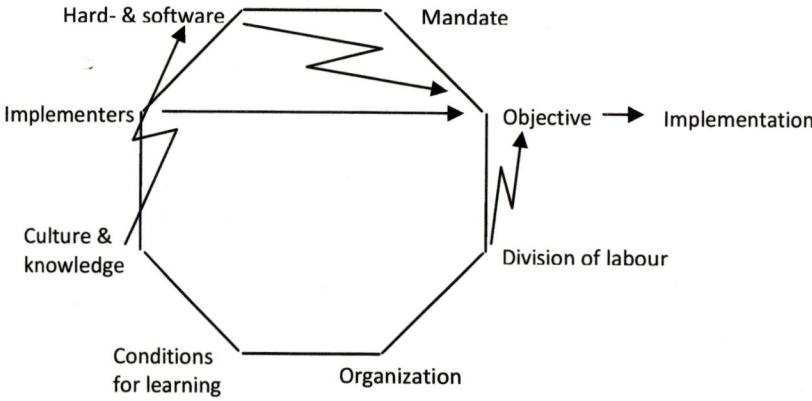

Figure 12: Prominent contradictions in the mandate-driven implementation case

Hard- & software – objective contradiction
The main inhibiter in the implementation process was the performance and functionality of the system, which was poorly adapted to the work conditions of the hospital staff. Logging on could take up to three minutes, the response time of the system was slow and there were a number of critical errors despite the fact that the unit was by no means a pioneer adopter of the system. Furthermore, the office based nature of the system did not correspond well with the nomadic work style of doctors during ward rounds and nurses' administration of medicine. The frustration showed clearly in the interviews:

Nurse I: The computer is designed to be used in an office but the nursing staff are nomads really. We don't have one work station and that is also what makes the system troublesome to use. We have to shift workstation all the time and therefore we constantly have to type in the same information as well as log on and off.

Senior consultant: To be perfectly honest I think the system stinks, and the reason why I think so is that this EHR module is not designed in a way to support a rational workflow in an orthopaedic surgical unit.

As a consequence, many, especially the doctors were disappointed with the system.

Doctor I: It's the equivalent of having looked forward to getting a new car and then receive an Eastern European Skoda - It is a car, and it does run, it will get me from A to B, but maybe there could have been a nicer way to do it

The impression did however vary depending on professional group, familiarity with the system and time of use.

Nurse I: I have heard some people say that this is it, we won't use it anymore. Which is as it should be, it's important to have confidence in the system. But the way that it runs now – I don't think anyone would dream of returning to the old system.

Despite the lack of enthusiasm about the system, the mandate seems to have overruled the above mentioned inconveniences making the users go out of their way to use the system as prescribed, even though, one year into the implementation process, there was still no proof of the benefits of the system use with regards to reduction of medication errors or higher efficiency. Actually the patient flow, which is directly related to the allocation of funds to the unit, had decreased as a result of the implementation.

Senior consultant: I don't see that I gain any benefits from the system, on the contrary. As for the unit, we don't experience any benefits either – If one were to imagine, that we had spent the same amount of resources on the old system, where we dictated our observations and secretaries typed them into the healtht record, then there would be considerably less errors than we see today. Back then no one cared about the medication, it was prescribed and that was the end of it. Nowadays we have a nurse employed full time ensuring that no errors are made in the EHR system

Division of labour – objective contradiction

The introduction of the system in the surgical unit also had an impact on the division of labour between doctors and nurses. The workflows in the system corresponded well with the formal division of labour prescribed by the law, where the doctor is supposed to personally register the medication he prescribes. However, occasionally, the informal division of labour in the unit had experienced nurses performing routine administrative tasks for the doctors when these were unavailable. With the new system, this was no longer possible, which caused frustration among the doctors who were now forced to perform more administrative tasks themselves. The issue was further accentuated since the performance of administrative tasks was more time-consuming with the EHR, not only due to inexperience with the system but also because accessing and navigating the system took more time than writing prescriptions on a paper form or dictating them to a digital recorder.

Main responsible for the implementation at hospital level: A big problem is, that it takes longer for a doctor to prescribe medicine in the EHR than it did with the old system. And this is not only because some are still not proficient in their system use, it simply does take longer.

The increased burden of administrative tasks led to a great deal of dissatisfaction among the doctors, who were for the most part surgeons who did not consider the ordination of medicine the most important part of their job to begin with.

Senior consultant: We do not spend the same amount of time on medication as they do in other parts of the healthcare system. It is just something that has to be done and it is not uncommon that a doctor gives someone else his password and have them register the medicine. To an orthopaedic surgeon, medicine has low priority, but the EHR requires a big effort to keep the information up to date

Culture & knowledge – hard- & software contradiction

As most people involved with the design, development and implementation of software know, there is actually nothing unusual about bugs and inconveniences being discovered when new software is taken into use. Predicting how design will match working conditions is difficult and unforeseen consequences, both workflow related and technical are the rule rather than the exception. However, in the area of medical science, errors may cause the loss of lives and therefore innovations usually go through many years of research and testing before they are introduced into practice. As the amount of bugs and inconveniences in the beginning of the process showed, this was clearly not the case with the electronic health record, and this cultural difference in expectations to innovations was most likely another reason why the EHR was met with so much resistance within the unit, where it was perceived as unprofessional and potentially life threatening.

Senior consultant: If one was to imagine that this [implementation process] had been a medical study, it would never have passed the ethical board. It has grossly disregarded patient safety to begin with. The version of the EHR system that we started out with was potentially life-threatening. So the only reason we're using it is because this was dictated on county level.

No contradiction between mandate and culture

As the above review of the main contradictions shows, there were quite many reasons for the clinical staff to be dissatisfied with the EHR. Naturally, there were positive aspects of the implementation as well. Many thought for instance that the system gave a better overview of the medication a patient was given, and the increased accessibility of the information was praised, especially by the nurses. However, after one year of use, the system had still to prove its worth in the unit. According to a review performed by the implementation responsibles, it had not yet helped reduce medication errors, but rather eliminated some causes of errors only to introduce new ones. There were no indications that the work in the unit had become more efficient either and, as mentioned earlier, the system had even resulted in a decrease in the patient flow in some parts of the unit.

The reason why individuals usually decide to take a new piece of software into use is that they see the benefits of it, and are therefore willing to go through the trouble of changing their ways. Since this could not be said to be the case in the orthopaedic surgical unit, there must be some other explanations for the swift implementation, and the obvious answer, besides a well planned training and support structure ensuring the necessary conditions for adoption, is the mandatory approach. That the mandate has played an important role in the process is equally obvious when asking the participants.

Nurse responsible for implementation: I'm sure that if we'd had the choice to reject it, it would have been rejected, due to the number of influential people saying that this ERH is simply not good enough [...] and now we're using it none the less. But it has been necessary to use force, stand firm and say that this is it, this is the way we're going to do it

It is equally interesting to observe, how the resistance was primarily directed at the actual inconveniences in the daily use of the system, rather than the strategy of implementation, about which most participants were generally positive. The mandatory approach in itself seems to have had no negative influence on the sense of ownership or willingness to use the system

Doctor: Management should be allowed to manage. It's what they're there for and I would expect them to decide on these things [implementation of IT systems]. I would think that they were incompetent if they didn't promote new initiatives.

Nurse 1: It's probably due to the culture within the nursing area. We're so used to the constant level of change that if we're told to do something, we do it

This is most likely because the authoritative approach is generally accepted in the health care environment, and as such almost taken for granted to a degree in which the clinical staff would probably be surprised if initiatives of this nature were presented as voluntary. Or, to be more precise, the clinical staff is used to make decisions within their own domain of expertise and leave decisions outside these areas to others.

Nurse responsible for implementation: In our world, decisions are dictated from above – we have to do it – we may object, but there's no room for discussion, it's just the way it is, it's a political regime.

The exception to this rule was the senior consultant, who generally did not like having the use of the EHR dictated by management.

Senior consultant: Usually, none of the innovations that we take into use are dictated by management. Typically, we're the ones discovering when new technology or treatments are available and decide to try it out. If you want something to grow, it has to come from below

The pervasive use of the system and relative low degree of serious resistance such as refusals to use the system were however not only a consequence of a well supported implementation process and widespread acceptance of the authoritative approach but also of a general idea of necessity amongst doctors and nurses who believed that, sooner or later, the unit would have to use an IT system for this kind of registrations

Doctor: EHR [as an idea] we can't live without, and there's no question it's here to stay, because that's the way to go, but I do think that we could wish for a better system

Likewise, they were highly aware of the large scale of the process and the importance of the EHR for the Danish health care system in general.

Nurse 2: I think it [the mandatory approach] is the way to implement something this big, once it has been decided that this is the way to go. Because it's not just something we decide in our unit. It has to work at the county level and on the country level as well. I think making this kind of decisions at the top level is a necessity.

This explanation is also why the benefits of the EHR can not meaningfully be assessed on the unit level but have to be seen in a broader perspective. Still, this is not the same as blindly accepting the inconveniences introduced by the system to some units as a casualty of war. When the common sense that usually ensures that good initiatives are adopted and bad ones are rejected is dismissed, careful attention needs to be directed to the actual consequences of the implementation for the local work environments. This is probably why both managerial and clinical staff stressed the importance of good feedback channels and receptiveness on the part of management during the implementation process.

First of all, despite the hierarchical organization and general acceptance of the management's right to enforce centrally made decisions, the hospital is also a political organization with many influential and highly indispensable, specialized professionals. The feedback channels create a room for dialogue, thereby making the mandate conflict less with the senior consultants' rights to rule their own units.

Hospital manager: In a place like this one, filled with health professionals, you may scream and shout —issuing circulars and orders will get you nowhere, unless you initiate some kind of dialogue.

Secondly, the feedback channels are a means to ensure that inconveniences are discovered so that the mandate is not enforced regardless of the organizational consequences.

Nurse responsible for implementation: We have to listen to what the users have to say instead of acting as if everything is just fine. I might have a positive impression of the EHR system, but I have to listen and be open minded towards the users' complaints.

There are cases where the system proves unfit for practice and needs to change, other cases where workarounds have to be devised to make the solution fit and yet other situations, where the most reasonable solution is to discontinue the use of the system.

Discussion

User driven or management driven implementation? That question was one of the points of departure for this paper and the two cases we have analyzed had their offspring in each side of the dichotomy. The university case started out with a strong belief in user driven implementation and innovation. The EHR case started out with a strong belief in management drive and little belief in user driven implementation and innovation – at least it seems so. As shown by the analysis, the two cases ended up a lot more alike than they started out. In the university case, some degree of management turned out to be needed to realize the (full) potential of user driven implementation and innovation. In the EHR case, some degree of user driven implementation and innovation turned out to be necessary for the implementation that started out as management driven to work around different challenges and succeed. The following discussion is organized in three major sections. The first two sections cover learning and user driven implementation and the role of management drive. The third and concluding section sums up the lessons learned in terms of implications for practices and research.

Learning and user driven implementation

Both cases indicate that learning *did* take place before, during and after the implementation process. In other words, (collaborative) learning seems to be a fact and not just a possibility in the organization. Orlikowski (1992) was on the verge of a similar conclusion when she concluded that groupware implementation could lead to cognitive organizational changes.

In the EHR case, it had proved valuable that the organization could adapt practice to difficult conditions prior to the EHR implementation and especially during and after the implementation due to the new tasks and the challenges to the division of labour. The organization did however move beyond some of the formal structures, work descriptions and perhaps even their mandate in the coping process. It remains unclear whether the EHR designers failed to realize that or someone saw the EHR design and implementation as an opportunity to reinforce the formal structure. In either case, the implementation process broke some of the existing coping strategies, but it also forced the organization to develop new strategies - a strategy development that would have been easier if the implementation process from early on had acknowledged the complexity and quality of existing practice. This is especially clear in the case of the *hard- & software – objective contradiction*. If the managers and designers had relied on a higher degree of user drive in innovation and implementation it is highly unlikely that they had ended up with a stationary tool for use in a nomadic style work practice. The most visible support for learning was the local EHR managers that supported users of the system, but they were not able to deliver a substantial feedback channel connecting users and designers.

In the university case, the individual members of the organization had also developed teaching, learning, administration and other practices to function as teachers, students, secretaries, managers and so on. These practices had developed over time within the culture and structure of the university. The implementation project aimed to build on existing practice by supporting a diverse set of activities initiated primarily by teachers in the early iterations of the project. When the mandatory platform Quickplace was implemented, the users were presented with a tool that offered one of the qualities mentioned by research on user driven innovation – it had resemblances with a user toolkit. It did however also have the qualities of a fully functional application. In this way, the ICT was open for the users to adapt in more ways. The pressure on the users to use the new tool in a specific way remained relatively low, but it did make some of the teachers question whether they, in the future, would be able to build on the tools and corresponding knowledge they had developed earlier. The analysis has also shown that different contradicting perspectives on how to teach and learn by means of the new tool arose. Whether this contradiction was productive in terms of facilitating learning remains unclear – no obvious resolution of the contradiction or change of practice in response to the contradiction is visible in our data.

In conclusion, we can say that neither of the two cases had a strong design and support for individual and organizational learning during the implementation process. The university case relied more on user drive in the implementation process than the EHR case, but as it turned out both cases ended up utilizing user drive to integrate ICT in a productive, daily practice.

Management driven implementation

The role of management stood out in both cases. Management did however play different roles. In the university case, management only played a role in the early iterations by allowing experiments in the organization. In the final iteration of the project, use of the new tool was made mandatory, but as mentioned earlier the mandate was by no means as strong as it was in the EHR case.

In the EHR case, high level management forced local management to take charge of an implementation process – implementation of a tool that the local managers in retrospect never seem to have believed in. The unfortunate result is a process and an implementation that has cost a lot of resources inside and outside of the organization – it may even have been a risk to patients in the hospital. It is however still not clear to the members of the organization what the gain has been even though the EHR has been accepted in the organization now. Since the cost efficiency in any sense of the term based on the statements of the members of the organization seems highly questionable, it is reasonable to conclude that, at best, top level managers have failed to communicate the implementation. At worst, they have thrown the organization into a process that failed and did nothing else but cost a lot of resources. However, lower level management and other members of the organization have managed to implement the new tool and apparently the EHR is now to a large extent accepted in the organization. In that respect, we cannot say that the implementation failed if success is defined as use and acceptance, but implementation should be about more than that. Implementation should also have real impact on quantity and/or quality of production or a higher degree of customer or employee satisfaction or any other positive impact seen from the point of view of the implementing organization or its surroundings. The EHR case indicates that a lot of positive drive can come from a management driven approach, but also that it is important to ensure good feedback channels and a responsive, open-minded environment – this to avoid implementing something that is impeding people from doing their work rather than helping them and it seems that the management drive behind the EHR implementation came close to doing so. The management failed to supply a system that helped the users and what was even worse they apparently failed to acknowledge that the system did not help – a situation that made the implementation very stressful to the implementers.

In the university case, management could also have played a role by taking an active part in resolving some of the contradictions. The part of the culture & knowledge – mandate contradiction that has to do with contradicting views on how to communicate in the organization is a good example. Management could have taken a more proactive role by managing conversations (Wenger et al 2002) about best practices for different kinds of communicative practices in the organization. By doing so the management identifies a challenge that needs to be met, but the solution is not imposed on the organization without prior negotiation and alignment of different perspectives. Among other challenges, the process of negotiation and alignment should deal with the fact that implementation of ICT often distributes gain from the implementation and workload during the implementation unevenly.

Christiansen and Nyvang (2006) report from a case that has many similarities with the present. They identify a similar need for management, coordination and alignment of different initiatives in the organization to give more attention to user driven initiatives in different parts in the organization to integrate and succeed as a whole. This leads us to stress that some degree of management is not necessarily an opposing alternative to user influence. As such, the main issue becomes selecting a mix that fits the organizational culture and the local premises of the implementation process in a way that exploits both the users initiative and knowledge of which changes improve their work situation and the ability of the management to give priority and resources to the change process in a demanding daily work context.

Conclusion

We will conclude by outlining two primary outcomes, the theoretical and the analytical contributions of the paper and as a secondary outcome suggest directions for future research.

The primary, theoretical outcome is the revision of Spinuzzi's model of the activity system and the conclusion that implementation processes are closely intertwined with learning processes in the organization. The review of existing literature has thus led us to suggest that an activity theoretical and ecological approach is taken when it comes to understanding implementation of ICT in organizations. It is useful because it shows that the implementation process does not take place in a void. On the contrary, it takes place under the influence of a set of mediating artefacts including hard- & software, mandate, culture & knowledge, conditions for learning and division of labour. To get a deep understanding of the challenges and possibilities of implementation processes, it is important to take mediating artefacts into account – most importantly the mediating artefacts that contradict each other. The contradictions are important drivers of further development of the implementation and drivers of learning processes in the organization.

The primary analytical outcome is the documentation of continuous and perhaps even unbreakable links between user and managerial drive during implementation of ICT in organizations. We have shown that the implementation process is also a learning process that connects with earlier learning and points towards future learning. Learning on the behalf of all parties involved has thus been brought to the forefront of implementation processes in a more substantial way than seen been before in the implementation research.

No matter whether the approach is primarily user- or management driven, it is also imperative to realize that implementation requires an effort in the organization. If users are supposed to be a productive and responsible part of the implementation process, they must be given the necessary mandate, conditions for learning and resources to do so. The ecological approach has however also revealed contracting views and interests and management can play a productive mediating role by managing conversations, communicating decisions through the organization and keeping feedback channels open for individual members or groups to share their views on the implementation.

We suggest additional research on implementation of ICT in organizations from an ecological perspective and a learning oriented approach to further develop research based knowledge about the complex relation between user drive, management drive and learning in implementation processes. In particular, the research should aim to develop knowledge about the implications for practice to support managers in the process of designing implementation projects in organizations.

References

Argyris, C. (1999). *On organizational learning.* Oxford: Blackwell.

Bakka, J. F., & Fivelsdal, E. (2004). *Organisationsteori - struktur, kultur, processer* (4. ed.). København: Handelshøjskolens Forlag.

Beyer, H., & Holzblatt, K. (1997). *Contextual design: A customer-centered approach to systems designs*. Morgan Kaufman Publishers.

Bøving, K. B., & Bødker, K. (2003). *Where is the innovation? The adoption of virtual workspaces*. Paper presented at the The diffusion and adoption of networked information technologies. IFIP WG 8.6 working conference, Copenhagen.

Christiansen, E, & Nyvang, T. (2006). Understanding the adoption of TELEs - the importance of management. *The European Journal of Education*, 41(3/4), 509-519.

Dahlbom, B., & Mathiassen, L. (1993). *Computers in context: The philosophy and practice of systems design*. Cambridge: Blackwell Publishers.

Engeström, Y. (1987). *Learning by expanding*. Helsinki: Orienta.

Engeström, Y. (1999). Innovative learning in work teams: Analyzing cycles of knowledge creation in practice. In: Y. Engeström, R. Meittinen & R.-L. Punamäki (Eds.), *Perspectives on activity theory*. Cambridge: Cambrigde University Press.

Engeström, Y., Meittinen, R., & Punamäki, R.-L. (Eds.) (1999). *Perspectives on activity theory*. Cambridge: Cambridge University Press.

Gallivan, M. J. (2001). Organizational adoption and assimilation of complex technological innovations: Development and application of a new framework. *The DATA BASE for Advances in Information Systems, 32*(3), 51-85.

Hippel, E. v. (2001). Perspective: User toolkits for innovation. *The Journal of Product Innovation Management, 18*, 247-257.

Jeppesen, L. B. M., M. J. (2003). Consumers as codevelopers: Learning and innovation outside the firm. *Technology Analysis & Strategic Management, 15*(3), 363-383.

Land, F. (2000). The first business computer: A case study in user-driven innovation. *IEEE Annals of the History of Computing, 22*(3), 16-26.

Larman, C. (2003). *Agile and iterative development - a managers guide*. Boston: Addison Wesley.

Nyvang, T. (2007). Teachers implementing ict in higher education. In: L. Dirckinck-Holmfeld & A. Lorentsen (Eds.), *Virtual learning environments. New ways of learning in higher education*. Aalborg: Aalborg Universitetsforlag (under publication).

Nyvang, T. (2006). *Implementation of ict in higher education*. Paper presented at the Networked Learning Conference 2006, Lancaster.

Nyvang, T., & Johnson, N. A. (2004). *Using activity theory framework (atf) to build an analytic bridge across the atlantic: Two cases of information and communication technology (ict) integration*. Paper presented at the SITE 2004, Atlanta.

Orlikowski, W. (1992). *Learning from Notes: organizational issues in groupware implementation*. Proceedings of the 1992 ACM conference on Computer-supported cooperative work Toronto, Ontario, Canada.

Rogers, E., M. (1995). *Diffusion of innovations*. New York: The Free Press.

Spinuzzi, C. (2003). *Tracing genres through organizations - a sociocultural approach to information design*. Cambridge, Massachusetts: The MIT Press.

Thomke, S., & Hippel, E. v. (2002). Customers as innovators: A new way to create value. In: *Harvard Business Review, 80*(4), 74-81.

Vliet, H. v. (1993). *Software engineering - principles and practice*. Chichester: John Wiley & Sons Ltd.

Von Krogh, G., Ichijo, K., & Nonaka, I. (2000). *Enabling knowledge creation*. New York: Oxford University Press.

Wenger, E. (1998). *Communities of practice - learning, meaning and identity*. Cambridge: Cambridge University Press.

Wenger, E., McDermott, R., & Snyder, W. M. (2002). *Cultivating communities of practice - a guide to managing knowledge*. Boston, Mass.: Harvard Business School Press.

224 Interaction & Communication

Local IT-Support: Values, Characteristics, and Selection Methods

Anne Marie Kanstrup & Pernille Bertelsen

> Local IT-support can be a valuable and effective strategy to support implementation and use of IT in organizations. The paper puts this argument to e-Government and through reports from two case studies of local IT-support, the paper presents characteristics of good, local IT-support and suggests a method for identifying qualified candidates for IT-support positions in organizations.

Introduction

As pointed out by Rose (this book), technology cannot dance alone. Nyvang and Poulsen (this book) describe how different strategies can be used in order to make technology 'dance' with employees in an organization with different outcomes. Similarly, studies of e-Government from the Digital North Denmark in the years 2001-2004 report that "some strategies perform better than others, but the picture shows that different implementation strategies work in different settings – there is no single best approach to e-government" (Remmen 2004). This paper is based on the argument that no matter which strategy is chosen for implementation of e-Government (or more generally IT) in organizations, the employees have to be supported locally. The aim is not to present local IT-support as a strategy for IT-implementation in organizations (for such arguments see e.g. Aasand, Mørch, and Ludvigsen 2004). Rather, the aim is simply to draw attention to the fact that IT-support is an almost invisible factor in the work with IT-implementation and use in organizations: it is a rather unstudied phenomenon (Kanstrup 2005) and it is difficult to account for (Kanstrup 2004). This is despite the fact that local IT-support always exists in organizations – people seek support if not by a formal support function then by colleagues (Govindarajulu 2002). However, the quality of local IT-support varies and will be at its best if it is acknowledged, formalized and subsequently prioritized

(Kanstrup 2004). From this outset, this paper points to the potential of local IT-support to improve the implementation and use of IT in organizations. First, the paper will present arguments for the value of local IT-support and second, present characteristics of what is termed good local IT-support (elsewhere "participatory IT-support", Kanstrup & Bertelsen 2006). Third, the paper will present a method for identifying and selecting local IT-supporters in-house. Conclusions summarize and reflect on further studies.

Values of local IT-support

The value of IT-support is both found in economic numbers and in studies of the quality and use of IT-support in organizations. With regard to economics, surveys report that "TCO[1] models vividly show that, within distributed systems, labour costs far exceed the initial acquisition costs of the computing equipment" (Castellani et al. 2005) or more precisely that "End-user time spent on non-job-related PC activities accounts for more than 40% of a PC's total cost" (Cappuccio et al. 1996). As summed up by Nardi, efficient use of software calls for IT-support: "You have to support people if you want them to get to those more efficient features of the software" (Kanstrup 2004). Returning to the studies of e-Government in the Digital North Denmark, it is noticeable that e-Government solutions did not decrease the workload in the organizations of the studies. Rather, it is reported how "especially the counties – but also a majority of state institutions and municipalities – have experienced positive benefits such as adjustments of work procedures and new competences. However, when it comes to release of resources (another word for higher efficiency), more than 50% of state institutions and municipalities have only had few or no resource savings" (Remmen 2004). Despite main objectives on efficiency, the primary goal seemed to be better service and as reported "One of the interesting answers is that nearly 3/4 on national level and 2/3 of the municipalities in North

---

[1] TCO is short for Total Cost of Ownership: a method used to assess effectiveness of IT in organizations. The measure is relevant in relation to local IT-support since it focuses not only on "hard costs" such as purchased hardware and software which are relatively easy to trace in budgets but also on "soft costs" beyond mere acquisition such as IT-support – "operation costs" this is called holding areas such as support, training, upgrading, virus, etc. (Castellani et al. 2002 & David et al. 2002).

Jutland found to a high or to some degree that the benefits from e-government will be too small compared with the costs" (ibid.). It is reasonable to believe that it will take several years before a clear picture of the effects of e-Government can be presented. As reported by Remmen, "A frequent answer to the question about the results of the e-government projects in the Digital North Denmark is that it is too early to measure" (Remmen 2004). However, implementation costs, use-costs, inefficient use of IT-applications, not to forget requirement specifications are all costs, which fall on the organizations (vs. software enterprises). For that reason, knowledge on how to deal with IT-support at a local level is needed.

With regard to the quality of IT-support, recent studies of more than 2000 IT-users in US enterprises report that "the main part of IT-users are dissatisfied with the IT-support that they receive" and that "dissatisfaction increases the more the users are in contact with IT-supporters" (Morris 2005). Studies of helpdesk-support in organizations show that "users use helpdesk support only minimally", instead they seek IT-support from colleagues since "local staff understand better" (Govindarajulu 1996 and 2002). These studies all raise questions on both how to organize IT-support in organizations (local vs. centralized), and on what good IT-support is (qualifications of IT-supporters and help-systems). Nardi's studies of local IT-supporters coined "gardeners" (Nardi 1993; Nardi % O'Day 1999) and Åsand, Ludvigsen, and Mørch's studies of local IT-supporters coined "super-users" (2004) are some of the few but yet very good answers to these questions. These studies emphasize the importance of local IT-support describing how knowledge about local practice is just as important as knowledge about technology in order to provide good IT-support. Returning to the studies of e-Government in the Digital North Denmark, it was acknowledged that e-Government is ideally 20 % technology and 80% organizational change, and in early phases it is more likely a fifty-fifty percent relationship which, since the pressure of start-up phases is described like a "80-80%" relationship by project managers (Remmen 2004). Central is, however, to acknowledge the importance of support through not only technical assistance but also in relation to organizational change. Bygholm (2001) has made a division between different learning levels when it comes to local IT-support:

- Object level: knowing what (e.g. knowing what this type of software application is)

- Tool level: knowing how (e.g. knowing how to use this application in my work)
- Practice level: knowing why (e.g. knowing why we implement e-Government systems in the organization).

Bygholm points out that when implementing IT in organizations it is not enough to support object and tool knowledge, i.e. it is not enough to teach end-users 'how to push the buttons'. IT-implementation requires that we work with and discuss the use of IT at an organizational level raising questions in and to an organization about the values and norms of good technology use. As pointed out by Nardi and O'Day (1999), "why questions" and especially the importance of local actors as local IT-supporters are important in order to bring technological development, implementation and use to a local action-level. And that is what will be perused in the following: presenting the actions of local IT-supporters and their value, not only to an object and tool level but also to a practice level, that is: contributing to both the 20 and the 80 percentage relationchip important for IT-implementation of e-Government.

Characteristics of local IT-support

Point of departure for studying IT-support is an understanding of IT-support as design. IT-support is productive design at a local level designing practices for good technology use. Consequently, IT-support is elsewhere referred to as "local design" (Kanstrup 2005) highlighting both the local level of the IT-support under study (vs. centralized helpdesks) and the "design-in-use" perspective emphasizing "the incompleteness of any technical artefact ... and the need for its continual adaptation and further development" in use (Dittrich 2002). In order to define this design perspective, specifically Winograd's definition of design has been used in that it brings the search for integration and use of technology to the forefront emphasizing that: "If we want to make technology that really *works*, we need to move from a constructor's-eye-view to a designer's-eye-view taking the system, the user, and the context all together" (Winograd 1996). The main point here is "*all together*" emphasizing that design is not only about working with the system, i.e. working with the users or the context in isolation. Design is working with all these work areas "all together".

Analytically, Winograd's definition of design is used as a description of the work areas for local IT-support. This means defining work areas of local IT-support as "the system, the user, and the context". These work areas are combined with 'ways of working' broadly defined as the local IT-supporter's "doing" and "being", inspired by ethnomethodology (Garfinkel 1967) and its focus on members' methods for 'doing' and 'doing being' (Sacks 1984). This combination has resulted in the development of a matrix (table 10) used to form an analytic synthesis of studies of local IT-support (for elaboration see Kanstrup 2005).

Ways of working / Work areas	Doing	Being
System		
User		
Context		

Table 10: An analytic tool for understanding characteristics of local IT-support

The Case Study

The case study of local IT-support consists of a primary case, which has been *the* case providing insight and understanding of this type of work supplied with a secondary case used for "testing" (inspired by Strauss & Corbin 1998) the understanding developed from the primary case. The primary case is a nursing aide school in Denmark followed during the years 2001-2004. The study took place in one particular class at the school: the "IT-class" as the teachers called it where teachers and students worked with virtual learning spaces in order to develop the IT-competencies of the students as well as their reading and writing skills. A secondary goal for the teachers in the project was to try out new methods of teaching. They wished to combine and support the problem-based learning pedagogy of the school with technology. At the beginning of the project, all students in the class (about 50) were provided with a laptop and a palm pilot. Wireless network was installed in all rooms at the school in order to increase the students' flexibility and ability to work online. Microsoft Office with Windows2000 was installed on all laptops together with an e-mail programme, a calendar, and an application for synchronizing LotusNotes and the palm pilot. Lotus Quickplace (a web-based software application from IBM designed for team collaboration) was used as a virtual learning space.

The case study was carried out as fieldwork by collection of data during visits, (video) observations, interviews, diaries, and mail and phone correspondence primarily with the IT-supporter. At the first visit (autumn 2001), the IT-class entered the third week of experimentation. At that time, they encountered several technical problems, especially synchronization problems with the network and Quickplace. At the second visit (February 2002), they still faced technical problems regarding synchronization of Quickplace. At the third visit (August 2003), the project was near its end. The teachers were generally satisfied with the results and the technical problems were almost forgotten.

From the first visit, the importance and value of the work of the local IT-supporter, Kurt, was clear. During this first visit, Kurt was absent for several hours due to meetings with the central IT-department of the school but his name kept coming up. Almost every time students and teachers faced technical problems they said: "We will solve it when Kurt returns" or "Let's wait and see what Kurt says", etc. An interview was conducted with two of Kurt's colleagues who described, among other things, how the idea of using IT in teaching came primarily from Kurt, "he is the one who got the idea of making an IT-class". Kurt was employed partly as a teacher and partly as a "pedagogical IT-supporter" (a title referring to an education for teachers on how to support colleagues and students in IT-use at schools, see Andresen 2002). He was the initiator of the project and worked hard to support the integration of the technology into the organization. Seeing Kurt in action, and especially seeing some of the results of these actions, made him a good example of local IT-support. Thus, the second visit to the case focused narrowly on Kurt's IT-support. The third visit was an interview with both Kurt and his colleagues, however, primarily discussing Kurt's IT-support-work in the project, and, in the summer 2004, Kurt was interviewed about his IT-support-work and reflections on the analytic results of the study at that time.

The analytic results from this case study were tested in a secondary case: an institute of language, speech and brain disorders where video communication systems were used for training of aphasiacs. The local IT-supporter in this case,

Suzanne, was another good example of local IT-support analyzed through her personal diaries on her IT-support work during 2002-2003.

Analytic results

The matrix below presents analytic results from the case studies of local IT-supporters work and a rough outline of the characteristics of local IT-support:

Ways of working / Work areas	Doing	Being
System	Taming the system: working with *the system in use* & working with the system with empathy	Being emphatic towards IT: IT-support as a call and trajectory: *Believing in the good that system can do for the users and context*
User	Engaging users: *making work with the system visible* & sharing responsibility	Being collaborative: representing the other and *being through others*
Context	Connecting and dividing: *opening the way for why-questions* & removing prejudices	Being communicative and reflective: *balancing between practices* and between battle and cooperation

Figure 13: Analytic results/characteristics of local IT-support

The main point from this analysis is the synthesis, which points to the 'all-togetherness' as the key in local IT-support: the local IT-supporter's ability to work with the system, the user, and the context all together. The local IT-supporter's ability to "work it all together" appears from the matrix as a whole but also from each work area pointing out to the other areas. Examples are found in the local IT-supporter's work with the "system in use" or in his effort to "make the system work visible for the users" or in his "balancing between practices" of technicians and users, management and employees, teachers and students, etc. In other words: the matrix must be seen as a unity in order to get the picture of the characteristics of local IT-support. By describing each work area for the local IT-supporter, this is made even more visible:

- The local IT-supporter's work with the system is characterized by "working with the system in use" and by learning about the system through "empathy". This is seen in Kurt's and Suzanne's constant relating the system to the use practice. E.g. when errors occur, technicians are seen working with these errors as a technical matter focusing on "IP-errors" or "server-errors" whereas Kurt and Suzanne talk about the errors in use e.g. "we have a group of students who cannot synchronize". The attitude towards technology is similar to the attitude towards users, which is characterized by an empathy seen in the IT-supporters' effort to understand and tame the system. This empathy and effort is based in a belief in the good that the technology can offer the users and the context, grounded in the local IT-supporter's own trajectory. For instance, Kurt has a history of reading and writing difficulties caused by dyslexia. He has experienced and believes that IT can help this problem, which many nursing aide students also have. His engagement in IT is not based on a technical interest only but in a belief in the good that the technology can bring to practice.
- Similarly, characteristic of the local IT-supporter's work with the users is the effort to make them part of the work with the system. This means that users do not go for a walk or a cup of coffee while the IT-supporter works with technical difficulties, errors, etc. on their computers. On the contrary, the users are asked to take part in the work with the system. The local IT-supporter describes and discusses the IT-problems with the users, how they might be solved, how difficult they are, etc. At the first visit, this looked like users sitting next to the local IT-supporter while he worked on solving the problems. But during the second and third visits, a clear development was seen especially in the users' effort to try to solve technical problems themselves before calling for help. The local IT-supporter's work with users aims at engaging and guiding them towards independency. It is about being collaborative by sharing ownership and responsibility and the work with users is a top priority to the local IT-supporter who finds his/her being through others/users,

meaning that the gain is not found in his/her own but in others'/users' development.

- The local IT-supporter's work with the context balances between connecting and dividing being communicative and reflective. It is about translating between different practices (connecting practices and being communicative/translating) and about finding a way for the technology in the context (dividing labour and being reflective about the practice and its members). It is a work with obstacles for the integration of the system such as users' disbeliefs in the system and technicians' prejudices about users, which the local IT-supporter handles primarily by opening the way for 'why-questions' (Nardi & O'Day 1999). E.g. when students ask "why do we need these computers", the local IT-supporter answers "can you elaborate on that" (opening up vs. shutting down the discussion). The work with the context is a balance between practices (and their prejudices and different beliefs) and different strategies for integration of IT in the context. This means that the local IT-supporter is mostly found at the boarder between communities of practices from where (s)he makes relations and paves ways for the system into the organization.

These characteristics of local IT-support are of course not exhaustive but an abstraction of dominated forms of practice found in the data material of two cases. Thus, the analysis is a first step taken towards characteristics of local IT-support, which can be used for further research.

Identifying local IT-supporters

Methods on how to identify qualified candidates for local IT-support are almost non-existing. In its present form, the characteristics of local IT-support presented above can be used by organizations for reflection on critical skills of local IT-supporters. Another question is, however, how to identify these skills and how to organize IT-support in the organization. The above case studies tell the story of two people who became IT-supporters on their own initiative, which is a rather typical scenario: you "become" a local IT-supporter (Kanstrup 2004). In these two cases, the IT-supporters had exemplary skills but this is not always the case (Morris et al. 2005) thus the question on how to identify those with the right skills. Some institutions, e.g. the Danish primary schools and high schools have established educations for local IT-supporters on "pedagogical IT-support" (Andresen 2002). This arrangement is, however, far from practice in most organizations (in Denmark). Taking hospitals as another example, we also find use of local IT-support. But despite the fact that several hospitals in Denmark use local IT-supporters to implement the first generation of Electronic Health Records (EHR) systems, there is no written evidence that document how to identify such IT-supporters in the health sector. The following is an attempt to create awareness of this need and a debate on which criteria to use to identify relevant IT-supporters that have the right qualifications as well as trust among colleagues.

Two prepositions have been governing the process:
- The staff knows very well who among themselves they trust to back-up the colleagues when a new IT system is being introduced.
- It is possible to ask the staff – either from pre-defined criteria or by their own judgement – to appoint colleagues to become potential local IT-supporters by the development and use of a simple selection tool.

In other words, the following case study presents the idea that local IT-supporters with local competencies can be identified by asking the staff. This knowledge, together with the characteristics of local IT-support presented in the previous case study, may be useful for management when they establish the IT-support team in their organization.

The Case

Due to political pressure, transition from paper based patient records to Electronic Health Records (EHR) at Danish hospitals is a priority task these years. It is a process that requires all staff to learn how the new EHR system works, and hence a challenge to the hospital management. The need for training of all staff before implementation places the hospital management in a dilemma: thorough introduction of all employees to EHR results in high implementation costs and is very time consuming. On the one hand, it is the responsibility of the management to ensure a careful EHR training off all staff to avoid fatal failures after implementation. On the other hand, a thorough introduction for all staff results in increased expenses on top of the implementation and operation costs for the individual hospital, expenses which many are not able to find in their current budget. In Denmark, the implementation cost is a burden for the hospital and not for the system providers. As an attempt to solve this dilemma, several hospitals which have already implemented first generation EHR systems, have pointed out a number of local IT-supporters to receive training in the new EHR system. When the local IT-supporters have received training in the system they are deemed capable of supporting colleagues whenever they need assistance with the EHR.

The empirical example referred to in this paper has been developed in collaboration with the EHR project manager at Skejby University Hospital, Denmark. At this hospital, the implementation of the EHR system is planned to be supported by two types of local IT-supporters; the co-ordinating IT-supporters as well as ordinary IT-supporters.

- A co-ordinating IT-supporter is often a new, recruited position at each department or ward (depending on size). The time allocated to co-ordinate IT-support depends on the size of staff at each department.
- Ordinary IT-supporters are staff employed at the ward, appointed by the ward management or volunteering to receive extra training in how to operate the EHR system. It is a colleague that has responsibility for a key task in line with the many other key tasks that are usually divided among the hospital staff.

In this relation, it is important to pay attention to the fact that local IT-supporters can be found in various forms and/or at various levels in organizations. The local IT-supporters in the cases presented first are educated to handle local IT-support (Andresen 2002; and Suzanne even started on a master in ICT and learning). They manage the IT-implementation, operation, and maintenance and work together with both end-users, management, and technicians and primarily with building bridges between these different stakeholders. In the following case study that is a "co-ordinating IT-supporter" as opposed to an ordinary level where the local IT-supporters work closely together only with end users. It is the ordinary type of IT-support, which is in focus in the following. Figure 14 shows the organization of the EHR-implementation in the case study. Here, it becomes obvious how the co-ordinating IT-supporters refer to a project manager and how ordinary IT-supporters (shortened 'OS') work only in relation to a section/sub in the ward.

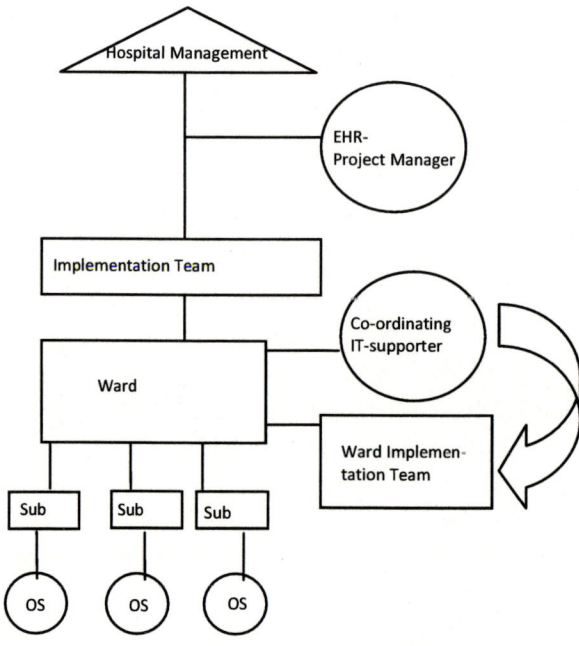

Figure 14: The organization of the EHR-implementation

In Danish hospitals, there is a tradition of distributing different key tasks to members of the staff who show an interest and these tasks often lead to a salary bonus.

The IT-support task at hospitals must be covered 24 hours/7 days a week and all clinical tasks and professions are involved in the use of EHR. Consequently, more than one IT-supporter needs to be identified for each department or ward.

Methodological Framework

The method developed and tested in this study is sociologically founded and takes its starting point in the actor-network theory where relevant actors and social groups are identified through the use of the methods; "roll a snowball" or "follow the actor" (Bijker 1995). This starting point is linked to a method that was originally developed to identify "indigenous knowledge specialists" (Mundy 1996), which is a sophistication of "Sociometry", a sociological method originally developed by Moreno in the 1930s (Moreno 1937).

For the specific purpose of this paper, the term 'indigenous knowledge' is defined as *context dependent knowledge* that is being developed, changed and used by a limited group of people and being carried on to e.g. new staff that over time are being integrated in the same unit. It is a knowledge which the individual belonging to the unit can bring into other contexts, but here the knowledge will have a different meaning, because it will be used separately from the context and practice where it was developed. To put it differently, to be an indigenous knowledge specialist is in this way a term we use about staff that posses a knowledge about the organization they work for, its individual members and the context in which their unit performs. As such we do not talk about a knowledge that can be acquired after two weeks in a workplace, but rather about knowledge that takes time (months or even years) to develop.

It is a prior assumption that a doctor or a nurse at a hospital ward possesses several different forms of knowledge in order to be able to carry out his or her job (note formal, informal, tacit, context dependent). Here, we are testing an employee-oriented method that take into account the knowledge held by the different professions but also the cross disciplinary and context dependent knowledge that is in play among staff at a hospital ward. Applied to the healthcare sector in Denmark, an employee-oriented method takes its point of departure in recognizing the importance of a context dependent knowledge. When an organization wants to appoint local IT-supporters, the community of practice and knowledge on this practice become important factors as they are the result of the practice, which over time has been developed at – in this case a hospital ward. It is this context-dependent knowledge, which the sociometry and snowball methods seeks to involve in order to give the management an optimal basis from which they can appoint local IT-supporters.

The Snowball method is used to identify relevant actors in a distinct context. A putative key person is identified and asked to identify others who (s)he believes will have knowledge about the topic under investigation. Thus, the unit of analysis is not known in advance. The following people appointed are interviewed and they again will identify other informants whom they believe will be able to contribute with knowledge about the topic under investigation. The snowball is rolling. The actors are followed one by one until the necessary information has been achieved or no new points are being made.

Sociometry is a method developed to measure the degree of relatedness between people. It works different from the snowball methods by operating inside a well-defined and identified group or unit of investigation:

"A useful working definition of sociometry is that it is a methodology for tracking the energy vectors on interpersonal relationships in a group. It shows the patterns of how individuals associate with each other when acting as a group toward a specified end or goal." (Hoffman 2001). The method is based on the presumption that people make choices in their interpersonal relations. They choose where to sit, who they like and dislike, who are important to them and how they think individual persons in a given group perform. In order to make sense out of these many choices, they can be illustrated in a pattern. It is not a rigid method with fixed procedures and rules, but in contrast a method that can be modified and made appropriate to the concrete context (Moreno 1937).

In this study, the method has been tested to form the basis for identifying IT-supporters at a hospital ward. As mentioned previously, one of the assumptions was that the staff does have an opinion on colleagues suitable as IT-supporters. They also seem to have an opinion on who hold the qualifications that enable them to help the rest of the staff.

The figure below is an illustration of the methodological framework containing snowballing, sociometry, and context dependent knowledge.

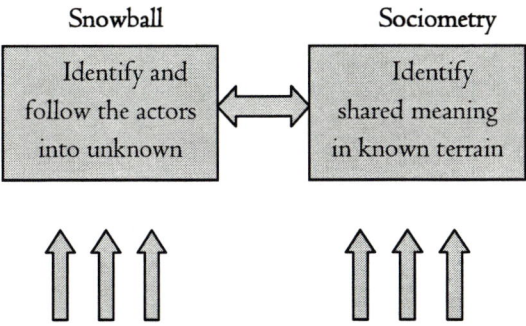

Figure 15: Methodological framework for identifying local IT-supporters

The Empirical Test of the Method

During the empirical test, the method has been used to identify potential local IT-supporters at two wards at Skejby University Hospital. Exactly how the method is applied in other places can be flexible and depends on the IT-support qualifications agreed on by the staff and management. It has been our objective to develop a method that can be applied in the healthcare sector in general.

The method starts by asking the staff whom among their colleagues they think of as being the most suitable for the IT-support task. Each informant is asked to name three colleagues (among all staff disciplines). If they only point at one person there is a risk that they either point at the secretary or one from their own profession. If they point at more than three there is a risk that the decision is made on a too loose foundation.

A member of another ward can collect the information (to avoid a positive or negative impact from the interviewer). Depending on how well the required qualifications have been discussed and agreed on, they can be introduced before the question is asked, e.g. the characteristics of local IT-support presented in the section above. The clearer the management is on what they expect from the local IT-supporters the larger the chance that the right people are identified for the position.

The method can be applied in two different ways depending on whether all staff is interviewed or whether a staff segment is consulted in two or more steps.

Variant 1
All staff at the ward is asked to name three colleagues. The local IT-supporters are found among the persons mentioned by most colleagues.

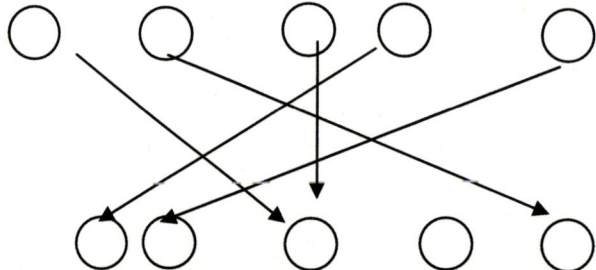

Figure 16: Identifying (a) candidate(s) by looking for the one(s) mentioned most by colleagues

Variant 2
Three people (e.g. one from each profession or in seniority rank) are asked to point out three potential IT-supporters.

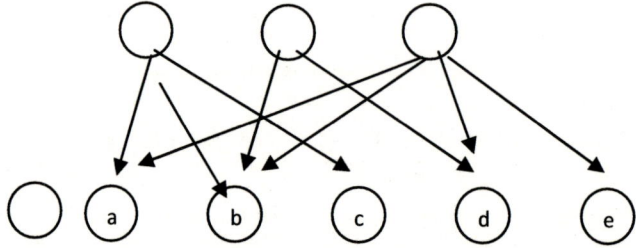

Figure 17: Identifying a candidate by first looking for three potential candidates

a – e are further questioned and asked to point out three IT-supporters.

Local IT-Support

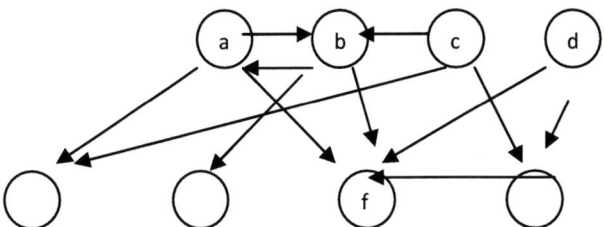

Figure 18: Identification by snowballing: asking the three candidates in figure 17 to point out three candidates

If the aim at a ward is to identify three local IT-supporters it would then be interesting for the management to look at a and b, as well as f as possible candidates for the post.

If no clear picture has come up after two rounds, it will be possible to continue asking the people pointed out until the preferred number of candidates has been reached.

The information can be collected either by the use of an interviewer that makes sure to ask all staff at the ward or through a questionnaire survey administrated by the staff themselves.

Analytic results

The purpose of the development and test of an IT-support-identification method was to get beyond a situation where the management point out staff that they think have IT-knowledge, trust among the staffs, or whom they think the organization can spare.

The method has been tested at two hospital wards and the results were clear: in a fast and well-arranged way, it has proved suitable to identify the people who the staff recommended as most qualified. An unexpected result was that we, by selecting three of the answers from the large sample and those three they each suggested as potential IT-supporters, we reached the same result as the large sample. It is the same people that come forward. This result suggests that the management in a well-arranged way, with a minimum of effort can get access to the staff preferences, and by doing so actually base their choice of local IT-supporters on the context dependent knowledge and the interpersonal relationships among the staff.

We have not investigated who the management would select if they should point out local IT-supporters on their own and therefore we can not tell if there will be any convergence between those preferred by the management and employees respectively. It is of course important that the employees have some knowledge about the IT-system under implementation to be able to point out people with the right competence. The principals for the clinical operation of the system should be clear to everyone. In the present test, the informants were told that they could point at people from other professions than their own and most informants did so. In addition, the fact that we did a survey of employees' perspectives in relation to the implementation of EHR assisted in putting EHR on the agenda at the ward level.

Conclusions

The paper has presented two case studies, which brings knowledge to a rather unexplored area in IT-work: IT-support with focus on local IT-support. The first study has presented characteristics of local IT-support. Here, the main point has been the local IT-supporters' ability to work with the system, the user, and the context all together. The second study has presented a method for identifying local IT-supporters in organizations. Here, the main point has been that local IT-supporters can be identified by asking the staff in a well-arranged way, with a minimum of effort: asking nine gives the same result as asking 32.

In this way, the paper contributes with applicable knowledge for organizations when defining critical skills for local IT-support and when identifying qualified candidates from within the organization for the support position. However, we hope, that the paper will also contribute to bringing attention to the importance and value of local IT-support in relation to e-Government and IT-implementation more generally. Further research is needed both on the development of the presented characteristics of local IT-support from a larger corpus of cases but also from other perspectives. To mention some of the unexplored perspectives, we still do not know much about how to create conditions for local IT-support in organizations, how to organize and educate local IT-supporters in the best way, how to integrate local IT-support in the design process, or how to measure the effect of local IT-support on the productiveness of the system. And if users find support in several types of resources as argued by Govindarajulu (2002), we also need to consider how to create a 'web of resources' for IT-support. Recent research on remote telephone support from call centres has argued for bringing this global type of IT-support work to a local level by working on designing good on-line support systems that can be accessed directly by users (O'Neill et al. 2004 and 2005; Tolmie et al. 2004). These studies bring along another perspectives on how to perceive the organization of IT-support (from the focus found in this paper on the human actor to a focus on technological solutions for IT-support). It is a perspective which calls for further research on IT-support work as argued by these researchers in order to "provide a resource for design" (O'Neill et al. 2004). But it is also a perspective which shares the same problems as the 'human' support-system presented in this paper: the problem of how to design the 'local'. As described by Stevens and Wiedenhöfer, online help systems often fail due to contextualization problems – how to de-contextualize and how to re-contextualize – which are again problems that users can and do overcome by using local IT-supporters of either official or un-official status among their colleagues, family, or other 'locals' (Stevens & Wiedenhöfer 2006). In this way, the primary statement in this paper: the importance and value of local IT-supporters "local time and place knowledge" (Ostrom 1990) seem to be a central value and challenge to IT-support in general.

Acknowledgements
Thanks to "Kurt" and "Suzanne" for sharing their work as local IT-supporters. Thanks to Inge Madsen at Skejby University Hospital, Denmark, for co-operation and logistic support, and to Ole Busk for data collection.

References
Andresen, B. B. (Ed.) (2002). *IT-vejlederens håndbog* (The Handbook of the IT-supporter). Vejle, Denmark: Kroghs Forlag.

Bijker, W.E. (1995). *Of Bicycles, Bakelites, and Bulbs: Towards a Theory of Sociotechnical Change*. The MIT Press, Cambridge, Massachusetts.

Bygholm, A. (2001). End-user Support: A Necessary Issue in the Implementation and Use of EPR Systems. Paper presented at *MEDINFO 2001*, Amsterdam, Holland.

Cappuccio, D. et al. (1996). *Total Cost of Ownership: The Impact of System Management Tools*. The Gartner Group.

Castellani, S. et al. (2005). Total Cost of Ownership: Issues around Reducing Cost of Support in a Manufacturing Organization Case. *IEEE International Workshop on Business Transformation: towards a theory of business agility*, Munich, Germany, July 19.

David, J. S. et al. (2002). Managing your IT Total Cost of Ownership. *Communications of the ACM* 45(1): 101-106.

Dittrich, Y. et al. (2002). PD in the Wild; Evolving Practices for Design in Use. *Proceedings of the Participatory Design Conference 02*, Malmö, Sweden, 23-25 June.

Garfinkel, Harold (1967). *Studies in Ethnomethodology*. Cambridge: Prentice.Hall, Inc.

Govindarajulu, C. (2002). The Status of Helpdesk Support. *Communications of the ACM* 45(1): 97-100.

Govindarajulu, C. (1996). End-user computing support: Status and directions. *Proceedings of the 1996 Soutwest Decision Sciences*, San Antonio, TX, USA.

Govindarajulu, C. (2002). The Status of Helpdesk Support. *Communications of the ACM* 45(1): 97-100.

Hoffman, C. (2001). *Introduction to Sociometry*, http://www.hoopandtree.org/sociometry.htm).

Kanstrup, A. M. & Bertelsen, P. (2006). Participatory IT-support. *Proceedings from the Participatory Design Conference 2006: PDC2006*. Trento, Italy, August 1-5.

Kanstrup, A.M. (2005). *Local Design: an inquiry into the work practices of local IT-supporters*. Ph.D thesis, Department of Communications, Aalborg University.

Kanstrup, Anne Marie (2004). Talking about Technology - An interview with Bonnie A. Nardi. *IMPACT, an electronic journal on formalisation in text, media, and language*. Published 14.06.2004.

Moreno, J.L (1937). Sociometry in Relation to Other Social Sciences. *Sociometry*, Vol. I, 1-2 (Jul-Oct), 206-219.

Morris, M. et al. (2005). *How Do Users Feel About Technology?* Forrester Research.

Mundy, P. (1996). *Recording and Using Indigenous Knowledge, Identifying Indigenious Specialists* www.panasia.org.sg/iirr/ikmanual/.

Nardi, B. A. (1993). *A Small Matter of Programming - Perspectives on End User Computing*. Cambridge, Massachusetts: The MIT Press.

Nardi, B. A., & O'Day, V. L. (1999). *Information Ecologies - Using Technology with Heart*. Cambridge, Massachusetts: The MIT Press.

Nyvang, T. & Poulsen, C. R. (2006). Implementation of ICT in Government Organizations - User Driven or Management Driven? In: Kanstrup, A. M., Nyvang, T. & Sørensen, E. M. (Eds.), *Perspective on e-Government: Technology & Infrastructure, Politics and Organization, Interaction & Communication*. Aalborg Universitets Forlag.

O'Neill, J. et al. (2004). *Users solving technical troubles with a remote expert*. Ubicomp Conference, Giving Help at a Distance workshop, Nottingham, U.K., September.

O'Neill, J. et al. (2005). *Using real-life troubleshooting interactions to inform self-assistance design*. INTERACT, Rome, Italy, 12-16 September.

Ostrom, Elinor (1990). *Governing the Commons. The Evolution of Institutions for Collective Action*. Cambridge University Press.

Remmen, A. (2004). *Images of e-Government: experiences from the Digital North Denmark*. Presented at 'ICT and Learning In Regions': Concluding

International Research Conference for the Participatory Research on the Digital North Denmark. Aalborg, June 1-2.

Rose, Jeremy (2006). Technology and Government: extending the double dance Agency. In: Kanstrup, A. M., Nyvang, T. & Sørensen, E. M. (Eds.), *Perspective on e-Government: Technology & Infrastructure, Politics and Organization, Interaction & Communication.*. Aalborg Universitets Forlag.

Sacks, H. (1984). On doing 'being ordinary. In: J. M. Atkinson & J. Heritage (ed.), *Structures of Social Action - Studies in Conversation Analysis.* Cambridge: Cambridge University Press.

Stevens, G. & Wiedenhöfer, T. (2006). CHIC – a pluggable solution for community help in context. NordiCHI 2006: changing roles, October 14-18 2006, Oslo, Norway.

Strauss, A. & Corbin, J. (1998). *Basics of Qualitative Research - Grounded Theory Procedures and Techniques.* SAGE Publications, Inc.

Tolmie, P. et al. (2004). *Supporting Remote Problem-Solving with Ubiquitous Computing: Research Policies and Objectives.* Ubicomp Conference, Giving Help at a Distance workshop, Nottingham, U.K. September.

Winograd, Terry (ed.) (1996). *Bringing Design to Software: A New Foundation for Design.* Addison-Wesley Publishers.

Åsand, H. R. H. et al. (2004). Superbrugere - en strategi for ikt-omstilling. (Super Users – a strategy for IT-Change) In: A.M. Kanstrup (ed.), *E-læring på arbejde* (E-learning at Work). Roskilde Universitetsforlag /Learning Lab Denmark.

Authors

Pernille Bertelsen: Associate Professor at the Department of Development and Planning, Aalborg University. Her research interests are principally user-driven and concerned with health informatics and organisational change, workplace studies, problem based learning and development of participatory approaches for involvement of users in design and implementation of IT-systems. She is member of Virtual Center for Health Informatics (V-CHI) at Aalborg University.

Ann Bygholm: PhD, Associate Professor at Department of Communication and Psychology at Aalborg University. Her research is mainly based on theories on communication and cognition within the area of computer supported collaborative work, human computer interaction, and implementation and evaluation of information systems within the educational system and the health care sector. Ann Bygholm was one of the initiators behind the interdisciplinary Master of Information Technology in Health Informatics and Virtual Center for Health Informatics (V-CHI) which is a network of persons in the fields of research, development, production, educational, and clinical environments. she was part of Aalborg University's Participatory Research on the Digital North Denmark.

Ellen Christiansen: PhD, Associate Professor at Department of Communication and Psychology at Aalborg University. She is a researcher and teacher within the field of Human-Computer Interaction. Ellen has worked with participatory design since her PhD studies, which included a stay at the Swedish Center for Working Life in Stockholm in 1985-86. Theoretically, Ellen Christiansen is rooted in the cultural historical tradition from Vygotsky, and today she is working theoretically to expand and underpin the concept 'information ecology', while working empirically with interface design framed by user driven innovation.

Lone Dirckinck-Holmfeld: PhD, Professor at Department of Communication and Psychology at Aalborg University. Her research is within the field of Computer Supported Collaborative Learning (CSCL) and she is author and co-author of several books, reports and papers on ICT and learning and dialogue research. Lone Dirckinck-Holmfeld was head of Aalborg University's group on Participator Research on the Digital North Denmark.

Anne Marie Kanstrup: PhD, Assistant Professor at Department of Development and Planning at Aalborg University. Research and teaching is within the fields of systems design, Human-Computer Interaction, and workplace studies. Anne Marie Kanstrup's PhD was part of Aalborg University's Participatory Research on the Digital North Denmark and, since 2005, she has been research co-ordinator in Aalborg University's Centre for Digital Governance.

Ole Brun Madsen is Professor in Distributed real-time Systems and Head of CNP, Center for Network Planning, Co-director for CTIF, Center for TeleInFrastructure and head of the Networking and Security section at the Department of Electronic Systems at Aalborg University. He has been project leader for a number of national and international R&D projects and acted in high level advisory tasks within the European Commission on the R&D framework programmes in DGXIII and in United Nations UNDP activities. Present research is focused on Infrastructure Architecture and Modelling Tools for Network Analysis and Design. Ole was part of Aalborg University's Participatory Research on the Digital North Denmark.

Jeppe Agger Nielsen: PhD student at the Department of Economics, Politics and Public Administration, Aalborg University, Denmark. His research interests are mainly concerned with ICT and organisational change, and the use of ICT tools in democratic processes. He is author and co-author of books, articles and papers on ICT in the public sector and member of the Demo-Net – European network of excellence.

Tom Nyvang, MA in Human Centered Informatics, Assistant Professor at Department of Communication and Psychology, Aalborg University. Tom has been employed at Aalborg University since 2000, and is part of the E-learning Lab. He has authored and co-authored several conference papers and book chapters on e-learning. The main research area is the implementation of ICT in higher education with focus on the relationship between organisational change, development of ICT based infrastructures for learning and improvement of pedagogical approaches. Recently, he has turned his attention to implementation of ICT in other government institutions. His research is based mainly on socio-cultural approaches to development and learning (as known in socio-cultural activity theory) and theories of systems development.

Camilla Roseeuw Poulsen, MA in Human Centered Informatics, Aalborg University and author of the master thesis "Implementation of Electronic Health Records" for which she was awarded the Human Centered Informatics prize for the best MA thesis in the academic year 2005-2006. Camilla is currently working as Workflow Consultant at CCI Europe, where she assists in the implementation of advertising systems for newspapers worldwide.

Jeremy Rose: PhD and Associate Professor at the Department of Computing Science, Aalborg University, Denmark. He has worked with the PITNIT and SPV research projects in Denmark, in a variety of action research and consulting roles, and is active as a member of the IFIP WG8.2 community. His research interests are principally concerned with IT and organisational change, IT and societal change, the management of IT, and systems development. He has published in management, systems, eGovernment and information systems journals and conferences. He has been involved with research in computing in the public sector (in both England and Denmark) and is active in managing the Demo-Net European network of excellence. He was the founding director of the Centre for eGovernance at Aalborg University.

Esben Munk Sørensen: M.Sc. and PhD in Rural Development and Spatial Planning. Professor in Geoinformation and Land Management at Department of Development and Planning at Aalborg University. Formerly research-professor at National Centre of Landscape and Forest. Since 2005, Esben is Manager of Center for E-governance at Aalborg University.

Lars Torpe, Associate Professor at Department of Economics, Politics and Public Administration at Aalborg University. Research within the fields of democracy, political participation, voluntary associations and social capital. Author and co-author of several books and articles within these fields. He was part of Aalborg University's Participatory Research on the Digital North Denmark.

Christian Richter Østergaard, PhD., is post doc. researcher at Department of Business Studies, Aalborg University, Denmark. His research interests include the emergence of regional clusters and the evolution of the information and communication technology (ICT) sector. He wrote a PhD-thesis on the development perspectives for the ICT sector in North Jutland as a part of Aalborg University's participatory research group on the Digital North Denmark.